PRAISE FOR THE

COR

"If you're looking for a guide to ease the transition from flip-flops to wing-tips, a fine choice is **They Don't Teach Corporate in College**. Alexandra Levit does a great job attacking assumptions that high-achieving college grads drag into the workplace with them."

—Mary Eleen Slayter, *The Washington Post*

"Ms. Levit teaches newbies such practicalities as making a memorable first impression, networking without cringing, coping with difficult personalities, and learning to be an effective boss. The book is easy to read and loaded with common-sense techniques."

—Steve Powers, *The Dallas Morning News*

"We walked into our CEO's office to brief him on the Millennial employee panel we were planning with Alexandra. We brought a copy of **They Don't Teach Corporate in College** along to show him, but to our surprise, he already had a stack of them in his office. He gives them to promising young employees he happens to meet in the company."

—Amanda Tolino, Campbell's Soup, Inc.

"...workforce newbies need a boot camp like this to face up to the rigors of the working week."

—Abby Wilner, coauthor of *Quarterlife Crisis*

"Alexandra Levit has written a savvy, informative guide for first-timers making their way in Corporate America."

—Stacy Kravetz, author of *Welcome to the Real World*

"Her straightforward, practical advice is something that all colleges should recommend to their outgoing seniors."

—Amy Joyce, author of *I Went to College for This?*

"This book explodes with practical and relevant advice for young professionals who want to master the fast track yesterday."

—Harry E. Chambers, author of *Getting Promoted*

"There's only one thing I hate about this book: that I didn't have it when I was in my 20s! In a compelling and eminently readable volume, Levit lays out the secrets that it takes most of us at least a decade—and a lot of mistakes—to discover."

—Rachel Solar-Tuttle, author of *Table Talk: A Savvy Girl's Guide to Networking*

"I am a college professor, and I have been using **They Don't Teach Corporate in College** as a supplement to my supervisory management class. Alexandra Levit is right on the mark with this book. The students have really enjoyed reading it and have learned so much from it. I have incorporated this book into my class discussions, and the students will be more prepared for the corporate world because of it!"

—Mary Sakin, Farleigh Dickinson University

"Alexandra Levit writes with honesty and a refreshing bluntness about office mysteries that boggle young employees. Sprinkled with bullet points and real-world examples of corporate successes and gaffes, **They Don't Teach Corporate in College** can be referred to by twenty-somethings (and those who need a refresher) again and again."

—Beth Herskovits, *PR Week*

A Twenty-Something's Guide
to the Business World

They Don't Teach CORPORATE in College

Third Edition

Alexandra Levit

CAREER
PRESS
Pompton Plains, N.J.

THEY DON'T TEACH CORPORATE IN COLLEGE, THIRD EDITION
EDITED AND TYPESET BY KARA KUMPEL
Cover design by Howard Grossman/12E Design
Printed in the U.S.A.

To order this title, please call toll-free 1-800-CAREER-1 (NJ and Canada: 201-848-0310) to order using VISA or MasterCard, or for further information on books from Career Press.

The Career Press, Inc.
220 West Parkway, Unit 12
Pompton Plains, NJ 07444
www.careerpress.com

Library of Congress Cataloging-in-Publication Data
Levit, Alexandra, 1976-
    They don't teach corporate in college : a twenty-something's guide to the business world / by Alexandra Levit. -- Third Edition.
        pages cm
    Includes bibliographical references and index.
    ISBN 978-1-60163-308-8 -- ISBN 978-1-60163-484-9 (ebook) 1. Business--Vocational guidance. 2. Success in business. I. Title.

HF5381.L48 2014
650.1084'2--dc23
                                                            2013040937

For my husband and partner in life, Stewart Shankman, who reads every word.

Acknowledgments

They Don't Teach Corporate in College is the result of years of personal experience in the workplace, as well as valuable input from the following talented individuals: Jason Alba, Ken Blanchard, Harry Chambers, Diane Danielson, Judith Gerberg, David Gordon, Alison Green, Christine Hassler, Stacy Kravetz, Dan Pink, Lindsey Pollak, Linda Price, Karen Schaffer, Mark Schwartz, Rachel Solar-Tuttle, Neil Stroul, Bruce Tulgan, and Abby Wilner.

The hardworking folks who were essential in helping me turn a good idea into a published book include my agents, Alex Glass and Michelle Wolfson; my generous friend Peter Castro; my patient and wise lawyer, Josh Grossman; my editors, Diana Ghazzawi and Kara Kumpel; and the rest of the very competent and always responsive staff at Career Press: Ron Fry, Michael Pye, and Laurie Kelly-Pye.

I will be forever grateful to the dozens of professional twenty-somethings who inspired me with their personal stories, and to the thousands of readers who made the original and second editions a success and paved the way for this 10th-anniversary edition of *They Don't Teach Corporate in College*. I am also deeply indebted to the HR, recruiting, and training professionals, the university professors, and the corporate partners who helped spread the book's messages to large populations of twenty-somethings.

I'd like to thank my friends, my colleagues through the years, and my family—especially my husband, Stewart Shankman, and my father, Robert Levit—for keeping the faith and encouraging me each step of the way.

And finally, this edition is dedicated to my mentor and inspiration, the late Dr. Stephen R. Covey (1932–2012), whose thinking has shaped my entire career.

Contents

Preface to the 10th-Anniversary Edition

Dear Readers,

Ten years ago, a little book called *They Don't Teach Corporate in College* was written in a second-floor apartment in eastern Long Island, New York. At the time, I was working as a PR manager for a Fortune 500 software company and was engaged to my college sweetheart. My career had finally hit its stride after years of setbacks, and more than anything, I wanted to share the lessons I'd learned with twenty-somethings who were just beginning their business world journeys.

In 2004, there were no other books like *They Don't Teach Corporate in College*, and I was very fortunate that the content seemed to resonate with people. A new career was born.

Throughout the next 10 years, I became a spokesperson and researcher on issues and trends facing modern employees. I wrote for the *Wall Street Journal* and the *New York Times*, and worked with companies like American Express, DeVry University, Deloitte, Intuit, and Microsoft. I traveled around the world, from Budapest to Sao Paolo, sharing my learnings with audiences as small as 10 and as large as 1,000, and I consulted with the U.S. Department of Labor on an online course called JobSTART 101. Last, but certainly not least, I got married and had two children.

I wanted to get my message of career readiness out as widely as possible, because with the 2008 recession, twenty-somethings needed more help than ever. Young professional unemployment and underemployment soared. The most driven and qualified college graduates were sitting on the job market for years at a time, struggling with displaying an effective online and offline personal brand and competing with dozens of candidates for every available position. Even those who were gainfully employed experienced an unprecedented level of stress as their organizations flattened and downsized, technology accelerated, and work/life boundaries blurred.

When general hiring resumed to somewhat normal levels last year, the job market for young professionals remained stagnant. At least in part, the reason is an ever-widening skills gap. According to the Job Preparedness Indicator research conducted by my nonprofit organization the Career Advisory Board, only 15 percent of hiring managers feel that current candidates have the requisite skills to fill open positions. And college grads are some of the worst offenders, lacking highly desirable traits like basic business acumen and communication skills.

In honor of our 10th anniversary, I'm doing what I can to address this skills gap. This new edition is jam-packed with new content, including advice for navigating a business world that is increasingly global, virtual, entrepreneurial, and unpredictable. You'll hear current thirty-somethings sharing wisdom with their twenty-something selves, and will hear my take on the most frequent questions asked by *They Don't Teach Corporate in College* readers in the last 10 years. But, as I said back in 2009, life in the business world hasn't changed in the 80 years since Dale Carnegie talked about getting people to cooperate, so many of the original lessons are intact.

To all of you who have supported me from the very beginning, thank you so much. If it wasn't for you, recommending *They Don't Teach Corporate in College* to your friends, family members, colleagues, and managers over and over again, none of my work would be possible. Please keep in touch always!

Introduction

After I graduated from college, I was hell-bent on moving to New York City. I believed in the saying, "If you can make it in New York, you can make it anywhere." I was the type of kid who studied hard and got *A*s in school, and I didn't think I'd have any trouble skipping up the corporate ladder in one of the most intimidating cities in the world. When I landed a job in a top public relations firm despite having zero relevant experience, I thought the toughest part was over. I dumped my extra resumes in a recycling bin and eagerly awaited a paycheck that would scarcely cover my rent. I looked forward to worldly business trips, stimulating office brainstorms, and hanging out with my coworkers every Friday at happy hour.

Three years later, I found myself cringing at the words *corporate travel*, and I had never made it to a happy hour gathering because I was passed out on the couch every Friday night. One of my managers disliked me so much that I was convinced I had killed her in a past life. I held an entry-level position for 16 months while people with half my intelligence and work ethic lapped me. I saw a career counselor, book-marked job boards on my browser, and dreamed of a distant future in which I was happily ensconced in a job that merited getting up in the morning. My resume listed four positions in three years, because I was always on the lookout for a better opportunity that would bring the ever-elusive job satisfaction I dreamt of.

Desperate for help, I looked in Barnes & Noble for a book geared toward twenty-somethings struggling to survive in the professional world. I found a handful of titles on finding an affordable living situation, decoding tax forms, and allocating the right combination of funds to one's brand-spanking-new 401(k) plan. And I assure you, after painting these books with a yellow highlighter, I had the best damn 401(k) in the world. My 401(k) was so sound that I could have been a billionaire by the time I retired from my chief general manager, divisional senior vice president position at age 65!

Too bad I wouldn't last that long. The way I was going, I would be the corporate equivalent of the dinosaur in Darwin's natural selection process. In those days, I spent a lot of time in bars doing tequila shots and smoking cigarettes. I complained to anyone who would listen about the death of common sense in the workplace, and how my expensive undergraduate education was being wasted on clearing paper jams from the printers. When I probed my mother for answers, she told me that life wasn't supposed to be fair or fulfilling, and that I should learn to tolerate my job. My father shrugged and said he hoped I would become the first in a long line of suffering, worker-bee Levits to triumph in the business world...but he doubted it. My friends told me to go to law school.

The idea of going back to school was tempting indeed, and why not? We're comfortable with the concept of school. We know how the story goes: if you work hard, you get good grades and everyone is happy. The business world, however, is another animal entirely. Politically motivated and fraught with nonsensical change, the professional world is not a natural fit for graduates who leave school expecting results from a logical combination of education and effort. Suddenly, the tenets of success we were taught since kindergarten don't apply, because getting ahead in the business world has nothing to do with intelligence or exceeding a set of defined expectations. In our first corporate jobs, we come up against rules no one ever told us about. We feel lost. It's like we were whisked away on a spaceship and have landed on an alien planet where we have to eat oxygen and breathe vegetables.

So how did I survive it? Well, things started to turn around when I finally realized that the professional world is the same everywhere. I was bringing my misguided attitudes and beliefs about the business world to each new position, and I knew I wouldn't be successful until I changed them. So I stopped job jumping and started taking courses and reading books on practical self-improvement. I put myself under a microscope and took a close look at the persona I presented to the companies I had worked for. After polishing the package and learning how to promote it, I mastered human relations skills such as diplomacy, cooperation, initiative-taking, and networking. I also refined personal development skills such as organization, time management, and attitude adjustment. Eventually, I overcame the negativity that was making me miserable and holding me back in my career. By my late 20s, I saw results in the form of four promotions, and I could finally claim that I was—at long last—happy working in the professional world.

Throughout the years, as I've talked with young professionals, I've realized that my experiences are disturbingly common. Today's twenty-somethings technically have more occupational choices than their parents did and face escalating uncertainty about your careers. More than ever, twenty-somethings worldwide are seeking counseling, and job jumping due to stress and dissatisfaction has become the norm. For example, a recent study by the U.S. Bureau of Labor Statistics shows that the average young professional stays in a job under two years.

At the end of the day, the choice is yours. You can help NYU Law and Northwestern's Kellogg School of Management increase their applications by another 200 percent while you shell out more than $100,000 for several more years of school. Or, because you don't want to be in debt and eating with plastic utensils the rest of your life, you can learn to win the game of the professional world. Difficult as it may be, you must change your attitude about the education you left behind. A college degree is a piece of paper that gets you in the door for an interview—it may even land you a job. But if you want to get any further in the professional world, you have to treat your first job out of college like it's 1st grade. This new world is full of possibilities, but you must be willing to readjust your thinking cap and prepare for some tough lessons.

The business climate is tougher than it has ever been. I came, I saw, and I didn't go back to school. That's why I decided to write this book. By sharing the strategies that helped me succeed in my career, I hope to provide a helping hand to those just beginning the journey, and also to reassure those who have been in the trenches for some time already that it is possible to make sense of this upside-down world.

The contents of *They Don't Teach Corporate in College* are as follows: The first chapter serves as the insider's guide to job hunting, including proven techniques for surveying the field, meeting contacts, preparing promotional materials, interviewing, and deciding whether to relocate or work for free. Chapter 2 will help you transition to a new position, and suggests actions that will help you achieve the best possible first impression. The third chapter lays out strategies for getting to know a new boss, navigating the company's social scene, practicing cringe-free networking, and finding a mentor and sponsors. Chapter 4 describes critical skills such as goal-setting, self-promotion, innovation, problem-solving, and risk-taking, which will take you wherever you decide to go. Chapter 5 covers how to stretch the 8-plus hours a day you spend at work—everything from effective time and project management and organization to making every piece of communication count.

The sixth chapter is devoted to combating negativity, maintaining a positive attitude, and staying motivated in the face of difficult circumstances. Chapter 7 focuses on approaches for enlisting the cooperation of others, creating positive relationships, and coping with difficult personalities. The eighth chapter is a how-to on advancement, including mastering the performance review process, troubleshooting antipromotion situations, and coping with organizational change. Chapter 9 will guide you through your first experience as a boss, drilling down into specific techniques for starting off on the right foot with employees of varying generations and styles, delegating tasks, facilitating open communication, and resolving performance issues. The last chapter advises when it's time to move on, and offers suggestions for finding a new position and making a graceful exit.

To keep things interesting, you'll also hear from current twenty-somethings sharing their on-the-job adventures, as well as current thirty-somethings who wish they could go back in time and give their twenty-something selves some better career advice!

What's the best way to use this book? I suggest that you jot down on paper the concepts that resonate with you so that you can remember them later. Post your notes in your cubicle or office—anywhere you'll see them. Some of the ideas mentioned might seem like common sense, but you'd be surprised how rarely people act on them in real life. If at any point you feel as though all this is not worth the effort, just consider how much time you are likely to spend in the professional world. Assuming you work from age 22 to age 65, for 235 days a year, you'll be on someone else's clock for about 80,000 hours—a tenth of your life. Isn't it only fair that you do everything you can to create a rewarding job experience?

There's one more thing I want to emphasize before we begin: The strategies I'm about to discuss are "best practices"; that is, they represent the ideal way to handle particular situations. Although you should generally stick to these principles if you want to be successful, no one expects you to follow them to the letter every time. As human beings, it's impossible for us to be perfect employees. We can sing self-improvement mantras until we're blue in the face, but, at the end of the day, we will still have our areas of strength and areas where we can always do better. So don't be too hard on yourself. The best you can do is read through these 10 chapters and pick out the concepts from which you feel you can benefit the most. If you shut this book and take away one piece of advice that makes you more effective at work, then I will have achieved my purpose in writing it.

Chapter 1

Find Yourself, Find a Paycheck

Whether you're just coming out of school or are mid-career, searching for employment in the professional world is more challenging than any assignment you'll be given on the job. Not only do you have to decide exactly what to look for, but you also have to find a way in the door—and make that doorstop hold until you have an offer in hand. Fortunately, as in any game with rules, job hunting has its loopholes. In this chapter, I'll discuss how to take advantage of them as you're surveying the field, meeting contacts, preparing your promotional materials, and interviewing. I'll also touch on the sticky question of negotiation, and will suggest how to decide if you should relocate for a job, work for free, or hire a career coach.

The Panic Button

For me, preparing to enter the business world was a lot like being reborn. At the end of my senior year of college, I felt the same sense of discomfort that a baby must feel when leaving the safety of its mother's womb. I freaked out about being unemployed and having to move back home, so I stormed my university's career center and wreaked havoc on every job database I could get my hands on. I needed a job ASAP, and I was willing to take anything I could get, regardless of whether or not I was interested in the occupation. After all, it was only my first job, right? The media reinforced my belief that because I was 22, I wasn't supposed to have a clue. Alexandra Robbins and Abby Wilner, authors of *Quarterlife Crisis: The Unique Challenges of Life in Your Twenties*, define a quarterlife crisis as the "overwhelming instability, self-doubt, and sense of panicked helplessness faced by twenty-somethings as a result of constant change and too many choices." I became complacent, thinking that because I'd inevitably change my mind a million times, I might as well put off the soul-searching.

Even if this approach seems perfectly legitimate to you, I don't recommend it. First of all, prospective employers don't like unfocused candidates; they want to believe that you've been preparing to work for them forever. Also, switching careers multiple times just for the hell of it sounds like a lot of work to me. You need a lot of training and experience to become proficient in a career, and once you have a family to support, will you be able to afford to pursue the job you love at a $40,000 entry-level salary? Along those same lines, your 20s is the best time to get to a respectable level on the ladder. During these years, you don't have competing responsibilities, and you are accountable to no one but yourself.

Given these factors, wouldn't it be much easier to make the smartest career choice you can now? Don't get me wrong—discovering your true calling is not an exact science, and it's impossible to know what you will want to do 10 or 20 years from now. Some futurists even predict that people currently in their 20s will have several careers in their lifetimes that haven't been invented yet. Therefore, all of the self-reflection in the world will probably not result in a bulletproof career plan for the rest of your life. It's also possible that you will try a field you've researched and think is interesting, but will realize you hate it after a few months on the job. However, by doing a complete self-assessment while you're still in school or shortly thereafter, you will be able to decide on a path that provides the core skills and experience you will need to take you wherever you want to go in the future.

The Self-Assessment Journey

Start with a blank slate. This is easier said than done when everyone you know—especially your parents—has an opinion on what you should do now that you're all grown up. You also have to get past the issue of your college major. You might think that because you studied economics you have to pursue a career as a financial consultant. The truth is that even a business-related major will not adequately prepare you for the professional world, so why let it pigeonhole you?

Forget what you studied in school for a moment and make a list of your skills—otherwise known as the things you do better than most of your friends. Skills can be general or specific. (An example of a general skill is communicating well with people, and an example of a corresponding specific skill is that you present well in front of groups.) Next, sit down for a brief philosophical journey and reflect on the following questions:

+ What are your values?

+ What type of work would make you want to sit in traffic for hours just for the privilege of showing up? What would you be compelled to do even if you never got paid for it?

+ How do you prefer to work? How are you most effective?

+ What is your definition of success? What drives you?

+ Where do you see yourself in 10 years?

Use the answers to these questions to develop what Stephen Covey, author of *The 7 Habits of Highly Effective People*, calls a personal mission statement. To paraphrase Covey, the personal mission statement is your own big picture. It should include what you hope to accomplish in your career, and it should reflect the type of person you want to become. By thinking about what's really important to you and where you want to go in life, your efforts and energy will be directed toward a common purpose. Along with your list of skills, your personal mission statement should provide clues about fields to research.

Now go online and pore over material about occupations that correspond to your skills, interests, and personal mission. Once you've made a list of potential careers, ask the career center at your college or university to help you set up informational interviews with alumni so that you can learn more about each job field you are interested in. In these meetings, don't be afraid to ask specific questions about training requirements, responsibilities, salary, work environment, and opportunities for advancement. As long as you are polite, no one will fault you for wanting the real scoop. Plus, if a job is not as glamorous as it sounds, you will want to know that before investing more of your time and energy. If possible, sample your options by taking courses related to the careers that interest you, applying for internships in your target occupations, or visiting prospective companies so that you can get a real feel for the field you'll be pursuing.

If you've already been in the business world a few years, I suggest a healthy reality check before you jump over to another job. Revise or develop your personal mission statement and ask yourself if you're on the right track. Why aren't you happy in your current position? Is it your career choice, your work situation, or you? If it's the second or third scenario, read on. Hopefully this book will help you. If it's your career choice, though, this might be a good time to make an appointment with a career counselor, take a personality inventory such as the Myers-Briggs Type Indicator, or read a career assessment book such as *What Color Is Your Parachute?* by Richard Nelson Bolles. Even if you're mid-career, you can still find a job that works for you.

When you've collected enough data to make an informed decision about a particular field, imagine your career path over the next five or 10 years. Suppose you land a dream job in your chosen field. You'll want to set some preliminary goals for what you hope to accomplish once you get there. In determining aspirations and time frames, try to be realistic. If your objective is to be a millionaire by age 30, you are setting yourself up for disappointment. (For more information on setting goals, see Chapter 4.) You should also have a backup plan. What will you do if you can't find a job or if you don't succeed in your first career choice? Knowing you have something to fall back on will only increase your confidence level as you hold your nose and dive in.

No matter what direction you choose, you'll have to cope with some doubt and uncertainty. But don't let indecisiveness get the best of you. Staying unemployed for too long while you consider the perfect career move will drive you crazy and make prospective employers squirm. Make the best decision you can, act confidently, and never look back. If you do what you think is best, the pieces will most likely fall into place.

Your Professional Persona

The semester before I graduated, I flew home to look for a job.
I had been kind of lazy in college, and my parents didn't feel I was

ready for the professional world. They even told me to hold off on interviewing. I didn't listen, though. I bought a new suit, got a haircut, and practiced by talking to myself in the mirror for a week. When I went in to meet with employers, I pretended I'd been a smooth professional all my life. My parents met me for dinner one night, and they kept looking for traces of the former bum. I think they were in shock. My dad was like, "Well, I guess maybe you are ready."

Dan, 27, Rhode Island

In life, we get many chances to reinvent ourselves. Remember when you first arrived on campus for your freshman year of college? The most exciting thing about it was that no one knew what a [insert negative adjective of choice here] you were in high school. You taught yourself new habits and hobbies, and you bought yourself a new wardrobe. Maybe you even picked a new nickname. You had the chance to start over, as if your previous life had never existed.

Graduating from college is a similar opportunity, and, understandably, you probably want to spend the next few years figuring out who you are and what you want out of life. Should you decide to pursue a career in business, however, developing a professional persona will unquestionably serve you well. By *professional persona*, I mean the mature, competent, and friendly face you project to the work world. It doesn't matter what type of person you are in real life; just think of yourself as an actor playing a role while you are at work. So what if you still play drinking games on Friday nights or prefer a book to human company? You can still have a professional persona.

How will this help you? Quite simply, a marketable professional persona positively influences people's perceptions of you so that you can ultimately succeed in the world of work. I'm sure you've heard of big-time publicists who get paid megabucks to promote celebrities and make them look like the coolest people on earth. You can be just like those PR folks, only you have just one client to promote: you. It's pretty easy, but there is a catch: you must first learn to toot your own horn. Although there is a fine line between confidence and arrogance, learning to capitalize on your skills and assert your achievements is a must for career success. If you don't do it, no one else will, and you'll be out-promoted by people who know how to leverage their own contributions. Trust me on this. In the end it will pay off almost as handsomely for you as it does for the wealthiest of publicists.

Growing and maintaining a professional persona is hard work, because everything you say and do affects it one way or the other. The best way to make your persona stick is to clearly establish it at the beginning of your relationship with a company and consistently sustain it during the early phases of a new job.

You can start online. The first step is to do a Google search of your name—and alternate spellings of your name—and see what comes up. A lot of factors influence which pages appear first in a particular search engine, but you can help your cause by purchasing your name from a web domain company, such as GoDaddy (GoDaddy.com), and housing a professional biography, other credentials, and current contact information on a simple and clean Website. If you find yourself competing with other people who have the same name, you might also increase your share of online real estate by writing industry articles for third-party association Websites or community blogs.

Your social media presence should enhance, rather than detract from your professional persona. By now you are hopefully aware that social networks and blogs are not the private havens for friends that they used to be. You can pretty much count on the fact that your boss, senior managers, colleagues, and potential employers are looking at your online sites—privacy controls or no privacy controls. That's not to say that you can't have a little fun by including content that demonstrates you're a human being, but don't go too crazy with apps and games, and beware of getting too personal. Upload photos of friends, but leave out those of last weekend's drunken soiree.

If you love posting real-time updates on micro-blogging platforms like Twitter, Tumblr, or Instagram, please think very carefully before you send messages or photos out into the world. Trust me: your boss *will* find out that you're posting from a Cubs game when you're supposed to be out sick, or that you've been conversing on Twitter all morning when you have a critical deadline to meet.

All of your online profiles should be consistent, updated frequently, and crafted to portray the attributes that encompass a strong professional persona: trustworthiness, sincerity, reliability, enthusiasm, self-sufficiency, and loyalty. Keeping the idea of the professional persona in mind, let's move on to the mechanics of finding a job.

Scoping the Field

Getting a good job in today's economy requires more than just graduating from a good college and hanging out at recruiting fairs. You have to set yourself apart, get their attention, and make them want you.

You probably don't have a lot of time to make this happen. If you're unemployed, you might be cashing in the last of your savings bonds to make your rent, and you need a job ASAP. If you already have a job and are looking for another, you have only so many hours to inconspicuously surf online before your boss figures out what's going on. When you're in your 20s, employment is a catch-22—you need experience to get a job, but you must have a job in order to get that experience. Our forefathers relied on temp agencies to float them through the job-search process. Unfortunately, we don't have that luxury. These days, temp firms are more crowded than a Beyonce concert. You'll sit in their plush waiting rooms for hours, answering personality inventories on your smartphone and proving that you're Windows 8 compliant on an old, slower-than-DSL desktop.

Don't despair, though. Landing a job in the business world is quite achievable with a little ingenuity and preparation. Don't give them a reason to hire you; *dare* them to find a reason *not* to. This is where the concept of the professional persona comes in. Every interaction you have with a company—from your first written communication to your salary negotiation—should exude maturity, professionalism, and competency. You want the employer to say, "Wow, I've never seen a more together candidate. So what if the company is in a hiring freeze? I have to get her on board."

So where do you start? A good first step is to scout out openings commensurate with your level of experience. Here are some places to try:

+ Your college career center and/or alumni network.

+ Online professional networks such as LinkedIn.com.

+ Employment or recruiting agencies—a.k.a. headhunters, or people who get paid by a company to scout out desirable candidates.

+ Company Websites with job postings.

+ Local job fairs.

+ Trade associations.

+ Craig's List (craigslist.org)—hey, you never know.

Keep in mind that most job openings aren't advertised, because a lot of businesses prefer to hire from within the company or through word of mouth. If you're coming in from off the street, you could be out of luck. My friend Jake once tore through New York City in search of a job. In a week, he dropped 200 resumes at a career expo, signed with five recruiting firms, and answered dozens of online job postings. Boy, was he bitter when he was still unemployed after his month-long assault on the New York job market. Jake learned that, unfortunately, being proactive is sometimes not enough. Instead of working harder, work smarter. Use online resources, such as Hoover's (hoovers.com), and business trade publications, such as the *Wall Street Journal*, *New York Times*, *Forbes*, *Fortune*, *BusinessWeek*, *Business Insider*, and *SmartBrief* to target desirable companies in your geographic area. Then, prepare to infiltrate these companies by making the transition from outsider to insider. Here's how:

✦ Get to know individuals already employed at your target company who are in a position to hire you. (See "The Myth of Cover Letters" on page X.)

✦ Apply for an internship position that will land you inside the company and provide you with an opportunity to build your skill portfolio.

✦ Secure referrals from anyone you know in your chosen field—either people with years of experience behind them, such as old professors and your parents' friends, or recent graduates who will have sympathy for your plight and might also be more familiar with a company's lower-level job openings.

Using a combination of these approaches, you are much more likely to gain access to unadvertised job openings in the companies you desire. However, it probably won't happen overnight. Be persistent and don't fall into laziness, even if you're not seeing immediate results. Keep your expectations realistic and remind yourself of the end goal every day. Above all, don't doubt your own abilities. Ignore all of the folks who tell you that the market sucks and that you should take any available job, even if it's not what you want or need. Learn to take rejection with a grain of salt—it's all part of the process. If you take the right action patiently and efficiently, an opportunity will come along that's a good fit for your skill set.

Irresistible Resumes

From the time I was just out of college, employers have told me that I have a terrific resume. If you think this means that my experience has been equally terrific, think again. Hey, when I was applying for my first job, I didn't have any real experience. I imagined the employer scanning the page for something that mattered to him, and realized I had to make my few skills stand out in a way that would immediately grab his attention.

Leanna, 25, California

The purpose of a resume is to land you an interview. Amazon.com has a million books about the best way to write a resume so you can achieve that goal. In my opinion, though, writing an impressive resume is simple if you keep a few things in mind. First, employers never read a resume in its entirety, and I'm willing to bet that the average resume gets read in about five seconds.

My father once told me that employers like numbers and statistics—hard facts that show how a candidate is directly responsible for making a company more profitable. Now let's be real here. If you're still in your early 20s, the chances are not very good that you are at a high enough level to have had sole ownership of a project. However, the chances are excellent that you have had some measurable impact along the way. Did you help with a project that drove company revenue? Was there any piece of that project that you alone were responsible for? Let's examine how this strategy might work for a candidate who is pursuing her first corporate job, and also for someone who has worked in the business world before.

First Corporate Job

Let's say you didn't have corporate internships while you were in college, but you did sell ice cream at Baskin-Robbins for four summers. Maybe, while you were there, you helped the manager execute a campaign to draw in customers from a nearby shopping mall.

Original Statement: Passed out free ice-cream-cone coupons at nearby shopping mall.

Power Statement: Designed and distributed "Snack on Us" coupon targeted to mall shoppers, increasing store traffic by 25 percent.

See why the power statement is better? The original statement makes it look as though you were just a passive body handing out coupons, and the reader is probably thinking that anyone could have done that job. The power statement, however, reads as though you made a significant contribution to the Baskin-Robbins corporation by creating an innovative marketing campaign. Note that the wording of the power statement is still good even if you didn't make the flyer all by yourself. If you had any creative input whatsoever, saying that you designed it bolsters the perception of ownership. The "Snack on Us" labeling also suggests that you were responsible for branding the campaign. With one statement, you have completely changed the reader's perception of your role from ice-cream-shop cashier to small business entrepreneur.

Early Career Move

Suppose you worked as an administrative assistant in a large consulting firm. You were a member of a team that serviced a healthcare account worth $250,000 in monthly fees. Perhaps most of the real account work was left to the senior individuals on the team, but you were responsible for creating and managing the budget spreadsheets.

Original Statement: Created budget spreadsheets for healthcare account.

Power Statement: Managed finances for healthcare account worth $250,000 in monthly fees.

Maybe your contribution to this account was solely administrative. The first statement reads this way. The power statement, however, makes a reader think that you were responsible for managing an enormous amount of company revenue. It says to me that you are extremely trustworthy and that you have a head for complicated finances.

As you can see, the words you choose to communicate your experience make all the difference in whether your resume is considered average or fantastic. In public relations, we call this strategy "spinning," and if you don't think it will work for you, sleep on it. With a little creativity and positive positioning, the most mundane tidbits of experience can become resume jewels.

Spinning is one thing, but you should never lie outright on your resume or fake credentials. Now that this is becoming an increasingly common problem, employers are on high alert, and the risks far outweigh the potential benefits. Here are some other tips that may help your resume through the door.

+ Tailor a resume for each field you are pursuing. Read relevant samples online, and get someone in your targeted industry to review your resume draft and provide feedback.

+ Leave off the objective—it boxes you into a particular position, and it's too easy to sound insincere.

+ Choose the layout that best suits your situation:

  + **Chronological**: Employment history is arranged by the dates you worked for particular companies. (Use this format if you're moving within the same field.)

  + **Functional**: Employment history is arranged by skills and accomplishments. (Use this format if you're changing careers.)

+ Investigate what experience is required for your targeted position, and then illustrate how you fit the bill.

+ List titles that accurately reflect your job description, even if they're not official.

+ Focus on results rather than responsibilities.

+ Use action verbs to qualify achievements (for example, *coordinated* and *evaluated*).

+ Include a section for marketable skills (for example, computer and language skills).

+ Keep the document to one page.

+ Check for typos and inconsistencies in format.

Online services such as Vine (vine.co) and VisualCV (visualcv.com) allow you to take your resume information to a more sophisticated level, but don't let too many bells and whistles detract from the basics. Make sure that all forms of your resume have up-to-date contact information, including a cell phone number and email address. And yes, you need a voicemail greeting for your cell. Replace the cutesy one with a message that is tailored to your most important audience: your potential employer. (See Chapter 5 for voicemail greeting tips.)

The Myth of Cover Letters

Burning the midnight oil to write a spectacular cover letter to send with your resume is not the best use of your time. Why? It's critical that the right people read your materials, and that probably won't happen with a traditional cover letter and resume addressed to a human resources manager. Your resume could be better than Donald Trump's, but if it sits in Mr. HR's inbox for six months, it's useless.

A few years back, when I was looking for a job, I read two resume-writing books cover to cover. After I applied to a bunch of jobs using their advice, I received form letters from 20 percent of the companies and no response at all from the other 80 percent. Desperate, I tried the following method—and got a job offer the first time.

No matter what the recruiters say, the best way to land a job is to communicate directly with the individual who can hire you. It's easier than you think. The first step is to ask everyone you talk to if they know someone at your target company. Inevitably, you'll be chatting with someone at a party and will find out that her sister-in-law works for "Fab Company." Should you find yourself in this situation, don't waste time reflecting on the coincidental nature of the world. It's your lucky day! A lot of experts say that the best way to proceed from here is to ask your party friend if she would feel comfortable introducing you to her sister-in-law. I agree that this is a good idea in principle. The only trouble is, then you have to rely on the party friend to follow through. Instead, maintain control over the process by getting the sister-in-law's name and ask your party friend if she'd mind if you emailed her sister-in-law. She'll probably say yes to your request, because most people like to help someone out. Be sure to thank her profusely. Then go home right away and draft a cordial message resembling the one on page 31.

Ideally, you should use an email address from your own personal domain (such as alex@alexandralevit.com) and not something unprofessional (in other words, NOT awesomepossum@gmail.com). Mention the name of the family member you met at the party in the subject line so that your contact will open the message instead of deleting it with her spam. The tone of the message should not be wishy-washy or vague. Keep it short and sweet, ask for what you want up front, and be specific. Include a signature line with full contact information at the bottom.

Subject: Referred by Jenny Partygoer

Dear Ms. Sister-in-Law:

My name is Jill Jobhunter and I'm a friend of your sister-in-law, Jenny Partygoer. Jenny mentioned that you worked at Fab Company. I'm looking for a new position in Widget Creation, and I believe that Fab Company might be a good fit for my skills and experience.

Might you be willing to have a quick look at my attached resume, and potentially pass it on to someone in your Widget Creation department? I'd be happy to return the favor anytime. Thans so much.

Sincerely,

Jill Jobhunter
Widget Creator
Phone: (312) 555-1212
Email: Jill.Jobhunter@gmail.com
Website: www.jilljobhunter.com

So what happens if you've shouted Fab Company's name from the rooftops and you still can't make a connection to someone who works there? The situation is not hopeless by any means, but you will have to do a little more digging. Call around, look online (LinkedIn is an absolute goldmine), and query trade associations to find the names of people who work in your proposed department. You don't need to locate a senior manager—anybody with a similar job function will do. If you've found a name, but not a corresponding email address, check the company Website or call its reception desk to get the format for email addresses at that organization—you'll find they are usually firstname_lastname@company.com, firstname.lastname@company.com, or firstinitiallastname@company.com. Google the person to find out as much about him as you can, and then craft a short, friendly email introducing yourself and explaining what you're looking for. Here's an example:

Subject: Your press release on Fabcompany.com

Dear Mr. Smith:

I noticed that you handle Widget PR for Fab Company, and I was hoping you could offer me some advice. My name is Jill Jobhunter and I am a marketing communications executive with four years of experience promoting Widgets, and as I will be relocating to Atlanta this fall, I'm hoping you might have a few minutes this week or next to connect via phone and share your knowledge of the PR market down there. If this is a possibility, perhaps you could let me know the best place and time to reach you? I'm happy to return the favor anytime. Thanks so much.

Sincerely,

Jill Jobhunter
Marketing Communications Executive
Phone: (312) 555-1212
Email: Jill.Jobhunter@gmail.com
Website: www.jilljobhunter.com

In your initial communication with Mr. Smith, do not ask him for a job. Rather, gently probe him for information about career opportunities once you're chatting on the phone or have met in person. The point is to establish a personal relationship with Mr. Smith, because, even if he's not the person who would ask you in for an interview, you've now made it inside the company. Mr. Smith probably has the internal contacts to introduce you to the person who can hire you. Perhaps he will forward your information directly, or mention to several of his colleagues that you'll be contacting them.

Even if you can obtain an important person's phone number, I wouldn't call until you've exchanged a few communications via email. For one thing, the chances of getting a higher-level executive on the phone are pretty slim. If the exec doesn't know you, getting past her assistant will be like robbing a casino. Also, leaving a voicemail message has the unsavory intrusiveness of a cold sales call. In the beginning, stick to email—it really is your best opportunity to knock the socks off someone who matters.

Polished Interviews

I left my last job under pretty dismal circumstances. HR had failed to settle an ongoing dispute between me and my boss, so I quit. I was so depressed and unmotivated, I thought of leaving the professional world for good. But then I got an interview opportunity at a really prestigious company in the city, so I dusted off my resumes and went. My interviewer and I bonded immediately. We had been talking for about half an hour when she asked me why I left my last job. She was so nice and understanding that I felt perfectly comfortable telling her everything. I didn't regret it until I got the letter telling me they were hiring someone else.

Olivia, 23, Missouri

The key to stress-free interviewing is to prepare, but not too much. You want to do just enough research so that you know what to expect and can speak intelligently on the points related to your job function, and it helps to jot down a few "wow 'em" facts about the company that you would never know unless you did your homework; however, don't spend too much time on the company's Website that you end up sounding like Wikipedia in the interview.

It's in your best interests to find out as much as you can about the person or people interviewing you so that you know whom you're dealing with. A Google search will prove helpful in this regard. Determine in advance what type of interview you'll be having so that you aren't caught off guard. Will the meeting be one-on-one, or will you be sitting in front of a panel of executives? Will you be asked to consider a real-life business problem? Will any type of written or computer test be required while you're there?

I also recommend putting together an interview portfolio. A portfolio is an online and/or physical display of your business achievements that shows your level of commitment to previous positions. For example, as a marketing communications executive, my portfolio included press releases and business plans I'd written, magazine articles I'd contributed to, and print advertising campaigns I helped develop. A neat and professional portfolio can be an excellent tool to refer to during an interview. Most people outside of creative fields don't bother to create anything like this, but it really does speak volumes about your ability to package yourself.

Although it's a good idea to be conversational during an interview, be careful how much personal information you divulge. There is never a good reason to bad-mouth your previous employer, even if everything you say is justified. While he is listening to your sob story, your prospective employer is thinking how in a year you will be sitting in front of another interviewer complaining about his company. Don't be fooled by an interviewer who seems compassionate. Remember, the two of you are not friends, and the interviewer's first loyalty is to the company he's hiring for. If you are asked why you left a job, answer with a neutral statement, such as, "The commute didn't allow me to spend enough time with my family," or "I wanted to gain experience working in a different industry." Here are some other things to keep in mind as you undergo the interview process.

Pre-Interview:

+ Familiarize yourself with basic interview questions such as "Tell me about yourself." Don't forget doozy interview questions such as "What is your worst quality?"

+ Assess your own skills and career path in the context of the position.

+ Brainstorm three to five of your most important business accomplishments and practice succinctly communicating the challenges and results of each one.

+ Think of some appropriate questions of your own to ask the interviewer.

+ Be careful not to memorize your comments, or they will end up sounding scripted.

The Day of the Interview:

+ Dress in neat, formal business attire: Men should wear a dark suit, solid or pinstripe, with socks that match the pants and a belt that matches the shoes. Women should pair a dark suit with tasteful accessories and non-scuffed heels of a reasonable height.

+ Don't arrive too early or too late.

+ Carry a nice briefcase that looks worn, but not too worn.

+ Begin with a strong handshake.

+ Speak confidently, even if you feel like hurling from nervousness.

+ Avoid talking nonstop without taking time to listen sincerely.

+ Refrain from saying anything negative.

+ Pay attention to nonverbal cues—yours and the interviewer's.

+ Take a moment to think if you don't know an answer immediately.

+ Be prepared for standard interview add-ons such as personality and skills assessment tests and background checks.

+ Let the interviewer bring up the topic of money first.

After the Interview:

+ Write thank-you notes to everyone you spoke to.

+ Follow up with the interviewer for a status on your offer.

The Real Deal

My first job out of college was at a sporting equipment manufacturer. That kind of place attracts a lot of "jocks" and wannabe "jocks." I came into that environment as the smart kid from a good school, and these people felt it was their right to harass me as much as they wanted. I really couldn't relate to my coworkers because they were all married with children. Also, for them, it was just a job, and I was genuinely interested in the technology I was working with. It was a terrible fit. I didn't know until I left that job that the workplace does not have to be like that. At my new company, I found people with similar interests and was able to enjoy my work much more.

Frank, 28, Florida

Many companies have their human resources representatives conduct interviews, but you should try to meet with—or at least speak with—the person who will be your official manager. The reason behind this is pretty simple: if your personalities clash or if you have fundamental differences in the way you work, you need to know immediately so that you can determine if you want to pursue the opportunity further. I'm not saying that one conversation will accurately reflect how your boss will act on the job or that problems won't arise later that were impossible to predict. However, if you hate the person on sight, you should consider whether it's a smart move to work for her.

While you're interviewing, you should also talk to existing employees at the company—preferably those in the department you want to work for. Tactfully learn as much as you can about the organizational culture, or the working environment and politics. Think seriously about whether you could fit in, because you won't be able to have a happy and fruitful career in a place that makes you uncomfortable or doesn't meet your individual needs. Get a sense of the overall mood and morale of the employees, and listen carefully to what they say—and what they don't say. If you think that every employee is going to sing the company's praises just because you came up from HR, you might be surprised. I interviewed at a technology company that really impressed me until two of my potential colleagues told me to leave "before I got sucked in." I didn't take the offer, but I might have if I hadn't taken the time to get the insider's view.

A quick word about interview thank-you notes: Some people think email thank-you letters are enough, but I have to disagree. If you want the company to think you are a "go the extra mile" type of person, start by spending the extra minute it takes to snail mail actual cards.

Airtight References

You just had a successful interview, the employer is about to make you an offer, and then he asks for a few references to reassure himself that he wants to hire you. The operative word here is *reassure*. By the time employers get to the reference stage, their minds are usually made up, and they are just doing their due diligence. That said, you must assume that your references will be called, and, subsequently, grilled about your work experience. So, yes, your references have to be real people, and the contact information you provide for them must be accurate and up to date.

The best references are not your best friend's mother or your favorite elementary school teacher. They also do not include your current boss. I don't care how chummy the two of you are, you don't want your manager to know you're looking for another position. If you've never had a job before, you might ask an internship supervisor or a professor you've worked with to be a reference. If you have been employed, a friend you worked with in the past or a former boss from a job you left under good circumstances are good choices.

Do not give out references' names and contact information without talking to them first. Actually, you should contact potential references at the beginning of your job search and debrief each one on the types of opportunities you're looking for. If they agree to be references, speak to them again immediately after you've given their names to an employer. Let them know that the employer is going to call, and make sure to give them as many specifics about the position as you can. Is there an aspect of your personality, background, or experience that your references should emphasize in order to better your chances? If so, be sure to tell them. Providing your references with the key points you want them to mention will make it easier for them to help you.

Follow up with your references to determine if the employer called them. If they were called, get the rundown on the conversations, and then send each reference a thank-you note. If they weren't, don't freak out. I've heard of employers who ask for references just to make sure you have them—they have no intention of actually speaking with anyone. At any rate, send your references thank-you notes whether they were called or not. You never know when you might need them again.

One last point: It's not necessary to put "References Available Upon Request" on the bottom of your resume. Believe me, if an employer needs references in order to hire you, she'll ask for them.

Negotiation Prowess

The key to a successful salary negotiation is to avoid getting screwed, and to come out smelling like a rose in the process. You also want to make sure you get the most money possible up front, because once you are inside a company, salary increases are few and far between. In order to make this happen, you need to plan ahead. Before you go on an interview, you should have a good idea of what you—and the target job—are worth. If you've just graduated from college, you might not have much choice but to accept whatever entry-level salary the firm pays. If you're scouting for a new job, however, you should check Internet salary sites (salary.com, payscale.com, and so on) to see how much you can command given your level of expertise, your geographic location, and your years of experience. Next, call the target company's human resources department to find out the salary range of the available position. Finally, David Gordon, Director of Internship Studies at Columbia College of Chicago, suggests a few questions to ask yourself prior to discussing your salary with a prospective employer:

+ Are my personal salary requirements in line with the company's range for this position? If not, is there a chance to get more money?

+ What is the lowest salary I will consider?

+ What makes me worth more than what they are offering?

Gordon also notes that you should prepare for objections to your request for more money, including (1) you don't have enough experience, (2) other employees at your level aren't making that much, (3) the budget won't permit it, and (4) that's what they are paying new hires. Think about how you would respond to these objections in a way that continues the discussion on a positive note. Prepare to phrase your comments in the form of questions, keeping in mind that the end goal is to reach an agreement with which both parties are happy.

As I mentioned before, try not to be the first one to mention money in the interview, and avoid giving your salary range, if possible. When the interviewer asks you about your salary, keep your response vague, or ask what the company has budgeted for the position. If you must reveal what you're currently making, inflate the number slightly to account for bonuses, perks, or if you're due for a raise shortly. You should never lie outright about your salary, though, as this can come back to bite you.

After the employer makes an offer, remember to ask about other benefits that might add weight, such as stock options, bonuses, and vacation time. If you're happy with the total package, communicate that to the employer, and ask him if you can have 24 hours to consider it. Next, politely ask for the offer in writing. If you feel you need to negotiate for a higher salary, tread carefully. Gordon advocates the following techniques:

+ Reinforce how much you want to work for the company.

+ Put a human face on the situation.

+ Mention that other opportunities will pay your desired salary.

For example, you might say, "I'm really excited about this position and I think I'm a great fit for the company, but I don't think I could afford to take less than my minimum of $50,000. I have several other opportunities that are in my range, but I'd really prefer to work for you. Is there any way we could work this out?"

Remember that salary ranges are rarely fixed, and once the interviewer has decided she wants to hire you, she will usually meet your request for more money. However, occasionally you might find that great career moves come with a lower price tag. You might be wise to accept an offer that is less money initially, yet pays greater dividends in terms of growth and experience.

Should You Relocate?

When deciding whether or not to accept an offer, relocation may come up as an important issue. Careful consideration of the following three questions will aid your thought process.

1. Would you move there anyway?

If this job didn't exist, is the area in question a place you'd ever want to go? Think about what your regular daily routine will be like in the new location. Do the pace of life and the amenities appeal to you? How about the people, the culture, the weather, and the traffic? Remember that a job is only one aspect of your life, and even work that you enjoy won't be enough to overcome the distress of being stuck in a locale that's not a good fit.

2. How much will it cost you?

Your new organization may or may not pay relocation costs (moving company, temporary housing, and so on), but a more important issue is whether you can afford to live in the new city. How does your proposed salary compare with the cost of living? For example, $75,000 goes a lot further in Columbus, Ohio, than it does in Chicago, Illinois. Ideally, you should be able to pay your monthly expenses while saving a decent amount for retirement. In this day and age, living paycheck to paycheck is simply not sustainable.

3. What are your long-term opportunities in this new organization and city?

Relocating is serious business, and it's not something you want to do repeatedly in a matter of a few years. So before taking the plunge, you want to be sure that your new position offers strong professional development and the probability of advancement. In the event that things don't work out the way you hope, will you be able to secure gainful employment in your industry and at your level? No matter how great your new company is, you don't want to put all of your eggs in one basket, and your career prospects will simply not be the same in a rural or declining area as they are in a major metropolitan area.

Should You Work for Free?

At the start of your career, you might be considering taking an internship or volunteer position to break ground in a new industry, or working for free so that you can develop relationships with clients who may eventually pay you.

If this is your situation, you should be aware that unpaid internships have come under legal fire recently, with the U.S. courts ruling that media giants Fox Searchlight Pictures and Hearst Corp broke the law by not compensating their interns financially.

According to the U.S. Department of Labor, for an unpaid internship at a for-profit employer to be lawful, it should pass a six-point test. Among the requirements, the employer must derive "no immediate advantage from the activities of the intern," and the intern must not "displace regular employees, but (work) under close supervision of existing staff." In addition, the internship must be "similar to training which would be given in an educational environment."

That said, the protocol for non-profit organizations, small businesses, and consultants is far less clear, and working for free in these organizations may be a viable option for you. When deciding whether or not to work for no pay, you should first determine if you can afford it. What is your family's financial situation, and are you gainfully employed in another role? It's also smart to assess—specifically—how each position will deliver value in terms of your long-term prospects. Don't be afraid to ask the person with whom you are working for free. Contrary to what some believe, most people are not interested in exploiting workers and will be open to discussions about what's in it for you.

The proposed time commitment is an important factor too. Those who are employed should not devote more than 20 to 25 hours a week to an unpaid gig, or they risk burning out or short-changing the job that pays the bills.

If you have limited experience in the field, the person watching over your work during an unpaid gig may play it safe by giving you small tasks. Don't let her. Get involved with as many large, complex projects as possible, and jump at the opportunity to challenge yourself, master new skills, and be exposed to people who perform a variety of roles.

When the end of your volunteer stint draws near, think about whether you want to pursue a full-time, paid opportunity in the new field or with the contacts you've made. If nothing arises right away, actively keep in touch with the people you've met through email, social networks, or, even better, occasional in-person get-togethers.

Should You Hire a Career Coach?

Twenty-somethings ask me all the time if they should get a career coach. Usually this comes at a time when their job search is taking longer than they anticipated and they are starting to wonder if they are doing the right things.

My answer is usually that it can't hurt, but coaches cost money, so if you are going to hire someone you should get as much out of it as possible. Ask around for a referral or find one through the International Coach Federation (coachfederation.org). Before you sign on, review the best coaching practices on the ICF's Website to ensure that your coach is qualified and that you know what to expect from the process. Interview your prospective coach or ask for a trial session first so that you can determine if he is someone with whom you feel comfortable and challenged.

Give coaching the time and attention it deserves, and set concrete goals with your coach as quickly as possible so that you can begin feeling a sense of accomplishment. Don't shy away from discomfort, and keep the lines of communication open so that your coach can help you work through emotional roadblocks that may arise.

As the majority of coaching engagements last between six and 12 months, you and your coach should work together to determine an appropriate end point. If a coach has done her job well, then you won't be dependent on her and will be able to continue working effectively on your own.

Breaking Your Dependence on Your Parents

Back when I graduated from college, it was a sin—and an utter sign of failure—to move back in with the 'rents. But the times, they are a-changin'.

Thanks to last decade's recession, college students started moving back in with their parents in record numbers. According to various studies, the number of 18- to 34-year-olds currently living at home hovers around 40 percent.

Look, I'm not going to tell you to move out immediately if your financial situation is dire, but I *will* tell you not to get too comfortable. The longer you live with your parents, the more you delay your own progression into real-life adulthood. And if you want to have a spouse, children, and a healthy 401k, you don't have a decade to wait. Every personal and professional decision you make now should relate to the goal of getting your own place as soon as possible.

Whether you live with your parents or not, they are probably your friends, and you may well speak to them multiple times a day. It's terrific to have this kind of support system when you're getting a career off the ground, but do not let it go too far.

I am fond of the true story of an HR rep who had to throw out an application because the candidate's mother had accidentally written her name on it instead of the candidate's. Your parents should not be filling out your job applications, guys. They should also not be accompanying you to interviews, calling hiring managers to negotiate your salary, or stepping in when you have a problem with a colleague. In fact, as far as employers are concerned, your parents should be completely invisible.

If you are in the habit of asking your parents for advice on every major and minor decision, you should practice stepping away from the smartphone. As we'll talk about in Chapter 5, effective problem-solving is an important part of a successful career, and the longer your parents serve as a crutch, the longer you'll delay your development.

What I Wish I'd Known

One of my past jobs was at a retail behemoth with a cutthroat culture. During the interview, I kept noticing current staff being curt with each other, but I put it out of my mind because the company was really prestigious. I just wanted them to like me, and I didn't stop to think about whether I liked them. Of course I took the position and regretted it when, after a month or so, they began to treat me like they treated everyone else. Today I'd tell my 25-year-old self to pay closer attention to signals that a company isn't going to be a great place to work, and to remember that interviewing for fit should be done on both sides.

Luke, 38, Kentucky

Take-Home Points

✦ **Explore your career options.** Before putting yourself on the job market, take the time to fully investigate career options that will utilize your skills, interests, and personal mission.

✦ **Promote yourself.** Think of yourself as a publicist with the task of promoting you. Learn to capitalize on your skills and succinctly assert your achievements.

✦ **Learn to network.** Don't base your job search solely on advertised openings. Increase your chances of landing interviews by personally connecting with individuals within your target companies.

✦ **Create a professional persona.** Project a strong persona (your most mature, competent, and friendly face) throughout the job search, application, interview, and negotiation processes.

Chapter 2

Congratulations, You're Hired!

What a relief! Your job search is officially over. You've accepted an offer and have agreed to start the following Monday. Resist the urge to become complacent. Between now and the end of your first month on the job, it is critical that you skillfully wield your professional persona to make a stellar impression. Although it may sound intimidating, transitioning into a new work situation is fairly easy once you know what you need to do. This chapter will walk you through the actions you should take prior to your start date and during your first few weeks on the new job. Here I'll also cover some new-employee essentials that will help you be successful, such as decoding office lingo and getting past human resources.

The Start Before the Start

Maybe you're thinking, "There's nothing I can do until I actually get there, right?" Not true. If you didn't interview with the person who will be your immediate supervisor, contact her immediately. Send an introductory email, and while you're at it, ask her if she has any materials you can review that will better prepare you for your first day. Has your new company been in the news lately? Include a line in your letter that shows you've been keeping up. This short note will probably take 10 minutes to compose and will do wonders for your boss's preliminary perception of you as a competent and proactive new hire.

If your manager sends materials, be sure to read them carefully. Common sense, right? Well, sad to say, I was caught with my pants down when, on my first day of a new job, my manager asked me a question about the annual report he'd mailed. I'd only skimmed the report and didn't have it in front of me, so I choked. Maybe you are a better BS-er than me, but knowing the facts can never hurt—especially in a new work situation. Also, if your new manager mentions any important team meetings or conference calls that will take place before your first day, volunteer to join them via phone or Skype. This might be difficult to do when you're still sitting at your desk in your old company, but try to swing it if you can. Your new colleagues will be impressed to see you involved before you're on the company's clock, and, next thing you know, everyone on the team will be looking forward to your start date.

Camille Lavington, a personal marketing consultant and author of *You've Only Got Three Seconds*, says that when you first meet someone, you only have three seconds to make an indelible impression. The moment an individual sees you, he evaluates your clothing, hairstyle, grooming habits, facial cues, and posture. Without even thinking about it, he'll decide whether he wants to get to know you better and whether you are worthy of being taken seriously. No matter what you say from that point on, his opinion of you will be heavily influenced by his initial perception. Three seconds is not a lot of time. Plus, during your first day at a new job, you will meet a lot of people who are important to your future success. You will also have to cope with one major disadvantage that you can't do anything about: your age. Even if you alter your appearance or demeanor, you will probably still look like a twenty-something. Some people will expect you to act flaky, immature, or entitled because you are young, and the burden is on you to prove them wrong. Needless to say, you'll want to prepare for these challenges before you arrive.

Looking the Part

Like it or not, most of the professional world is conservative at heart. On your first day, show up wearing a clean and neatly tailored suit in an appropriate color such as black or navy blue, even if the rest of the company dresses in business casual. You might be overdressed, but I guarantee no one will criticize you for it. Rather, your colleagues will respect that you mean business, and your boss will be proud to introduce you around the company. Besides, isn't it easier to act professionally when you look the part? I know that when I'm sitting down to a meeting and I'm wearing khakis, I sometimes forget to cross my legs. I never do that when I'm wearing a suit. If your company is business casual, you can taper off the suit-wearing after a week or so. However, if the dress is mixed, I suggest staying with the suit. You'll be able to compete with the best-dressed people in the company, you'll appear older, and you'll look like a million bucks when you run into the CEO in the elevator. A colleague once told me that if I dressed like the VPs, I would become one faster because people would be able to picture me in a higher position.

I've also heard that women primarily look at shoes and jewelry when evaluating other women. Don't have a lot of money? I recommend investing in three good pairs of dress shoes and a few pieces of simple but high-quality gold jewelry. If you're afraid your commute will kill your feet, wear sneakers on the way to work and change before stepping into your office building.

The best advice I have for guys is to shave often, don't wear ties that scream for attention, and don't knock people over with your cologne. And forgive me for saying this, but lose any visible body piercings. I know it's not fair, but the fact is that a man wearing an earring has a certain connotation in the professional world, and something that tiny should not be allowed to compromise your professional persona. For the same reason, both genders should cover up obvious tattoos.

In recent years, twenty-something employees have been guilty of taking business casual dress codes to new extremes of casual. Folks, "business casual" should be defined as something you might wear to a place of worship—for example, a knee-length skirt, a short-sleeve blouse, and dress sandals for a woman and a pair of chinos and a polo shirt for a man. Jeans, flip-flops, T-shirts that advertise, and in general anything wrinkled, stained, torn, or too revealing of certain body parts should be reserved for a Sunday afternoon football game in your living room.

In addition to being vigilant about your style of clothing, you should watch your use of workplace accessories. Once upon a time, I carried a chewed pen around to all my meetings, until a coworker lightly asked me if my pen tasted good. I never made that mistake again!

Meeting and Greeting

The day I started a new job in event planning, my department was preparing for our annual conference in Philadelphia. We were on our hands and knees stuffing customer information packets the whole day, and by 7 p.m., my new suit was impossibly wrinkled, my stockings had a run, and I was flustered beyond belief. My boss told me our group head wanted to meet me, so I made a quick pit stop at the bathroom to freshen up and calm myself down. I took a deep breath and walked confidently into the group head's office, smiling and looking as relaxed as if I was on a cruise. Later, my boss told me that the group head was really impressed with me. I asked how this was possible, considering he had just met me, and my boss said that the group head felt that anyone who could be so together after such an insane first day must be a good find. That brief interaction set a positive tone for my relationship with the big boss from that point forward.

Marisol, 29, Maryland

Your first week at a new job will be a whirlwind of new people and situations. When I jumped from an office with 300 people to one with more than 3,000, I was so confused, I had trouble remembering anyone's name for a few weeks. Nevertheless, as I mentioned previously, the first few moments of interaction between you and other people will shape their appraisal of you. So when you are introduced to new colleagues, remember to make eye contact, smile, and shake their hands firmly. Ask them their names, and find out what they do for the company. Jot these things down quickly, along with anything else that might help you remember them. Engage in small talk freely if the conversation goes that way, staying away from thorny political issues that could get you into trouble. Show that you are interested in them by paying them sincere compliments or asking appropriate personal questions.

In these first conversations, the goal is to project enthusiasm, confidence, and an aura of respect—no matter whom you're meeting. I've seen new people come into a company and put their best face on for the executives, while disregarding everyone else. This is not smart. A professional persona is nothing if not consistent. Besides, you won't know who the company influencers are at the beginning. It's a good bet to pay special attention to administrative assistants. These individuals tend to have the executives' ears, and they know how to work the system. When meeting or dealing with "admins," be polite or even deferential. They may turn out to be the most important allies you have in the company.

If your manager doesn't send an email welcoming you to the department, it's a nice gesture for you to introduce yourself this way. The message should be no more than a few lines containing a brief summary of your background and stating how happy you are to be working there. Create an email signature, and add it to your outgoing messages so that your colleagues can note your full name, title, and contact information.

Decoding Office Lingo

If you thought everyone in the professional world spoke your language, think again. The business world's language is one of subtlety, filled with euphemisms and pet phrases to cleverly disguise what people actually mean. Because you wouldn't visit a foreign country without a translator app, I've provided some phrases here that should assist you at the beginning of your journey.

Phrase: "I've got too much on my plate."

What it means: This person has too much work to do or is trying to look as though she has too much work to do, so someone else will have to take on any new assignments.

Phrase: "I just wanted to close the loop."

What it means: This person has made progress on an issue you were involved in and is, thankfully, keeping you informed.

Phrase: "Let's assess the team's bandwidth."

What it means: This person is trying to find out how much work everyone has to do, probably so she can delegate a new assignment to the person who is least busy.

Phrase: "You and I are not on the same page."

What it means: This person does not agree with you or there is a communication breakdown regarding the best way to proceed with a project.

Phrase: "I'm in crisis mode."

What it means: The person is stressed about a matter that may or may not be urgent. Either way, she does not want to be bothered.

Phrase: "I'm just calling to touch base."

What it means: This person wants to give you an update on a project or needs to ask you to do something for her.

Phrase: "Don't forget to CYA." (a.k.a. "Cover Your Ass")

What it means: This person wants you to take action to ensure that you are not blamed for something.

Phrase: "FYI..." (a.k.a. "For Your Information")

What it means: This person is indicating to you that you will be held accountable for whatever information she is about to impart.

Phrase: "We're going to have to think outside the box."

What it means: This person has received instructions from higher up to make sure that a great deal of thought goes into a project, and the pressure is on you to come up with something creative that is different from what has always been done.

Phrase: "Someone dropped the ball."

What it means: This person is absolving themselves of responsibility for a failing project and is implicating someone else on the team. Hopefully the "someone else" isn't you.

Phrase: "You're on the fast track."

What it means: This person is telling you that you have great potential and will probably be promoted quickly.

Phrase: "Let's take it offline."

What it means: This person wants to talk with you privately in an effort to either keep things confidential or stop wasting everyone else's time.

Phrase: "Better keep this on your radar."

What it means: This person is implying that she plans to forget what she is about to tell you as soon as the words come out of her mouth. You, on the other hand, are responsible for keeping it top of mind and following up appropriately.

Phrase: "We need to first capture the low-hanging fruit before getting to the heavy lifting."

What it means: This person wants to get the easy stuff over with before moving on to actual work.

Phrase: "Let's leverage this best practice to add value and impact our bottom line."

What it means: Whoa, a quadruple whammy! You'll usually find jargon-filled sentences like these in strategic documents, such as business plans. For simplicity's sake, let's break this one down:

Leverage = recycle previous work

Best practice = how everyone else is doing it

Add value = justify a program's existence

Impact bottom line = make money

So in other words: "We must take advantage of the fact that someone has already come up with a working concept that everyone in the company buys into. You should use this concept to convince the higher-ups that your project will make the company money."

Settling In

When I showed up to my new office, there was a problem with my Internet connection, and I couldn't get my system up and running for the entire week. I was actually pretty annoyed, but there was no way in hell I was going to show it. I called the help desk a thousand times, and because I was always polite and grateful, I ended up being good friends with the guy. Now, whenever I have a computer issue, I know I'll be his first priority.

Micah, 23, Texas

Imagine being shown to your new office—a windowless cubicle. A dead plant is there to greet you, along with crumbs of dirt all over the carpet. The lightbulbs are burned out and you don't see your assigned laptop anywhere. Welcome to the business world! Don't be offended that your new organization didn't take the time to set up a nice workspace for you; just move on. The first thing to do (after cleaning up the crumbs, of course) is to procure your digital devices and ensure they are in working order so that people can get in touch with you immediately. Once your voice mail is functional, leave a short, friendly, and professional greeting. Speak slowly and block out as much background noise as possible.

Next, it's time to get some office supplies, so make your way over to the admin's desk. Proceed with caution. No matter what your level in the company, do not assume that it is the admin's responsibility to order your supplies. Ask her how you can order them, and see what she says. Pouting if you have to do it yourself is not a good idea. Look at it this way: at least now you can get those nifty dry erase markers you like!

Hooray, now it's time to decorate! Just keep in mind that, although your cube or office is the space you work in, it belongs to the company. It's fine to place a few framed photographs on your desk and/or pictures on the walls, but don't overdo it. Put all other personal items, including personal paperwork, in a single desk drawer that you can lock at night. You never know when your boss will need something from you after hours, and will take it upon himself to come looking for it. Also, be careful how much food you keep in your cube or office. Laugh if you want, but you don't want to be the one blamed for the mouse that sends 30 colleagues screaming into the hallway.

Plan strategically how you want to organize your desk. I know a lot of people who believe that having a cyclone of a desk makes them look as though they are so busy that they just can't keep up with the work raining down on them. That may be true, but it also makes them look terribly disorganized. Being neat and efficient is part of your professional persona, so even if you're the brilliant "absentminded professor" type, you might want to modify your habits. Create practical online and offline filing systems that allow easy access to regular materials and can be used readily should a coworker need to take over a project. Remove documents from your mailbox and email inbox as soon as you are finished with them, and write notes using the old-school dry-erase board or the new-school Evernote (evernote.com) to avoid a sticky-pad explosion. I think you'll find that keeping order is easy if you start at the beginning, before documents start flooding in.

Espionage

Whether you're thrown headfirst into a project or left alone to stare at the walls of your cubicle, the most important thing you can do at the beginning of a new job is to pay attention. You don't have to be a CIA operative to harness the power of smart observation. Simply keep your eyes and ears open, and you will become an expert at mastering the organizational culture of which you are now a part. I know you're eager to let the company know who you are and what you're all about, but keep in mind that the most successful employees are the ones who effectively assimilate into their company's culture.

Do your best to lay low in the beginning. Take the time to study every aspect of your new organization, including how people present themselves, how they work together, and how they interact with executives, managers, and clients. What are the written and unwritten rules of engagement? It's particularly useful to watch how employees conduct non-company business during the workday so that you can get a sense of how personal breaks, email, and phone calls will be tolerated. As you learn, begin to adapt your behavior and work style to suit the work environment.

Examine your company's Website, annual report, and recruiting materials for clues about its mission, goals, image, and values. Is your company more focused on forging ahead in the market or delivering superior customer service? Is the culture guided by competition or cooperation? Is it more important for employees to be solely focused on hardcore business realities or to be well-rounded in their professional and personal lives? If these things are difficult to determine through written materials, you may need to scope out your work area. On my first day at a Fortune 500 company, for example, I noticed a book of photographs on my boss's desk. The book, which my company had produced, featured pictures of children in the on-site daycare center. The following week, area schools were closed. I was not surprised to see my colleagues bringing their children into work for a company-sponsored holiday camp. In no time at all, I had become aware of the importance of family in that culture.

Remember that although the professional world is the same in many ways, cultures vary dramatically from organization to organization. Just because it was perfectly acceptable to order snacks for an afternoon brainstorming session at your old place of business doesn't mean that your new boss will consider this to be a legitimate expense. Developing a good understanding of your new company's culture will unquestionably serve you well as you look for ways to make a contribution.

Operating the HR Machine

The first time I had to fill out a W-2 form, I had no idea what I was doing. I was too embarrassed to ask about it at orientation, so I just fudged it. Unfortunately, come tax time, I owed the government a whole lot of money because I had mistakenly put down that I had a dependent. I wasn't planning on this expense at all and I ended up having to borrow money from my parents.

Brian, 22, Louisiana

When you're grooming your professional persona for a multitude of new colleagues and spying on the company culture, doing right by the human resources department may seem like the least of your challenges. If you're tempted to think about it this way, just remember that HR hired you, and they also have the power to make trouble for you, if so inclined. Learning the ropes early in your career with a company won't take much time, but it will inevitably save you major headaches later on.

The New Hire Folder

On your first day, you will probably be asked to fill out a "Hello, My Name Is" sticker and show up to an orientation for new hires. This event will typically feature overly enthusiastic guest speakers, generic orientation videos, and a tedious page-by-page review of a mountain of paperwork. You will leave the building at the end of the day, head spinning, with an information packet. Your first instinct might be to toss it in the dumpster on the way to your car. But, instead, you must take the folder home and re-read every word. If your organization is tree-friendly and all of its new hire information is online, you are not excused. Pop open that browser and get to it.

HR has probably asked you to immediately sign a few legal documents. One will be a tax form that the company needs in order to pay you, a second might be a non-compete agreement (stating that if you leave the company you won't go to work for a competitor for a set period of time), and a third could be a confidentiality agreement (stating that you won't share the company's proprietary information). It's important to understand what these documents say, so ask someone to help you if you have to. Getting these documents back to HR the next day will serve several purposes: You won't lose or forget about them, your assimilation into the community will be hassle-free, you will look like a responsible and efficient employee to the "Job Gods" in HR, and you will erase any chance of anyone going to your boss in order to collect your delinquent paperwork.

The new hire folder often includes an employee handbook that outlines company policies, such as initial performance review periods, compensation, dress code, smoking and drugs, sexual harassment, and company benefits. Treat this book as though it's your new best friend for a few days. Don't leave it on the train, and avoid the urge to stuff it in a desk drawer without reading it. Again, if it's online, you should still peruse it in detail.

True story: My friend Zach, who worked for a Fortune 500 telecommunications company, was fired after an HR representative caught him smoking on company grounds. Zach was outside the building at the time, but his company had a zero-tolerance smoking policy, which was covered in the employee handbook. Although his company's reaction was extreme, Zach was dismissed legally and couldn't do anything about it. The best way to steer clear of these situations is to know where you stand from the get-go.

The Perks

Time Off

Fewer aspects of your job are as important as the number of days you get to spend away from it, so you should read and understand your vacation policy up front. Many companies give a standard two weeks per year for new employees, but policies on personal days, paid holidays, sick and bereavement leave, and short-term and long-term disability leave vary. Some businesses also limit the amount of vacation time you can take during your first few months of employment. I accepted my first job six weeks before my college graduation, and, lo and behold, two days before I was scheduled to take off for the ceremony, I ran into a snag with HR because I hadn't cleared unauthorized vacation days ahead of time. By the way, unless you do not have any other choice, don't plan any vacations during your first three months with a company. Remember your professional persona and consider how jetting off to the Caribbean within weeks of your start date will look to company veterans who haven't taken a vacation in two years.

Flexible Work Schedules

The U.S. Bureau of Labor Statistics reports that about a quarter of employed Americans work from home some hours each week. In a recent study by the Families and Work Institute, 63 percent of employers said they allowed employees to work remotely, up from 34 percent in 2005. Even Marissa Mayer, the new Yahoo! CEO who banished telecommuting from company policy last year, can't stop this train.

Flextime arrangements might include part-time or compressed schedules (for example, the employee works 40 hours from Monday to Thursday and takes Friday off) and job sharing, in which a full-time position is split between two people. Teleworking or telecommuting, of course, means that, for at least part of the business week, an employee works from a remote location, often the home.

Talk with HR and/or read your orientation materials to understand how your organization's flextime procedure works. Note that even if the company doesn't have an official policy in place, if there are other people in your department who are already working flexible schedules, it shouldn't be unreasonable for you to hop on the bandwagon—provided you can honestly say you have the self-discipline to work productively without supervision. This last point is a critical one. You must know yourself and your job well enough to be able to accurately judge if telecommuting is a viable alternative.

In making an argument for flex time, always put the company first. For example, if you want to work from home one day per week, tell your boss that you plan to get more work done in less time due to the minimization of distractions and not having to commute. Ask for a trial of the new arrangement, and prove the cost savings by working much more efficiently on that home day than you do during your in-office days. Make sure that you are always accessible via email and smartphone during the business day, and report project status often so it's easy for your boss to keep tabs on you.

Medical Benefits

In our 20s, we're accustomed to abusing our bodies and getting away with it. Given that we never get sick and think we're going to live forever, it's easy to take health benefits for granted. However, because group insurance plans and flexible spending accounts (which allow you to deposit part of your salary, pretax, into a special account for medical expenses) are notoriously complicated, it's in your best interests to scope out the lay of the land in case you urgently need a health service. Familiarize yourself with the benefits you are entitled to and make sure you review your coverage in depth before heading to the doctor's or dentist's office. Trust me, it's well worth your time, because once you make a claim the insurance people decline to cover, squabbling with them quickly becomes a frustrating and time-consuming process. Also, playing tug-of-war with an HMO during office hours or inviting your HR benefits administrator to referee are not optimal strategies for minding your professional reputation.

Financial Benefits

Are there ways your company will contribute to your care and feeding beyond the bi-monthly paycheck? Yes, indeed. Most companies offer a 401(k), which allows employees to contribute a portion of tax-free income to a savings account. The company will also match a percentage of your contribution, which you get to keep if you stay there an allotted period of time. I could devote an entire book to a discussion about 401(k) plans, but instead I'll share a few tips for leaving your financial future in the hands of your new company:

- Pay close attention to the instructions for rolling over your retirement funds from one company's 401(k) plan to the next. Because you will likely have several jobs throughout the course of your career, you want your hard-earned savings to transition smoothly.

- Most plans offer a variety of fund-distribution options, so you should avoid placing 100 percent of your savings in your company's stock. In these uncertain times, your financial future should not depend on your company's stability.

✦ Find out how long you have to be employed with a company in order to be vested, or qualified to receive a percentage of your company's contribution to your retirement fund. This piece of data could make a difference when deciding whether to stay with a company three full years or two years and 11 months.

If you work for a public company (a corporation that issues shares of stock to members of the general public), you might be lucky enough to get stock options. A stock option gives an employee the right to buy or sell shares of company stock at a specific price for a specific period of time. You can typically get an excellent deal on your company's stock by exercising options—but tread carefully. Some employee stock purchase plans have stringent requirements for exercising options, including narrow windows during which you can buy or sell your stock.

Expense Reports

You might think this one is a no-brainer. You spend money on behalf of your company, and then HR pays you back, right? Unfortunately, business expense reimbursement can be fraught with peril. On the one hand, you want to get what's owed you. On the other hand, you must also care for your reputation by keeping company expenses down.

Because navigating most expense-report software programs is a chore, get to know your company's tools before you have items to submit. You should also find out early if job-related expenses must be charged on a particular credit card, or if you are required to use certain vendors in order to be reimbursed. When traveling or eating out on the company's dollar, choose the middle-of-the-road option instead of the most expensive. Most importantly, don't pad your expense reports. Read your policy in detail to determine what you will be reimbursed for, and don't submit anything that doesn't meet these requirements. And please don't lie. As enticing as it is to take your significant other out to dinner on the company after you return from a business trip, don't do it. The $50 you will spend today is a drop in the bucket compared to the months of salary you'll lose if you're caught.

Access Plans

Depending on your position, your new company might offer to pick up the tab for your smartphone and/or tablet. Joining the company plan can save you big bucks, but you should be prepared for calls and minute usage to be monitored. By paying for your devices, your company assumes that you will be using them for business. If you regularly run up international and roaming charges calling your family in Greece or your friend who owns a dude ranch in Montana, you should probably keep a personal phone as well.

Now that you understand your company's policies, it's time to bid adieu to the Job Gods and get to work. In general, the less HR is reminded of your existence, the better. Think of HR as a sleeping baby you don't want to disturb. Go about your business doing what you're supposed to do, but keep the noise level to a minimum.

On the Clock

During my first week at a financial consulting firm, I didn't have much work to do yet, so I decided to run out and catch up on the errands I'd missed while I was job hunting. I guess I ran over my lunch hour a few times, but I knew I'd be working 80 hours a week soon, so I didn't worry about it. Sure enough, within a few weeks, I was so busy I always ate lunch at my desk. So naturally, I was pretty surprised when my boss brought up attendance as an item of concern in my initial review. That first week, he'd seen me leaving the office a lot during business hours—but he hadn't paid attention to anything since then!

Kyra, 24, Ontario

One of my favorite managers used to say that perception is reality, and there is nothing stronger than a perception formed on the basis of a first impression. Whether you have a clock-watcher as a boss or not, it's crucial that you are on your best behavior during your first month at a new job. Be aware that everyone is watching you, so make sure to arrive on time for work. It's not a bad idea to be seen eating lunch at your desk a few times so that your coworkers keep that image in their minds. If you do go out, don't run over the allotted hour, and refrain from midday workouts at the gym until you're well established at the company.

At the end of the day, carefully watch what time people in your department leave the office. You should aim to depart at the midpoint. You don't want to be the first one out the door, but if you're the last one, you'll set a precedent that you are willing to work late for the rest of your days at that company. Also, because many employers think they are entitled to work twenty-something employees to death, make sure your boss and colleagues see early on that you have a life outside business hours.

In this age of instant accessibility, flexible workplaces, and virtual teams, it may seem ridiculous that anyone should be chained to a desk between 9 and 5 every Monday through Friday, but if your company is one that's still rigid about physical attendance, you may not have a choice. My friend Harry told me that his company's CEO stood at the window of his corner office and watched to see how many cars rolled through the gate one minute after 9 a.m. Remember that half the battle is showing up, so don't get caught on someone's attendance radar.

If you are fortunate to have a flextime policy, don't take advantage. Work the requisite number of hours, and while you're on the clock, either in the office or at home, stay busy doing the company's business. This includes resisting the temptation to be navigating between two Pinterest windows, your Facebook profile, and Spotify. I hear that you are an excellent multi-tasker, but your boss, who could be looking over your shoulder, doesn't know you that well yet. Staying away from distractions will be difficult in the beginning, particularly because most managers have no clue what to do with new employees—it's too late to involve you in an existing project, they do not trust you to handle anything that's on fire, or they do not have time to show you the ropes. Nevertheless, you don't have to sit at your desk twiddling your thumbs. Offer assistance to your managers and colleagues, and if anyone takes you up on the offer, make sure you do a better job than expected.

Inevitably, your days at a new job will involve administrative work in some shape or form. If you're a recent graduate, there is a good chance the company sold you on using your existing skills to do meaningful work. Therefore, you are probably insulted to be answering phones for the price of a college education. My best advice is to think of your time as an administrative assistant as a rite of passage. Everyone must do it, and by the time you emerge from your mountain of executive emails, you will appreciate the mundane tasks that go into running a business, and you will also have the knowledge and experience to contribute in a consequential way. If you're a mid-level employee and someone requests that you assist with administrative work, do it with a smile. Yes,

I realize that you paid your dues a long time ago, but that person might not know you blistered your fingers making 7 million photocopies as an admin. Trust me, you won't be doing it forever. Provided you command a higher salary than an admin, the company will want to leverage your skills elsewhere.

When your manager involves you in a project that includes coworkers, don't jump in and take over. Do more than your share of listening and ask for direction from your teammates rather than suggesting your own course of action. Nothing turns people off like a newbie who waltzes in and says, "Well, at my old company, we did it like this." The second this comes out of your mouth, people will think that if things were so swell at your old company, maybe you should go back. This is the last thing you want. For the sake of your professional persona, use your first projects as an opportunity to observe how things are done at your new company. You'll have your time in the sun soon enough.

During your first weeks, be especially careful about using company resources such as FedEx and international calling for personal reasons. Use any free time to research your position and brainstorm project concepts. Reading is fine too, but keep the content to industry publications, human resources material, or anything related to the company or your job. Show your boss what you've learned by sharing ideas, highlighting key points in printed articles, and asking questions. She will think that you are hungry and prepared to hit the ground running—which, my friend, is exactly how stellar reputations are made.

20 Tips for Road Warriors

Your new position may require business travel, and the first time your boss tells you that you're shipping out of town, you'll probably jump for joy. After all, this is exciting stuff. Not only will you be escaping the office, but you'll also be spending your company's dime to sleep in a king-sized bed by yourself and sample cuisine from a new city's finest restaurants. And don't forget about those free mini-shampoos in the hotel!

After a while, the magic of business travel wears off. You find that your trips away from the office involve working more hours, not less. You return, exhausted, with a bag full of dry cleaning and a week's worth of emails to catch up on. But for better or worse, business travel is a part of life for many corporate employees. Here are a few tips to make your trips more bearable.

1. **Revisit your company's expense rules.** Expense policies are riddled with fine print and change constantly. Some companies won't allow you to take a taxi to the airport. Others won't pay for your lunch because you'd be buying it yourself if you were in the office.

2. **Keep a bag packed at home.** You never know when you're going to need to travel out of town on short notice. Prevent frazzled, last-minute rushing around by keeping a travel bag packed and ready to go in your closet. Besides a suit and comfortable business shoes, include toiletries, regular medications, mints, business cards, and power cords for your devices.

3. **Remember your professional persona.** "Out of the office" does not mean "off the job." Resist the urge to let your hair down and party during a business trip. There's nothing wrong with having fun, but you should behave appropriately, no matter whom you're with or what you're doing. You never know who's watching.

4. **Review your itinerary ahead of time.** Go over your schedule to make sure you know where you're supposed to be at all times and how you're going to get there. Leave large time cushions in between each activity so that you can make it from one place to the next without having a heart attack.

5. **Sign up for a frequent flyer account.** Frequent flyer miles are the best way to make your business travel hassles pay off. For example, my husband and I went to Australia on miles we earned traveling for our respective jobs. While you're at it, make sure the credit card you use for business is linked to a frequent flyer program too.

6. **Print out important materials.** You never know when your laptop is going to decide to have a temper tantrum. Technology often fails us on business trips, so if you really need something for a meeting, carry both hard and virtual copies.

7. **Assign colleagues to share your workload.** Keep the machine running by making a detailed list of tasks you need covered while you're gone and delegating each one to a trusted colleague. Set up your email and voicemail systems with an "Out of the Office" message, complete with emergency contact information.

8. **Pack necessities in your carry-on bag.** Once your Samsonite disappears down the conveyor belt and into that black hole, you can't

control where it ends up. Of course, 99 percent of the time, your baggage will make it safely to your destination. Even so, have a contingency plan, just in case.

9. **Block out the noise.** A good night's sleep is imperative to your effectiveness on a business trip. Regardless of where you're going, assume that your hotel will be louder than a big city apartment building, and pack earplugs or download a white noise app like "Relax and Sleep" to one of your devices.

10. **Carry snacks and a bottle of water.** In the alternate universe known as business travel, something as simple as eating can turn into a complex task you can't be bothered with. In case you have to miss a meal, tide yourself over with a granola or protein bar. And don't forget to stay hydrated, especially when you're flying.

11. **Dress up, not down.** When you're attending meetings in unfamiliar surroundings, wear business-appropriate attire. Even if the folks you're meeting with are dressed casually, no one will fault you for being the only one in a suit. Pack your clothes in a garment bag and use the iron in your hotel room to keep your attire looking neat and wrinkle-free.

12. **Roll your laptop.** Save yourself an excruciating backache by rolling a carry-on bag instead of lugging it around on your shoulder. You'd be surprised how heavy all of that hardware can be after a day on the road.

13. **Fly during business hours.** Inevitably, taking a business trip means working longer hours anyway, so don't be a martyr and volunteer to take a red-eye flight. You're already stressed, so why should you be bone-tired too? Also, don't feel obligated to work during the flight out. Use the time to relax and mentally prepare yourself for the trip ahead.

14. **Pay someone to drive you around.** Even if you take pride in your sense of direction, do you really want to be bothered with navigating a rental car through the bowels of a strange city? If your company will allow it, stick to taxis or corporate cars. Just don't forget to carry extra money! In some cities, you will need to pay your driver in cash, so multiple or long trips will often cost more money than you may typically carry in your wallet.

15. **Check in at the office frequently.** Never allow your boss to think you've dropped off the face of the earth—even if you're super busy.

Drop her a text or an email to update her on your whereabouts, and don't let her catch you spending half a day gambling in the Las Vegas airport.

16. **Log on as often as possible.** Use Wi-Fi religiously so that you can keep on top of the endless stream of issues and action items back at the office. Even if your boss isn't expecting you to do this, you'll be grateful you did after you return to work when your trip is over.

17. **Check your watch and wake-up calls.** When you arrive in a new time zone, reset your watch and devices in order to avoid confusion later on. Also, don't rely on your alarm clock or the hotel's wake-up call alone to make sure you're on time for a morning meeting. Use both, just in case.

18. **Take advantage of the hotel's fitness center.** Running on the tread-mill or lifting weights is a great way to relieve stress and to work off those extra pounds you've put on from eating out every day.

19. **Have dinner with friends or family instead of your coworkers.** Does anyone from your personal life live in the city where you're traveling? Make an effort to get together instead of hanging out with the same colleagues you see all day. Business travel is a great way to catch up with folks you wouldn't get to spend time with otherwise.

20. **Extend your stay to do some sightseeing.** If your company is paying for you to fly to a city you've never visited, why not stay the weekend and treat yourself to some fun activities? There's nothing more frustrating than being in New York City from Monday through Thursday and spending the entire time in a convention center.

I've logged hundreds of business trips, and I still get stymied by some of these points. I'll never forget the time I arrived at JFK Airport only to find that my flight to Washington was departing from La Guardia Airport. If only I had reviewed my itinerary ahead of time! Learn how to travel smart, however, and your experiences as a road warrior can add a rewarding new dimension to your job.

What I Wish I'd Known

At the beginning of my career as a speech therapist, I was being supervised while seeing clients. One morning my alarm didn't go off, and when I finally woke up I realized that I wasn't going to get to my client on time. So I called my supervisor and just canceled. I was later penalized for this incident. Looking back, I'd tell myself to do whatever I could to see that client, even if it meant arriving a few minutes late. You always get more credit for showing up and doing your best than not showing up at all.

Naomi, 37, Chicago

Take-Home Points

+ Combat stereotypes. Prepare for the challenge of being stereotyped according to your age. Paying close attention to your appearance and how you introduce yourself to new colleagues will ensure that you come across as a mature professional.

+ Take your work seriously. At the start of a new job, no conversation or assignment should be taken lightly. Opinions formed from initial interactions are very difficult to change.

+ Observe your new organization's culture. Adapt your behavior and work style to fit within your company's boundaries. The most successful employees are those who assimilate quickly.

+ Remember that perception is reality. Be on your best behavior during the first few weeks at a new job.

Chapter 3

Working the Crowd

Now that you have the big-picture view of your new company, it is time to get to know people one on one. Establishing strong on-the-job relationships will drive your career growth and give you a reason to come to work in the morning. When you first meet new colleagues, it's hard to imagine having an informal lunch meeting with them or talking reality television in front of the watercooler. You might think that your fellow employees should approach you because you are the new kid. However, in most companies, the pace of business is so frenetic that you'll be lucky if people even notice you've arrived. It's your responsibility to make sure that you are professionally and socially integrated into your department, and you'll be better off if you take action sooner rather than later. In this chapter, I'll discuss strategies for getting to know your new boss and navigating your company's social scene. I'll also touch on how to practice cringe-free networking, how to scout out the antidote for business-world insanity—your mentor—and how to leverage executive sponsorship for the benefit of your forward momentum.

Getting to Know the Boss

My immediate supervisor was so disorganized that it drove me up the wall. He was so busy trying to find his way out from underneath his desk that he was unable to communicate any vision whatsoever. His style put me off so much that I started to get really bitter. Eventually I could see my attitude seeping into our interactions, and I think my boss could tell that I didn't like him. Soon he found subtle ways to let me know he felt the same way, and the next thing I knew, I was getting all of the most boring assignments. I didn't want to sabotage my career, so I tried focusing on my boss's strengths. I found that he was a great listener and that he could talk sports with greater finesse than my husband. By making a conscious effort to value what he brought to the table, I was able to turn things around between us.

Dvora, 26, Florida

There are as many different types of bosses in the professional world as there are people, and, hopefully, the manager you work for is a good fit for you. As the captain of your department's ship, your boss is responsible for the group's success, and, to a great extent, your own. As such, it's crucial that you get to know your immediate supervisor early and determine her priorities. During your first days in the trenches, observe your boss in action. If you can, shadow her for a day to see how she interacts with junior and senior employees, and how she handles different situations. Business consultant C. Sam Benson, in his article "Your Management Success," defines the following basic management styles:

+ **Aggressive:** competitive, decisive, direct; likes immediate results.

+ **Persuasive:** poised, optimistic, convincing; likes interacting with people.

+ **Supportive:** patient, reliable, a good listener; likes security.

+ **Analytical:** precise, prepared, plans thoroughly; dislikes mistakes.

It's difficult to slap a label on a complex person you barely know, but thinking about your boss's management style will help you determine how to proceed with the best chance of success. You may have heard that there are documented variations between male and female bosses. Supposedly, women are more nurturing, collaborative, and relationship-focused, but they may react emotionally when they feel threatened or insecure. Men are presumed to be more generous and easygoing, but they tend to favor individual work on tasks and an autocratic approach to decision-making.

There has also been a lot of talk about generational differences among the various age groups that currently comprise the workforce. In his book *Managing the Generation Mix*, author and generational expert Bruce Tulgan defines the generations as follows:

1. **Schwarzkopfers:** Born before 1946 (now few and far between), their strengths are loyalty, dependability, responsibility, altruism, and a strong work ethic. Other generations can count on these seasoned workers for everything from a historical perspective to an important document. Their attitude is "take charge" and "do what's right."

2. **Baby Boomers:** The huge Baby Boom generation, born between 1946 and 1964, experienced a child-centered upbringing, a focus on individuality and youth, and a distrust of anyone in authority. Older Boomers admit they're competitive and self-centered, but have a strong commitment to the mission of their organizations. Younger Boomers see themselves as cautiously loyal and more realistic about life and work.

3. **Generation X-ers:** These independent, driven go-getters, born between 1965 and 1977, are accustomed to taking care of themselves. Not obsessed with climbing the corporate ladder, these free agents are energetic, creative, and adaptable as they make lifestyle choices that contribute to their wellness, happiness, and health.

4. **Generation Y-ers/Millennials:** Born after 1977, Y is the most outspoken and empowered of all the generations. Influenced by education-minded Boomer parents and fueled by their facility with technology, Gen Y-ers are poised to be lifelong learners. They're socially conscious, have high expectations of organizations, and are constantly looking for ways to improve how things are done.

As members of the Generation Y/Millennial generation, you may have noticed that some of these broad characteristics accurately describe you, your colleagues, and your managers. However, as you get to know your boss, I urge you not to put much stock in generalizations. I think you'll find that the way your boss operates will depend almost exclusively on her unique personality, and that gender or age seldom play a major role.

It's a good idea to set up a one-on-one meeting with your new boss right away. You will need to be proactive about this because, in the crazed atmosphere of the professional world, your boss may be too harried to make the suggestion. If necessary, block an hour with his admin or ask him to grab a quick lunch in the cafeteria. New York City career counselor Judith Gerberg suggests three strategies for this first encounter:

1. Express gratitude and enthusiasm.

2. Clarify roles and expectations.

3. Define the training and support you will need to do your job well.

Additionally, you'll want to leave the meeting with answers to the following questions:

+ What are your daily responsibilities?

+ Are there department meetings he would like you to be a part of? Are there particular people he would suggest you meet?

+ What is the best way to get in touch with him if you need something? (Does he want you to drop by his office? Is an email best? Is texting appropriate?)

+ How should you document your work? How often and in what format does he want you to report on project status?

+ How should you go about suggesting new ideas or processes?

+ How will your performance be evaluated?

If you can accomplish one thing in this initial meeting, make sure you and your boss agree on how to move forward. All of your efforts to impress him with your expansive knowledge of the field and your creative ideas will be fruitless if the two of you are going in different directions. Find out what he wants from you first, and then brainstorm ways to surpass his expectations. You can also establish a good rapport by making your new boss feel needed. Show him in the very beginning that you are ready and willing to be guided, and bond with him over the fact that he has some years on you, and therefore has a treasure trove of career advice to offer.

How else can you get started on the right foot? Here are some other hints.

1. **Be humble.** Don't approach your boss with a sense of entitlement, as though he is personally responsible for furthering your career. Instead,

focus on learning what you can do to make his life easier, contribute to your company's goals, and make him look good to his boss.

2. **Be realistic.** Keep in mind that your boss is a human being who is going to make mistakes. He is not trying to make your life difficult. The two of you are on the same team, so don't be overly sensitive or critical. Listen without judgment, make a sincere effort to understand your boss's position, and patiently explain your ideas. If you're unclear about something, ask for clarification rather than expecting him to read your mind.

3. **Be honest.** Admit if you do something wrong, and then ask your boss how you can rectify the situation. Don't allow yourself to get caught in a maze of lies or excuses that will result in a loss of credibility.

4. **Be respectful of your boss's time.** Appear in his office with a checklist of things you need to cover, and don't dwell too long on any particular subject. Your boss will be more receptive to meeting with you if he knows you'll be in and out of his office quickly.

5. **Be self-sufficient.** Only approach your boss with a problem or complaint if you've explored all options for resolving it yourself. When you do approach him, be prepared to have a solution at hand that you could implement with his help. Choose your battles wisely, and decide carefully if bringing an issue to your boss's attention is really necessary or if you would be better off letting it go.

6. **Be friendly.** Encourage your boss to genuinely like you. If he expresses an outrageous political opinion or offers unsolicited advice about your personal life, nod and smile. You don't have to agree, but you don't have to disagree either. Your boss's feelings should be protected at all times. Compliment him on his tie or presentation, if it's appropriate, and thank him profusely for any efforts on your behalf. Do personal favors for him and brownnose all you want, but make sure you do it sincerely. Your boss will smell phoniness a million miles away—and believe me, he won't appreciate it. Even if your boss isn't someone you'd choose as a friend, focus on the things about him you do like, and do your best to establish a positive working relationship.

7. **Be a "can do" employee.** When your boss asks you to do something, accommodate him, if possible. The words "I don't have time" should never escape your lips. If you know something needs to be done, do it without being prodded, and if your boss asks for help in a group

setting, be the first to volunteer. Your boss will quickly come to see you as a huge asset to the team and as someone he can count on.

There's one important caveat to the "can do" mantra: You have to set reasonable boundaries for your new manager. There is a fine line between being a hard worker and letting people take advantage of you. Some managers, even good ones, fall victim to the "gofer" syndrome. If you've ever tried in vain to track down the guy who fills up the kitchen's cappuccino machine, you know what I'm talking about. The gofer syndrome involves a stream of barked orders to the tune of, "Do this, do that, get me this, get me that, tell this person ABC, and get an answer from that person on XYZ." Pretty soon, you're spending so much time on silly errands that you don't have time to get any real work done. Cure your boss of the gofer syndrome by telling him that you're happy find the cappuccino guy if he will give you permission to de-prioritize the report you're working on for the CEO. Your boss will see for himself how he should best utilize your time.

Also, don't let your boss catch you staying until 10 p.m. or obsessively responding to email within five minutes on weekends unless you want her to expect that behavior from you for the duration of your career. Along those same lines, you shouldn't impose a performance standard on yourself that is impossible to maintain. If you return all of your boss's messages immediately and complete assignments way ahead of deadlines, you run the risk of disappointing her when you can't deliver.

One more piece of advice: Get to know coworkers who report to the same manager quickly so that you can probe them about your boss's pet peeves, preferences, and expectations. Be careful how you phrase your questions, though, because you don't want to launch a discussion that criticizes your new boss in any way. Ask a colleague to fill you in on the chain of command in your department. Use this information to introduce yourself and explain your function in the office to your boss's boss and the other managers with whom you'll be working. Establishing strong relationships with the department higher-ups will accomplish the dual functions of making your boss look good and strengthening your overall position in the company.

The Work Social Scene

*When I moved to San Francisco to start a new marketing job
in the cosmetics industry, I really wanted to make friends with the*

younger people in my department. I tried to get to know the girls who worked in the cubes around me, but they were such a tight-knit group that I thought I was back in high school. Every time I'd ask one of them to go to lunch, she would come up with some excuse, and then later I would see her leaving with one of our other colleagues. Then one day, I saw the girl next to me thumbing through a bridal magazine. I walked up to her and asked her about her wedding. She was more than happy to talk about it, and when I told her I was from St. Louis (where she was getting married), she couldn't stop asking me questions.

Preeti, 24, California

Imagine being stranded on a desert island with your coworkers. Scary, huh? But when you think about it, you spend just as much time with them at work as you would if you were all breaking coconuts over your knees in the South Pacific. Therefore, if you want to enjoy your job, it's in your best interests to make friends with some of these folks. Work friends will be there when you want to grab a bite at the restaurant down the block or take a quick turn on the treadmill at the gym. They'll be there when you need to commiserate about a project or vent about a new company policy. They may even be around when your world changes forever, such as when my colleagues and I watched the September 11 terrorist attack on the World Trade Center. Work friendships make the professional world bearable, and you shouldn't try to make do without them.

The ideal time to scout out potential work friendships is at the start of a new job. When your boss introduces you to the other members of your team, make a note of people your age who look friendly. Take them up on their offers to help you. Maybe you already know how to order business cards, but there's no harm in finding an excuse to talk to your new coworkers. If someone asks you to get a cup of coffee, go gladly, but don't jump at the chance for a friend so quickly that you end up spending all of your time with one particular person. Because you're unfamiliar with people's allegiances, you need to avoid aligning yourself with a single colleague or group of colleagues. In your first month, you should aim to know a little about a lot of people rather than the other way around.

Once you're established in the department, make an effort to get to know potential work friends personally. This can be intimidating and even somewhat difficult if your office is full of cliques. It's possible that a group of your coworkers will go out to happy hour and leave you sitting at your desk feeling like the new kid in third grade all over again. The only way to break through work social groups is one person at a time. Zero in on the most approachable person in the group, find out what interests him, and then weave these things into a conversation. For example, if you see that your next-door neighbor has a Nerf basketball net in his cube, you might ask him if he caught the Final Four game last night. People love to talk about themselves, so encourage potential friends to tell you about their lives. Listen to what they say, and talk about yourself only if asked. Doing someone a favor is also a good friend-making strategy. Suppose one of your teammates is frantically looking for a last-minute pet sitter while she goes out of town on business. If you live in her neighborhood, graciously offer to feed her cats. Your teammate won't forget this act of goodwill, and will be likely to view you favorably in the future.

Sometimes team members will be nonresponsive to your gestures of friendship. Don't take it personally. Your department's culture might encourage people to keep to themselves, or you and your coworkers might not have much in common. If this is the case, expand your search to the rest of the company. Perhaps you should get to know the girl from accounting a little better. What about that guy who always rides the elevator with you in the morning?

In addition, check with human resources to see if your company sponsors out-of-office activities, such as sports teams, travel clubs, or volunteer and charity initiatives that allow you to express your sense of social responsibility. Sign up for "extracurriculars" that catch your eye, and commit to attending events. Once you're there, find someone you know, and ask him to introduce you around. Remember, as with everything in the business world, new work friendships require follow-up. When you meet someone interesting, think of an excuse to drop him an email afterward. You'll remind him who you are and encourage him to make contact again.

A word on dating at work: Don't go out with someone in your company unless you can handle seeing that person every day if the relationship doesn't work out. Definitely avoid dating your boss or anyone on your immediate team. Even if you end up marrying that person, it won't be worth the career complications. The best idea? Get your colleagues to introduce you to their single friends!

Work Friends vs. Real Friends

I will never forget the day I was standing on the corner of 43rd Street and Broadway in New York City with my coworker Laura. Laura and I had been through a lot together in the year we had worked on the same public relations account team. We had coped with ego-obsessed executives and unreasonable clients, and we had implemented innovative and creative ideas neither of us knew we had in us. Nearly every day, Laura and I had lunch together to dish about our projects and the latest goings-on in our personal lives.

Standing on the corner, I said to Laura, "I'm so glad you're one of my closest friends."

She looked at me strangely. "Alex," she said. "There's a difference between close friends and people you talk to at work. You know that, right?"

Laura's response may have been a little harsh, but it taught me an important lesson about work friends vs. real friends: it's easy to mistake one for the other, especially when you're struggling to establish a social life. In school, making friends is as simple as walking over to the dorm room next door and plopping down on the bed. After college, however, there are no such opportunities. Because you might be too busy to go out and meet new people, the tendency is to target your coworkers. It makes sense. After all, they might be the only people you know who are your age, and you see them for eight hours every day.

Although many people use work as a springboard for building strong friendships outside the office, I wouldn't assume your colleagues are your new best friends just because you take your coffee breaks together. Laura was right—there are differences between close friends who will be there for you through life's tough times and people you hang out with while you happen to be stuck in the same building. You can spare yourself disappointment later on by noting the differences between a work friend and a real friend. Here are some questions to ask yourself:

+ If your friend left the company, would you still be in touch with her in a year?

+ If you had a personal emergency, would you consider asking your friend for help?

+ Do you hang out with your friend outside the office? (Weekday lunch, happy hour, and business trips don't count.)

+ Have you met your friend's significant other? What about her friends outside the office?

+ If your friend received the promotion you were banking on, would you be genuinely happy for her?

+ If you ran into your friend in the grocery store, would you be able to talk to her for 10 minutes without mentioning work?

+ Have you seen where your friend lives?

+ Do you and your friend have anything in common besides your age and your job?

If you answered yes to most of these questions, you might have found yourself a real friend at work. Take care of this relationship by making a concerted effort to spend time with your friend outside the office. You and your friend should also avoid working together too closely. Similar to living with close friends, being in business with them can sometimes be disastrous. Whether we like it or not, people can behave differently when money, power, and careers are at stake. For example, suppose you and your friend pair up for a high-profile new business project. Your friend could be the kindest, most generous person in the world after quitting time, but she might take all the credit and do none of the work. You don't want to put yourself in a situation in which you must choose between your friendship and your career.

If you're lucky, someone you meet at work could turn into a friend for life. It happened to me. My friend Kathryn and I started our PR careers in the same department many moons ago, and she later was the maid of honor in my wedding!

On the Outside

A few years ago, I was working for a dot-com. My younger co-workers smoked pot a lot, and I knew they thought I had a pole up the you-know-what for always turning them down. I really wanted to get along with them, so one night while we were away at a conference, I got high with them in a hotel room. I thought there was no way our boss would find out, but somehow she did. She told me she expected more of me as a senior manager. I was lucky I didn't get fired.

Kim, 29, Washington

Happy hour, team lunches, holiday parties, you name it—there are plenty of opportunities to socialize in the corporate world. Partaking in these outings gets you out of sterile "Cube City" and allows you to pretend you actually have a life. The thought of free food alone is enough to put you in a good mood. So by all means, go to these events and have a blast. Just keep a couple of things in the back of your mind.

It's tempting to let loose with your colleagues, especially when you're out of the office. However, you should never let alcohol (or drugs) get the best of you. Remember how your college roommate said you were the biggest blabbermouth on campus after you'd had a few? Just think of what you might have to say about your job, your boss, and your coworkers if you get smashed with them. When your boss waves his corporate credit card, it's easy to get caught up in the excitement of free rounds on the company, so you should prepare for this situation in advance.

A few hours before you go out to the restaurant or bar, eat a hefty meal and drink plenty of water. Once you're there, do not get drunk. It's tough enough to maintain your professional persona when you're perfectly sober, but when alcohol steals your inhibition, you might find yourself saying and doing things you'd ordinarily consider big no-no's. I'm not going to say you can't consume alcohol, because we're all adults. In fact, if you repeatedly shun drinking in your colleagues' company, you might be perceived as weird or a loser. The key is to find the middle ground. No matter how much peer pressure comes your way, you should stick to one drink (two if you have a high tolerance). Pretend it's Pepto-Bismol, sip it super slow, and it will last the whole evening. Take heart—you can still party with the best of them; just save it for your best friend's tapas party or your Friday night poker game.

The good news is that drinking is not typically the focus when the boss takes the team out for lunch. The bad news is that you have to watch more closely what you say and do, because people are actually paying attention. When the group arrives at the restaurant, don't sit next to your manager at the big table. You'll look like a brown-noser to your coworkers. Plus, if conversations split off, guess who you'll be stuck talking to? Also, don't be the first one to order. Note the price of your colleagues' entrées and whether they are ordering drinks, and then follow suit with a selection that is perfectly in line with what everyone else is having. And, roll your eyes if you must, but I have to put it out there: Watch the table manners. Remember the dating rules your mother told you when you were getting dressed for your prom? Avoid talking while you're chewing, don't fix your hair at the table, and don't order anything you have to eat with your hands or is a stain waiting to happen. If the group is sharing dishes, don't hog, and put your smartphone away even if everyone else has theirs out. Eating out with the team is different from eating out with your friends. Relax, tell jokes, have fun—but don't forget that business is business, and you're still on the clock.

And finally, there comes a time each year when the professional world becomes a symbol of cheesy sentiment and material excess. Yes, it's the holiday season. And while your coworkers are turning your floor into a red and green monstrosity, and the mailroom guys are lugging a 10-foot-tall menorah into the lobby, you are probably deciding whether to go to the company's annual holiday party. For the sake of your career, you should make an appearance. And because your company is going to spend your raise on a dancing Christmas tree whether you enjoy it or not, you might as well make the best of the situation. Mind your professional persona, and dress appropriately for the occasion. If you're allowed to bring a date, treat someone you love (or someone you owe a favor) to a catered meal. If not, use the opportunity to get some face time with higher-ups you wouldn't get to meet otherwise.

Your department might also have its own party. Relax—these are fun! Spare yourself stress by finding out in advance about the company policy on giving gifts. Hopefully, your department favors the grab bag—a convention in which each person in the group puts one small wrapped gift in the pool, and then leaves with someone else's even smaller wrapped gift. If you're supposed to shop for your entire group, however, keep your gifts thoughtful but slightly impersonal. You're not required to give your boss anything, but it is a nice gesture. You should always buy the group admin something as a token of your appreciation for all of her help during the year. Departmental holiday parties often have a potluck component as well. Don't panic while your coworkers are competing to see who can cook the best holiday fare. Go to the grocery store and buy a $2 package of Duncan Hines chocolate chip cookie mix, spend 10 minutes baking the stuff, and pass the goodies off as homemade at the party. I guarantee your colleagues will say your cookies are the best they've ever tasted.

Conversation Taboos

When we're in our 20s, it's natural to think that the world revolves around us. In the business world, this attitude can lead to paranoia. Suddenly, you're afraid to talk to anyone lest he stab you in the back or underhandedly take credit for your ideas. Understand, though, that your colleagues are too busy with their own agendas most of the time to worry about getting you in trouble. So instead of staying up all night worrying whether or not your cagey workmate is going to spread rumors about you, follow these simple work conversation rules and rest easy.

1. **Don't spread gossip.** This one is first because it's the toughest to avoid. Dishing the dirt at work is fun, especially if you're bored. Listen all you want, but refrain from contributing to conversations that could compromise someone's reputation. Damaging stories spread like a conflagration, and being nailed as the source can be a career killer.

2. **Don't swear.** Nothing taints your professional persona as much as foul language. There are people all over the business world who spew curse words, and maybe your boss is one of them. If you're tempted to join in, remember where the phrase "potty mouth" came from. In the professional world, you don't want to look or smell like you were anywhere near the potty, so don't sound like it either.

3. **Don't be politically incorrect.** Just because we all crack up when Jon Stewart makes fun of PC in the workplace doesn't mean we shouldn't take it seriously on Monday morning. Realize that people are ultra-sensitive about issues of political correctness and that, as far as work is concerned, you should have no opinions. If you've noticed certain stereotypes to be true, keep your observations to yourself, and make sure to steer clear of racist or sexist jokes.

4. **Don't talk about sex, drugs, or politics.** I don't care how liberal your office is or how convinced you are that your colleagues will understand your point of view, if you wouldn't discuss it with your grandmother or your religious leader, mum's the word at work.

5. **Mind cultural sensitivities.** If you know you're going to be working in a foreign country or interacting regularly with people of varying nationalities, read up on the business customs and social etiquette in those regions so that you behave appropriately. For example, countries have different practices regarding giving gifts, asking personal questions, and standing in close physical proximity. Don't assume that people understand slang just because they speak English, and never badmouth a country you're working in or the culture or practices of foreign colleagues.

6. **Don't share secrets.** Really need to keep it a secret? Don't tell anyone. If you need to preface a statement with "promise you won't tell a soul"

or "don't tell anyone I said this," you shouldn't be saying it. The only people you can trust with secrets at work are the folks who fall into the "real friend" category we talked about earlier, and even then you should be wary. Think about it: Would you trust each friend in your close-knit college clan with a secret that could ruin your reputation if it got out? Exactly. If you absolutely must tell someone that you're looking for a new job, for example, call your mom.

Working Your Net

I still can't stomach the whole networking thing. I was recently at a conference where I saw a guy who graduated from my school a few years ahead of me. I'd read something about him in the alumni magazine. He had an amazing job in my field, and I wanted to go talk to him more than anything. In the end, though, I was too self-conscious. Why on earth would this guy want to help me, and what right did I have to ask him anyway? I didn't want to feel like a slimy car salesman, so I left. I knew I probably blew a great opportunity, but I just couldn't make myself do it.

Manuel, 25, Colorado

A popular misconception among twenty-somethings is that networking is about getting a job. In reality, it's much more than that. Michael Alexander of FindAMentor (findamentor.org) defines networking as "working a net to catch information." It's about establishing relationships that provide you with valuable feedback and allow you to make educated decisions. You do it every day without even realizing it. Let's look at an example: Suppose within days of your move to a new town, your car breaks down. How would you handle this situation? Would you fire up Yelp and take your car to the first mechanic you see, or would you ask your colleagues for a recommendation? The second option is an example of networking. Think about why many successful businesses don't need to advertise. They obtain new clients by word of mouth—otherwise known as networking!

The purpose of business networking is to gain information, increase your visibility in your field, and establish personal connections that will help you move forward in your career. Even if you're happy with your job, you should always be looking ahead to the next one. How do you use networking as a tool to prepare for your career's future? There are a few steps involved in this process:

1. **Expand your business networks before you actually need to.** Judith Gerberg, career counselor and director of Gerberg & Co. in New York City, recommends looking beyond your company for business contacts so that your networking will have lifelong continuity, regardless of the specific jobs you hold. She suggests joining professional organizations in which you have a genuine interest and attending at least one activity a month. At the same time, you should habitually ask people in your circle if they know anyone who might be a good contact for you. At its core, networking should be fun. If you seek out people who care about the same things you do, you'll enjoy networking and won't view it as a chore.

2. **Know what you want from your contacts and what you can offer them.** Many people dislike networking because they think that asking a stranger for help is an imposition. Remember that it's human nature to want to help someone, and I think you'll find that most people will be receptive, provided you approach them the right way. If you know you're going to be meeting potential contacts, don't just drop a pile of business cards in your briefcase and call it a day. Prepare for networking conversations in advance by considering what you need from the contact. Will a phone conversation do, or would you like to meet your contact for coffee or a meal? Additionally, Rachel Solar-Tuttle, coauthor of *Table Talk*, says that because networking is collaboration, every time you ask for something or meet with a potential contact, you should think about how you can help him in return. Listen to your contacts carefully so that you can glean insights about how you might assist them. Remember that networking is like karma—what goes around comes around.

3. **Contact the person.** When approaching a potential contact, be friendly, respectful, and brief. In Chapter 1, we talked about how email usually achieves better results than a phone call, but if you are attending a networking event, an in-person conversation is often the best option of all. No matter how you make contact, always keep in mind that the person is doing you a favor. If he's in the middle of something, don't interrupt, and be conscious of his time commitments. When you sit down with your contact one on one, offer to pay any expenses associated with the meeting, and remember to send him a thank-you note afterward. Another important point: don't be a stalker. Practice what I call the 3/6 rule—contact the person three

times over a period of six weeks, and if you don't hear back, move on to someone else who will be more open to helping you.

4. **Follow up with your contact regularly.** After a successful first networking meeting, it's your responsibility to keep the lines of communication open. Did your contact give you any advice or suggest a course of action? If so, touch base every so often to remind him who you are and to keep him apprised of your progress. Be aware of his career moves, and make sure he stays informed of yours. Invite him to get together again, and, during the holiday season, send him a card with a nice note.

Even the most natural networking interactions can be challenging if you're shy. You might not like asking people for anything, whether it's for advice about a particular industry or for a piece of gum. I overcame my anxiety by talking to potential contacts about the aspects of my career I feel most strongly about. Should a networking opportunity present itself during an impromptu conversation, I make a conscious effort to be myself and stick to subjects I know well. When making a networking call, I jot down a few notes so that I won't forget what I want to say. I schedule time for these in the morning when my energy level is high. I also make it a point to stand up during each call, because I tend to sound more professional when I do so. After several years of practice, I'm still nervous talking to people I don't know. However, every time I do it and experience a positive outcome, I gain a little more confidence. I promise that you will too!

Networking Tips I Hadn't Heard

Last year, when my friend Ben Casnocha sent me a copy of his new book, *The Start-Up of You*, I knew that I was going to read something innovative about networking. After all, Ben wrote it with Reid Hoffman, the cofounder and chairman of LinkedIn, and if anything has changed the game of networking in the 21st century, it's LinkedIn.

I was not disappointed. Here are four networking tips from Ben and Reid that I hadn't heard before, despite having read endless material on the subject. Start using them today, before you actually need them and before everyone else gets in on the secret.

1. **Start your own association.** Convene influential friends and colleagues with similar interests to share ideas and resources. Offer thought-leadership and high-level conversation so that it's more than

just a networking group. Meet on a regular basis, in a convenient location. This is a great way to keep relationships strong and receive great insights in the process.

2. **Create an "intriguing people" fund.** Automatically funnel a certain percentage of your paycheck into a bucket that pays for coffees, lunches, and the occasional plane ticket to meet new people and shore up existing relationships. Pick a person who is a weaker tie but with whom you would like to have a stronger alliance, and for several months, invest time and energy into building the relationship via shared knowledge and offers to help.

3. **Connect the dots in your network.** Pair individuals together who have similar interests, and make introductions via email. You may not benefit immediately, and that's okay. Then, think about a challenge you are dealing with and ask an existing connection for an introduction to someone who could help. Jumpstart the process by offering a small gift—such as a relevant article—to the person you want to meet.

4. **Do the layoff test.** If you got laid off from your job today, who are the 10 people you'd ask for advice on what to do next? Reach out to them now, when you don't need anything specifically. Have lunch, coffee, or even a phone call. You never know what gold nuggets might come out of an informal conversation without an urgent agenda.

Using Social Networks

I've been on Facebook since I was a freshman in college, and even though I'm about to graduate, I thought about leaving my profile up as is. After all, it took me a long time to put that thing together and I'm kind of proud of it. But now my career counselor is telling me that I should be using my social networks to meet people who can help me find a job for next year, and she's convinced that employers will actually be looking at what I have up there. I think I liked it better when Facebook was just open to your college network.

Jenson, 22, Iowa

Social networking is the grouping of like-minded individuals online, and it's is a terrific tactic for gaining access to respected individuals you probably wouldn't have the opportunity to interact with otherwise. Most of you probably belong to Facebook, LinkedIn, Twitter, Instagram, and Snapchat already, and there are tons more platforms that are both general and specific to particular industries.

Assuming you want to use social networks to bolster your career relationship–building activities, Diane Danielson and Lindsey Pollak, authors of *The Savvy Gal's Guide to Online Networking*, recommend that you start by researching where your colleagues and potential contacts hang out. Most networks also allow you to search by industry without signing up. For example, say Danielson and Pollak, if you're looking for decision makers in the healthcare industry, go to a networking site's search page and put in a job title (such as "healthcare CFO"). They also suggest taking a moment to check out the networks your friends and colleagues invite you to join.

Getting started on most social networks is pretty easy. You register for free and then create a personal profile that includes information such as your work history, organizations to which you belong, your interests and hobbies, awards and honors you've received, and the types of people with whom you're interested in connecting. One of the best things about them is that you'll never have to trouble yourself maintaining your address book again, as your online networking contacts will update their own information as needed.

As I briefly discussed in Chapter 1, make sure your social network profiles effectively portray your professional persona. And yes, this includes monitoring your friends' pictures and comments that appear on your pages. Among some other helpful tips from Danielson and Pollak:

+ **Meet first, ask later.** When meeting people in a social networking setting, it's best to develop a genuine personal connection first, and then broach the subject of how you and your new contact might help each other.

+ **Deliver what you promise.** Do not try to make friends by promising follow-up you may not be able to deliver (such as guaranteeing a meeting with your boss or client). Overpromising and underdelivering is a quick way to lose friends and alienate new contacts.

+ **Manage your expectations.** It's unlikely that any one single networking encounter will result in obtaining a new job or new customer. Approach each connection with a specific, more tangible goal in mind, such as securing a second meeting or gaining some valuable insight or information.

- ✦ **Use keywords galore.** Most people looking online for service providers search by keywords, whether in a search engine such as Google or within a social network, so make sure to incorporate all the keywords someone might use to find you into your profile (such as "database programmer, or "linguistics expert").

- ✦ **Publicize links to and from your profile.** Include a link to your professional profile as part of your email signature line so people can click on it and learn more about you. Within your profile, include the URLs of articles you've written, organizations you belong to, and events where you're speaking.

- ✦ **Take advantage of all your network has to offer.** Each week, set aside 30 minutes to explore the network and its different services. For example, the first week, you might look for people from your alma mater.

- ✦ **Peruse before you post.** Each online platform—whether a social network, microblog, or other content sharing site—has written or unwritten rules of engagement. Spend some time seeing how others operate so that you can effectively blend into the community.

- ✦ **Watch your tone.** Social networks and other online platforms tend to be sensitive toward posts that come across as condescending or sarcastic, and those that could be perceived as personal attacks. And when participating in global communities, keep potential cultural differences top of mind.

Before we move on, let's look at the offerings of the most prolific business network, LinkedIn.com.

The Mechanics of LinkedIn

As the site says, LinkedIn is an online network of millions of experienced professionals from around the world, representing hundreds of industries. When you join, you create a profile that summarizes your professional accomplishments and helps you find and be found by former colleagues, clients, and partners. By establishing a network consisting of your connections and your connections' connections, you are automatically linked to thousands of qualified professionals. It's a painless means to get introduced to advantageous contacts through people you already know, create new relationships, identify service providers or subject-matter experts, land jobs, and close deals—in short, a networking dream!

In his book, *I'm on LinkedIn: Now What???,* author Jason Alba suggests the following best practices for making the most of your LinkedIn participation.

✦ Make sure you are showing enough information on both your public and private profiles. LinkedIn allows you to view your profile as others see it when they are not logged in. If you want to advertise who you are and why you are valuable, make it easy for people to learn about you without having to sign up or log in. Also, make sure your public profile URL is appropriately descriptive (mine is *www.linkedin.com/ in/alexandralevit*).

✦ If you don't have your own Website, use your LinkedIn profile as an online resume. Put the URL in your email signature and in blog comments or online articles you write.

✦ LinkedIn's Jobs section shows you the connections you have within particular hiring companies. Use this information to network with these individuals directly instead of sending a resume to HR.

✦ Request recommendations from people you've worked with successfully in the past, and write them endorsements in return. Potential clients and employers are much more likely to contact you if you can prove that others have been satisfied with your work, product, or service. Don't go too crazy with recommendations, though, as their credibility has been sorely tested recently as people have amassed too many. They also don't take the place of having references that can be called.

✦ Join relevant LinkedIn groups to expand your search visibility, and consider complementing a LinkedIn group with a GooglePlus group for enhanced communication. The ability to search for new contacts within a LinkedIn group is particularly useful if you have a small or non-diverse network.

✦ Stay informed about the things you're interested in by following channels related to your job and industry. You can get articles from influencers and top news sources while building your community in a particular space.

Entering the Blogosphere

For almost a decade now, career experts have been buzzing about the necessity of having a blog. Their rationale is that everyone who's anyone is out there participating in the online conversation, and if you don't have something constructive to contribute, colleagues and employers won't be as impressed with you. Personally, I don't think it's realistic—or even a good idea—for every employable person in the world to go out and start a blog. For one thing, the blogosphere is cluttered enough as it is, and blogs that have no real purpose for existence will just muck things up even more.

You should write a blog because you have a unique opinion on an issue based on your own life experiences, not because you think it will make you more marketable. If you blog for the wrong reasons, no one will read it, and, for all of your efforts, you won't increase your visibility. Secondly, not everyone is cut out to write and/or maintain a blog that requires a concise outpouring of coherent thought several times a week. Lots of people love it, but, to many others, it sounds like the modern version of Chinese water torture.

If you're determined to use the blog medium to become an established expert in your field, or a credible potential hire who'll appear attractive to employers and recruiters, realize that a professional blog is no place for irrelevant musings or runaway diatribes. For example, my readers come to my blog, Water Cooler Wisdom, expecting concrete career advice from the perspective of someone with a consulting practice that helps employees survive in the business world. Tough as it is for me to accept sometimes, they have no interest in hearing about my day—unless I can use the story about the crazy guy I met on the subway to make a point about career success.

There has also been a recent backlash against bloggers who are cavalier with facts or attribution of sources. Be careful of this, and also read other bloggers in your field and cite their work so that the opinions you express are not just your own. Think about what your readers really and truly need to know, and then scout out facts and tips that answer their burning questions. Tie your posts to current events and news headlines, and populate your blog with enticing titles and frequently searched keywords so that it's easier for new readers to find you. Network with other bloggers in your space (even the high-profile ones!) by commenting on their posts, and in return, answer comments on your blog in a timely fashion.

My final thought on this is that if you just want to write, you don't have to reinvent the wheel with a brand new blog. There's no shortage of established outlets just for twenty-something writers that would be grateful for your contributions!

Recruiting a Mentor

You may have heard that the best way to advance in your career is to find a good mentor. A mentor is a person, usually older than you, who can advise you on matters relevant to your career, and who offers support and direction as you progress in your field. Obviously, having a mentor is a good idea, but he won't come to you. You have to seek him out and proactively establish the relationship. Doing this is easier said than done, because the best mentors are typically not your direct supervisors, and you may need to look outside your immediate department. Organizational psychologist Neil Stroul recommends that you observe powerful individuals in your company and approach someone who possesses a "generosity of spirit," a natural willingness to go out of his way to help others. Ideally, this person will have already passed through the part of the career path that you are currently on, and will have achieved success by making smart decisions and learning from his experiences. He will be someone you like and admire, and someone whose values you share.

Once you target a potential mentor, how do you ask for his help? First of all, approach your mentor-to-be as you would any other networking contact: by preparing in advance. You should determine what you are looking for and devise a tentative schedule for how often you would like to meet. Make sure your expectations are reasonable, because the potential mentor is unlikely to agree if he thinks he will have to meet with you every week or act as a referee between you and your boss. When contacting the person, briefly explain why you are seeking his guidance. Compliment him sincerely, and ask if he would be amenable to an in-person meeting. Upon sitting down face to face, reiterate your thanks, and lay out your vision for the relationship. Read the person's reaction. Hopefully, he will be as enthusiastic as you are, and the two of you can set up a timeline for future meetings. But if he isn't, now is the time to find out. You don't want a mentor who is meeting with you out of a sense of obligation.

Michael Alexander of FindAMentor offers some tips for making the most of a mentor relationship:

- ✦ Ask lots of questions.
- ✦ Practice listening.
- ✦ Answer questions truthfully. (When the truth is withheld—even a little—the information provided by your mentor may not be accurate.)
- ✦ Filter information consciously before accepting it as true and right for you.

- Understand your mentor's desire to help, and take feedback you don't like in stride.

- Respect your mentor's time constraints and other commitments.

Don't forget to show your mentor the appreciation he deserves for giving you the benefit of his experience. Follow up on your commitments to him, and brainstorm ways to help him in return. For example, one of my early mentors was a senior vice president at my PR firm. One of her favorite hobbies is yoga, so when she wanted to write an article about it for a healthy living magazine, I volunteered to edit it. Also, consider helping someone else. What's the best thing you can do when you've been fortunate enough to find a good mentor? Become one yourself! By sharing your wisdom and expertise with someone less experienced, you can give back some of the goodwill your mentor showed to you.

Securing Executive Sponsorship

If you've already wrangled a mentor, why do you need a sponsor? *Working Mother Magazine* says it best: "Sponsorship often gets confused with mentoring, but the two roles are different. Mentors provide advice, and such relationships can be formed among peers, bosses, and junior staff. By contrast, sponsors are senior executives with the clout to advance their protégés."

Men are better at embracing this notion of sponsorship, whereas women shy away from it—preferring instead to cement mentoring relationships where the focus is not advancement. Mentors don't actively advocate for a protégé's promotion, but sponsors do. This may partially explain why there are so few high-ranking female executives.

The ideal sponsor-protégé relationship should be based on mutual trust and admiration. In order to be most effective at providing the internal support that you need, your sponsor should ideally be a level or two above your boss. Avoid a political snafu by enlisting your boss's help to identify potential sponsors, and get his advice on the best way to approach the more senior executive.

Of course, in a perfect world your sponsor will find you. He will know your work and will reach out voluntarily. This happened to me last year when I first began work with a new partner company. If it weren't for this individual, I would have had more trouble navigating the organization, and would have nowhere near the level of success I have there today.

What I Wish I'd Known

In one of the first jobs I landed out of college, my role was to help monitor and analyze corporate credit card spending. I noticed that a certain higher-up had unusual spending related to another higher-up, and gabbed about it with some colleagues over drinks. A couple of months later, my boss called me into her office. My jaw hit the floor when she told me that she'd heard about the information I'd divulged. Mercifully, she did not fire me, but gave me a stern warning about confidentiality. I wish I could tell my 23-year-old self to avoid careless gossip. You never know if you can trust the people you gossip with. If they do it with you, they will do it to you.

Tracy, 30, Texas

Take-Home Points

✦ **Get to know your immediate supervisor early.** Determine her priorities, find out what she wants from you, and brainstorm ways to surpass her expectations.

✦ **Master the work social scene.** In your first month, aim to know a little about a lot of people rather than the other way around. Once you're established in the department, make personal connections with potential work friends.

✦ **Understand the different types of friendships.** Know that there are differences between close friends, who will be there for you through life's tough times, and work friends, with whom you hang out while you're stuck in the same building. Adjust your expectations accordingly.

✦ **Expand your business networks.** Business networking is a valuable tool to gain information, increase your visibility in your field, and establish relationships that will help you move forward in your career. Seek out new contacts and potential mentors whom you like and admire, as well as those whose interests you share.

Chapter 4

Be the Master
of Your Plan

At 22, I had been an overachiever all my life. Naturally, I expected to experience success beyond my wildest dreams at my first company. I was going to go in there and kick the corporate world's ass. As soon as they saw what I was made of, I was sure they'd make me the company's youngest vice president. I put so much pressure on myself to know everything right away that I nearly collapsed under the weight of my own unrealistic expectations.

Your first jobs are not meant to be the be-all and end-all of career stardom. How can you master the skills it takes to get ahead without putting in any time in the trenches? That's like saying you could win an Olympic gold medal in swimming without learning to doggie paddle first. Look at your first post-college positions as temporary stops on your career path instead of permanent ones. You are getting paid to learn everything you can so that snagging the next job isn't quite as challenging. This chapter will describe how to make the most out of your first job, knowing that you probably won't stay there forever. I'll start by sharing how you can set goals that further your personal mission. Next, I'll discuss strategies for adding value to your company, including how to better understand your business, how to come up with new ideas and sell them in your organization, and how to promote your successes. Finally, I'll advise you how to develop critical career skills such as risk-taking and problem-solving, which will be useful no matter where you go or what you do. As you're reading, imagine your current organization as a training ground to practice everything I cover.

Setting and Achieving Goals

My first job at a nonprofit organization was nothing like I thought it would be. My responsibilities didn't remotely resemble what we discussed in the interview. I was eager to be out in the field helping people. Instead, I was stuck behind a desk every day. I was really depressed until I asked myself, "What can I take away from this that will help me get where I want to go?" When I took a step back, I realized that I first had to understand the mechanics of how a nonprofit works—and I wouldn't be able to learn that out in the field. I had to spend time doing exactly what I was doing.

Tamika, 24, Washington, D.C.

Let's be realistic. Most junior-level jobs in the professional world have a low glamour factor. As I talked about briefly in Chapter 2, twenty-somethings are often required to pay their dues regardless of their education, and there's a chance your responsibilities have nothing to do with what the interviewer promised. I'm willing to bet that they're more administrative, less creative, and less empowering. This situation can be frustrating, especially if you're used to accomplishing much in a short period of time. You'll be much happier if you look at your time on the bottom rung as an opportunity, instead of lamenting the tragic turn your once-promising life has taken. Keep in mind what's really important to you and use this situation to acquire valuable skills and experience that will take you there. The easiest way to do this is to set specific, reasonable, and attainable goals for your present position that correspond to your long-term career strategy.

In his book *Getting Promoted: Real Strategies for Advancing Your Career*, Harry Chambers defines goal-setting as a positive statement that proclaims your expectations of growth and achievement. You want your goals to motivate you rather than discourage you, so they shouldn't be too ambitious. Instead, make them just tough enough so that you'll stay involved, constantly putting forth effort and reaching for that brass ring. Devise meaningful career goals by considering the following:

+ What you're going to do.

+ Why you want to do it and how it furthers your personal agenda.

+ When you're going to do it.

+ How you'll know when you've done it, and how you'll measure your success.

For example, a few years ago, I set the following goal for leveraging my present job responsibilities to further my big-picture agenda:

+ **Current Role:** Work with Web conferencing company to coordinate weekly conference calls between the New York and UK offices

+ **Big-Picture Agenda:** Serve as the lead on a global PR account team

+ **Goal:** Master protocol for conducting global account team status calls

  + **What I'm going to do:** In addition to setting up the calls, ask the VP for permission to listen and take notes.

  + **Why I want to do it:** By observing how global team account management is done, I will be better equipped to do it myself in the future.

  + **When I'm going to do it:** Talk to the VP on Monday and arrange to participate in calls starting next week.

  + **How I'll measure my success:** After I've listened to several calls, ask the VP if I can create an agenda for, and give project status on, an upcoming call.

Increase your commitment to your goals by writing them down in a list, and then sit down with your boss to review it and ask for his feedback. Do your personal goals align closely with your company's goals or the goals your boss has set for you? Are your boss's expectations practical given your level of experience and expertise? Are your own expectations reasonable? For example, does your boss concur with your goal to manage a client relationship self-sufficiently within six months, or does he feel that you'll require an additional year of mentoring before you'll be ready to take on that responsibility? Don't leave this initial meeting until you and your boss have agreed on your goals leading up to your first scheduled performance review. He will be impressed with your conscientiousness, and voilá—you'll be on the path to that promotion months sooner than if you'd waited for the formal review process.

Types of goals vary, depending on the specific job. Every twenty-something should aim to build a wide range of transferable skills (such as public speaking, client relations, sales, marketing, project management, and finance) that will add value in any job and that are not likely to become obsolete. Use your time on the job and your company's resources to achieve goals related to transferable skills, even if such goals are not directly related to your daily job responsibilities. My friend Joanne wanted to move from her position as a research coordinator to that of a sales representative, and provided the following example.

+ **Transferable Skill:** Public speaking.

+ **Goal:** Improve presentation ability.

> + **What I'm going to do:** Teach three internal training courses on blog monitoring.

> + **Why I want to do it:** I want to practice speaking in front of a group so that when I move to a sales rep position next fall, I will be qualified to conduct client presentations without supervision.

> + **When I'm going to do it:** Throughout the course of one training semester (six months).

> + **How I'll measure my success:** I'll work with the training coordinator to compare my evaluation sheets from the first and third courses. I'll know that I was successful if my scores improve.

Even after you've learned the basics, practice honing existing skills and acquiring new ones. Your development never stops if you want to stay marketable. Keep a running list of all the job responsibilities you have and the projects you work on, and create a portfolio of work samples. Learn all you can about your company and your field. Because the business world moves at the speed of the Internet, spend a few minutes each day reading Websites, blogs, and news outlets focused on your company and industry. Regardless of your position, keeping your finger on the pulse can only help you.

Want some other ideas? Sign up for as many professional and leadership development courses as your company offers for your level, and take advantage of job rotations or temporary assignments in other departments that may be available. Join company committees or projects outside your daily job responsibilities, and seek additional education in the form of certifications or online courses/webinars.

Independent of your manager's involvement, you should take the time to evaluate your goals and reflect on your progress every three to six months. Mark Swartz, a career columnist for the *Toronto Star*, recommends taking a regular inventory of what's working and what's not. Ask yourself the following questions, and answer honestly.

+ Are my current goals still valid?

+ Have any new goals emerged?

+ Are my priorities still in order?

+ Have new priorities changed the emphasis of my efforts?

+ Do my planning and daily activities support my goals?

+ Am I on the right track to get where I want to go?

Finally, be positive. Focus on how far you've come instead of how far you have to go. Take time out to pat yourself on the back. Eat your favorite dessert, buy the better seats at a baseball game—whatever, as long as it's a real treat. By acknowledging your progress toward reaching your goals and concentrating on how close you are to achieving them, you'll be more likely to go the distance.

Earning Your Keep

When I was an account coordinator at a financial consulting company, there wasn't much I could do to help the senior members of my team close new business. But then, one night, I went to a dinner party that my mother was throwing for some of her friends. One of the guests had just gotten divorced and was looking to overhaul her portfolio. When she mentioned this, I saw an opportunity and recommended my firm. Back at the office, I made sure one of our senior reps followed up, and this woman was so impressed with our response and ideas that she hired us to do all of her financial planning. It turns out this woman was quite well off, so a little effort on my part turned into a lucrative piece of business for my firm.

Melanie, 25, Arizona

Because you're reading this chapter, chances are you're blazing a trail of ambitious fire. You probably can't wait to make your mark on the company and prove to everyone you're worth 10 times what they're paying you. Well, hold on there, partner. Taking initiative in order to add value is an excellent idea, but there are a few things you'll want to consider first.

At a new job, size up the turkey before you carve yourself a piece. Realize that no one is expecting you to make a sizable impact within a month of your start date. Actually, going out of your way to make a big splash could be perceived as presumptuous and might incite jealousy among your new colleagues. You should also assess your boss's personality before you jump right in on projects. Although most managers appreciate independence, some like to maintain tighter control over the group's work and will be insulted and/or threatened if they feel you're taking too much initiative. Bottom line: in the beginning, when looking for ways to prove your worth, you'll be safest if you start small.

Ask yourself what your company or department needs, and think about how you can use your unique set of skills and talents to provide it. So what if you're hardly a Renaissance man or woman? You're still new blood. Can you offer a fresh perspective on a vexing problem that has been plaguing your managers for months? Can you find a way to do something faster and more efficiently?

When I started a job in corporate communications, I discovered that my company lacked templates for certain documents, such as launch plans and activity reports. My colleagues weren't against the idea of creating templates; they'd just never thought of it. They created every new document from scratch because that was the way they'd always done it. I recognized that I could make a contribution by introducing the templates I used at my last job. However, I didn't want to appear as though I was forcing my methods upon my new company, so I started by casually incorporating the templates into my individual projects. Eventually, my teammates figured out on their own that the templates were huge productivity-savers. Instead of feeling offended or threatened, my colleagues and manager began to see me as an asset.

Remember that you have to give your company more than you take out in salary and benefits to be considered a worthwhile investment. In the financially driven business world, it's not about effort, it's about results, so you're better off concentrating on areas that directly impact your company's bottom line. Bruce Tulgan, founder of Rainmaker Thinking, Inc., recommends focusing on opportunities that present themselves, even if they're outside your official job description. For example, you might not be in sales, but you can help your company generate new business just by talking to people about what you do. You networked your way into the job, now go out and do it on behalf of your company!

Many twenty-somethings are entrepreneurs at heart and believe they have to stop working for an established company in order to fulfill their dreams. This is not necessarily so. If you're lucky, your organization is one that supports *intra*preneurship—the practice of entrepreneurial skills and approaches by or within an established organization. Employees, perhaps engaged in a special project within a larger firm, are encouraged to behave as entrepreneurs even though they have the resources and capabilities of the larger firm to draw upon. Intrapreneurs focus on innovation and creativity and transform good ideas into profitable ventures. In her article for the UK's *Times Online*, Clare Dight offers these suggestions for budding intrapreneurs:

+ Once you've identified a good idea for a new or improved process or product, seek a network of peers and sponsors to help you evaluate it and get it off the ground. It might be a more senior manager who can open doors or someone with technical expertise who has know-how and credibility.

+ Do your homework and prepare a business plan. When pitching your idea, address your audience and speak in terms they understand.

+ Don't try to do it alone. Teamwork and team capabilities are an essential part of corporate entrepreneurship.

+ Don't be afraid to make mistakes, and be comfortable with yourself and your abilities.

+ Know when to let go. Even if you're convinced your idea will make the company billions, if you can't sell it, move on to something else.

I'm not going to lie to you, starting an intrapreneurial project out of thin air is going to be more challenging than, say, joining an existing committee whose job it is to generate fresh product ideas. You should wait until you've been around a while and have proven yourself as a smart, capable employee, and even then it takes guts, because there will always be some higher-up whose mission is to preserve the status quo and who thinks that you, as an intrapreneurial twenty-something, have some nerve. Your best bet is to put together a bulletproof case that clearly demonstrates how your concept will benefit the company, and to share it subtly and modestly, one person at a time, until you have enough supporters to counter the naysayers.

How to Better Understand Your Business

As a twenty-something who hasn't been out of school too long, there is a lot you probably don't know about the field you have chosen to pursue.

In order to acquire the right knowledge, you might pretend that you're preparing for an interview: If you were heading over to your company to meet people there for the first time, you would do your research in advance. You would want to know current details on the business's mission, vision, and goals, as well as its operations and challenges. As an outsider, you might check out the Website, the most recent annual report, financial and product press releases, and your favorite business news outlets. You would skim industry and trade publications online.

As an insider, you may have access to the firm's strategic plan, which you should try to get ahold of if you can. This document will usually list key goals as well as development, communications, and staffing plans, and you do not need to be a highly placed executive to map it to your daily responsibilities. And the more granular you can get, the better. If you work with the marketing department, for instance, ask for a copy of its individual annual plan and budget, competitive analysis, and any status reports it regularly delivers to the CEO.

If there is an area you know little about, such as accounting, human resources, or procurement, introduce yourself to someone who has worked in the group a long time and ask if she can tell you more about that aspect of the business and what she does on a daily basis. Ask how her group measures success and what skills hiring managers look for in her area.

Far too often, companies encourage a top-down flow of information, which means that your point of view is handed to you by the CEO, and then your boss. Step out of your box by joining internal task forces or committees and attending executive briefings where you get to hear a different story. If your boss is going to a senior leadership meeting, ask if you can attend and take notes.

Possessing a solid understanding of your ideal customer has a direct relationship to your level of understanding about your own business. And of course, it will also help you better serve that client and snag future clients like him. Approach a client with whom you have a great relationship and have built up rapport and trust, and tell him that you want to do an informal survey so that you can improve your results. Take the client to lunch or dinner and ask about his company's present situation, including strengths, weaknesses, opportunities, and threats. Get his take on the company's leadership, operations, human resources, and marketing strategy. Let the conversation flow freely, but do not demand confidential information or spend too much time on information you could have easily found online.

Finally, it can never hurt to enhance your business acumen in general. If you don't already have a business background, coursework in areas in which you lack experience may make sense.

Turn on Those Lightbulbs

I blog several times a week, and have been writing in the career advice and leadership development space for more than 10 years. How many ideas have I had to brainstorm to write about? You do the math. It's a lot. Some days I'm feeling especially creative and can generate insights from all sorts of places, but other days it's a struggle to put forth a single interesting thought. I've developed a few idea-generation strategies that you can hopefully use to add value in your role.

+ **Convene with nature.** Looking at open water and feeling the sand under my feet takes me out of my head and allows me to experience the moment. As I rest calmly, I'll watch the other people in my vicinity and wonder what they do for a living and what's going on in their lives right then. More often than not, a nugget of inspiration will arise.

+ **Do a mindmap.** Wikipedia has a great visual representation of a mindmap that crystallizes the concept better than my words can, but essentially a mindmap is a non-linear diagram that aids in brainstorming around a central thought or idea. During times when your brain is all over the place, a mindmap is a helpful graphical tool for organizing and structuring information into a coherent form.

+ **Piggyback on others' ideas.** My daily newsfeed includes posts from *Harvard Business Review*, *Psychology Today*, and TLNT.com, among others. I often find that another expert will discuss a subject or make an argument on which I can put forth a unique point of view.

+ **Make an opinion list.** Jotting down the issues you feel strongly about will usually result in fodder for your work life.

+ **Read business book summaries.** I get about three new business books in the mail every week, and I don't have time to read all of them. I recognize, however, that I may be missing a lot of great material, so I check out Soundview Executive Summaries (summary.com), which provides easy-to-digest, key takeaways from the top business books of the year, and helps me keep up to date on what's being discussed and why.

Selling Your Ideas Internally

Once you have a great idea you have to sell it. This is actually the toughest part!

The first step is to build your reputation in advance, which (hopefully) you are using this book to do. In order to diminish the perceived risk of an unusual or out-of-the-box idea, the person proposing it has to be a proven entity. That means that you're established at the organization and have done well there. Your boss trusts you and you are on the short list of employees with whom everyone wants to work.

To get an idea to fly internally, it has to be more than just cool. It has to resolve a critical issue that is currently costing your company money, or it has to have the potential to make the company a lot more money. Therefore, you must think through your concept thoroughly before approaching your manager and other higher-ups. At every stage, ask yourself the question, "How will this benefit the organization?" Include as many sample metrics as you can (for example, estimated productivity or sales increases, or higher client satisfaction ratings).

A picture really is worth a thousand words. Talk with fellow employees and/or customers and create a video that showcases the support behind your idea. The video can include "man on the street" interviews, your idea in action, or both. A well-executed piece also shows viewers that you know how to get things done and are willing to invest time and effort in the initiative.

Who are the other innovators in your firm? Track them down and ask about their activities. How did they go about selling their ideas internally? What worked and what didn't? Do they consider the organization supportive of intra-preneurship? Can they be of assistance when it comes to evaluating the idea and finding the right strategic and technical resources to get it off the ground?

Do you work with any consultants or agencies? If so, get their feedback on how to sell the idea. After all, consultants sell to people all the time, including those who don't possess a good understanding of their business. Chances are, they will have some great suggestions and tools for positioning the concept the right way and overcoming potential objections.

You should be prepared for many of your suggestions not to be implemented. This is because, in the business world, a lot of the important decisions are made at a high level. You should not consider your visibility efforts a failure if your ideas are nixed before they see the light of day. The goal is to show the higher-ups in your department that you consistently make worthwhile contributions.

Ownership

While working for a Fortune 500 software firm, I attended an annual staff meeting. The CEO tossed a beach ball into the audience, and everyone watched for five minutes as the ball was batted back and forth. Finally, the CEO called for quiet and asked for the ball to be returned to him. He held it in front of us for a moment before speaking again. "I'm going to throw this ball again," he finally said. "And this time I want someone to catch it and hold onto it. I want you to treat this ball as if it were one of our customers. Instead of passing the inquiry to another person, own the issue yourself."

"Beach ball management"—or bouncing a request over to a colleague because it's not your responsibility to handle it—is all too common in the corporate world. I think e-mail forwarding was invented for this purpose. If someone asks you a question and you don't know the answer, make it your business to find it. I realize it's easier to pass on the request and forget about it, particularly if the person asking is not someone you need to impress or if the request has nothing to do with your area. But if you take that extra step to ensure your department or company is perceived in a positive light, you will add value and stand out as a team player.

Sometimes when you answer the phone, an exasperated coworker or customer will be on the line. Quite possibly, you will be the fourth or fifth person this individual has been transferred to during a single call. Don't underestimate the importance of being the one who actually offers assistance and shepherds the issue through to a satisfying resolution. All it takes is one grateful person to e-mail your boss expressing appreciation for your efforts, and your reputation is made. If that isn't enough of a reason to do a good deed, consider the corporate "karma" factor: go out of your way to help someone today and the universe's system of checks and balances will see to it that you are rewarded later.

It's also imperative that you take ownership as it pertains to your job. Volunteer to take on tougher assignments whenever you can, and if you don't have much on-the-job experience yet, scout out small tasks that you can own. Treat every person you deal with as though he or she is your most important customer, and make sure to finish every project you start. If you encounter roadblocks, marshal your resources to get around them rather than letting a project languish. If a task requires you to follow up at a later date, stay on top of it and keep it on your calendar until it has been completed. You should never hear your manager say, "Whatever happened to that...?" Provide her with frequent updates so that she doesn't have to ask you for a status. You'll advance much more quickly when you can demonstrate the ability to manage projects with minimal supervision.

Who Knows What You Do?

I wasn't promoted, because I worked too hard, if you can believe that. I was so busy that I stayed in my cube all day, every day. People would come by to talk, but I was so consumed by what I was doing that I usually brushed them off. I didn't tell anyone what I accomplished because I thought it was obvious. One day my boss resigned and the head of the department gave the open position to a girl whose productivity was at least half of mine. When I got up the guts to ask why, I realized that the big boss wasn't aware of half the things I did. All he knew was that I kept to myself and wasn't perceived as a team player.

Claude, 28, Quebec

In Chapter 1, I talked about the necessity of showcasing your abilities and achievements in the business world, and suggested that you think of yourself as a publicist with the sole task of promoting you. It was easier to do this while you were interviewing, because all eyes were on you and you had your superiors' undivided attention. However, now that you are ensconced in an actual job, people are not as inclined to listen, and you have to compete with all kinds of noise to be heard. It's no longer enough to keep your nose to the grindstone and turn in a solid day's work. If you want people to take note of you and consider you a serious player, you must make your accomplishments visible.

This is not an easy thing to do, especially given what you were told throughout your 16 years of schooling. In high school and college, achievement was an individual endeavor. You were taught a lesson, you studied, you took a test, you got a score—and no one was the wiser. In fact, you were probably not encouraged to share your grades, particularly if they were good. You were equally successful, whether anyone realized it or not. The corporate world, however, is a whole different ballgame. Your promotability depends not on what you do, but on who knows what you do. Being insular is most damaging at the lower levels of your career, when you are unknown to 99 percent of your company. You could be sitting at your cube churning out work like there's no tomorrow, but unless someone in a position of authority is aware of it, you probably won't get anywhere.

So how do you share your contributions without being perceived as arrogant or boastful? The key is enthusiasm. If you emphasize your passion when describing an achievement, people will think you're just excited about it. An excited person appears earnest, and it's hard to be critical of someone earnest. Practice on your boss. It's okay if you mess up and start bragging uncontrollably, because your boss is supposed to know about everything you're doing and can't fault you for keeping him informed. But when informing everyone else of your successes, be as subtle as possible. Here are a few tactics you can employ without leaving your desk.

E-mail Example #1

Forward e-mails praising your work to your management, disguising them as modest FYIs and making the success seem as though it was a team effort (use "we" instead of "I").

To: Your Management

Subject: Progress With Fab Client

Text: FYI—looks as though we've made some good headway with Fab Client. Let me know how you'd like me to follow up. (Forwarded e-mail is below.)

E-mail Example #2

Ask people outside your department who appreciated your stellar work to let your higher-ups know about it:

To: Person Who Complimented You Effusively

Subject: Thank You

Text: Thanks so much for your kind words. You really made my day and I'm glad to be able to help. I know my manager, John Smith, would appreciate the input on how our group is doing. Would you mind sharing your feedback with him?

E-mail Example #3

Disguise your own success through a thank-you note to others who worked on a particular project with you.

To: Those Who Worked on the Project

Subject: Thank You

Text: I wanted to take this opportunity to thank Stew and Sean for their hard work on our new business proposals this week. Due in large part to their efforts, my team was able to land two new clients—Fab Client A and Fab Client B. Congratulations to all!

You might feel weird the first few times you do something like this. Unless you have a major ego, deliberately trying to make yourself look good is not going to feel natural. But trust me, you'll get used to it. As a mentor of mine once said, step out of your comfort zone often, and watch it get bigger every time.

Risk-Taking

I'm not a big risk-taker myself, so it probably makes sense that much of this book is about treading carefully through the jungle that is the professional world. However, there is a time and a place for everything, and I believe that if you learn to take calculated risks, you will be more personally fulfilled, and you will reap greater career rewards in a shorter period of time. Research cited in Gail Sheehy's book *Pathfinders* supports this point, suggesting that most truly contented people have taken substantial risks at some point in their careers.

Career author Harry Chambers defines risk-taking as the willingness to confront problems, recommend appropriate actions or solutions, and take responsibility for the ultimate outcomes. When you're a low man on the totem pole, putting in your two cents about anything may seem like a risk. You also have to be careful not to step on your colleagues' toes. For example, if your boss is around to handle a situation that falls under her jurisdiction rather than yours, chances are it's not appropriate for you to jump in and handle it for her.

When is a good time to take a risk that could jump-start your career? Because you can't plan for most opportunities (for example, your boss comes down with the flu and you must address a high-level executive's complaint in his absence), the best way to prepare is to learn in advance what would be considered an appropriate risk. This way, when you're presented with an opportunity in the midst of a stressful situation, you will be able to easily determine whether or not you should take the leap. Chambers suggests some risk-assessment questions to keep handy:

+ What is the challenge?

+ What is the potential upside? Will a positive outcome enhance your promotability?

+ What is the potential downside? Would the worst-case scenario have a negative impact on your current or future promotability? How much risk are you comfortable with? Would a lack of success be a permanent hindrance or a bump in the road?

+ How will you know if the risk starts to go bad? Will you be able to identify problems early enough to prevent career-damaging failure?

+ How will you handle a negative outcome? What is your contingency plan if the risk isn't successful?

You will likely face stressful situations in your career, especially when a risk presents itself and you must act immediately. In his book *Feeling Better, Getting Better, Staying Better*, world-renowned psychologist Albert Ellis says that you can assuage your risk-taking fears by preferring, rather than needing, a successful outcome. Realize that a bad risk won't kill you. Sure, you may lose, but you may also appreciably gain. Look at it this way: If you refuse to take risks, you will never get over your fear of them. Your career will be predictable and boring—and life is too short to live that way.

Also, keep in mind that how you react in a crisis tells others a great deal about you. If you're wishy-washy, you are likely to be perceived as ineffective, whereas if you take a confident stand, you will make a powerful statement about your career potential. Whatever you do, don't let on that you doubt yourself—nothing will cause people to lose respect for you faster. Even if you make a mistake, no one can fault you for courageously confronting a problem head-on. And when a plan doesn't work out, don't take it personally. A bad risk does not make you incompetent and shouldn't prevent you from taking similar actions in the future. Be honest, own up to your error, take stock of what went wrong, and make a note to do it differently next time. There is no better way to learn.

Problem-Solving

My market research firm had so many ineffective processes, it was amazing we made any money at all. I thought I was being help-ful when I showed my boss a spreadsheet detailing how many hours my colleagues and I wasted doing Internet searches. He immediately asked me what I proposed instead. I told him we should implement a software program to do the searches for us, but when he started in with more questions, I was at a loss. I guess I hadn't really thought it through. Looking back, I probably sounded like I was just complain-ing rather than actively looking for a solution to the problem.

Greg, 23, Massachusetts

Knowing how to resolve issues and act decisively on the fly are skills you shouldn't be without. Early in your career, you may not have enough account-ability to practice problem-solving on a regular basis, but if you take the time to master the process now, you will be all set when a curveball is thrown your way.

It's easy to say that a problem exists. Maybe you can even determine who's to blame. However, coming up with an effective solution is much more challeng-ing, particularly when you're navigating uncharted waters. Problem-solving abilities do not come naturally to many people. Some are born procrastinators, and others become so stressed that they lose their ability to think rationally. Either way, when confronting a situation that requires action, many people put off addressing the issue until the window of opportunity has closed. If you are faced with a choice, it is usually more effective to take the wrong action than to do nothing at all.

Let's look at the four steps of problem-solving with a potential scenario. Suppose it is just before Christmas. You work as a junior account executive at an advertising agency, and your client is a national bank. Your client contact informs you that the bank has had a sudden change in marketing management and wants your firm to pull together a presentation proposing some new creative campaigns. Unfortunately, the presentation is due just after the New Year, and your boss has already left for vacation. The future of an important client relationship is now in your hands. Yikes! What are you going to do? First, take a deep breath and don't let yourself get overwhelmed. You're going to solve this problem with a clear head, and you will come out looking like a superstar in the process. Here's how.

Step One: Define the problem in concrete terms.

What is the problem, specifically? In less than a week, with most of the team on vacation, we must overhaul our existing advertising plans and devise a slide presentation detailing a new, year-long creative campaign. I have neither the authority nor the expertise to create this presentation on my own.

Is this objectively a problem? Yes. I am not just panicking or exaggerating the criticality of this situation. The client really expects this presentation next week.

What can I gain by fixing it? This is a major opportunity to prove myself to senior executives in my firm and to develop a positive working relationship with my client without the interference of my managers.

Step Two: Generate as many possible solutions to the problem as you can.

What are the alternatives?

1. I could take the problem to the most senior executive in the office and let her handle it.

2. I could call my boss on vacation and explain the situation. Hopefully, she'll come back.

3. My boss recently experienced a similar crisis, and she brought in free-lancers to do the job. I could find their contact information in her address book and call them in to help.

4. I could coordinate a brainstorming session with the more competent account managers in the office and use the ideas generated to formu-late a presentable plan for senior management.

Are any of my potential solutions totally unrealistic? All of the options are realistic except for #3. At my level, I am not authorized to spend several thou-sand dollars to hire freelancers. I also cannot release control of the project to an external resource without senior executive approval.

Step Three: Evaluate each solution and choose the best alternative based on the pros and cons.

What are the pros and cons of Solutions #1, #2, and #4—my most viable alternatives?

✦ **Pros of #1:** Transferring responsibility on something of this magni-tude is perfectly legitimate. I won't have to put myself out. I can go home and enjoy my time off.

✦ **Cons of #1:** The senior executive might not perceive me as a can-do person because I am coming to her with a problem and no potential solution. I will also make zero impact from a visibility perspective.

✦ **Pros of #2:** My boss is probably the best person to handle this situ-ation. She has a long-standing relationship with this client, and she could probably do the job most effectively. Also, I would not be held personally accountable for the outcome.

✦ **Cons of #2:** Even though she'll understand, my boss might resent me for calling her during her well-deserved vacation. I will also lose the opportunity to showcase my problem-solving abilities and strong work ethic to my management and the client.

✦ **Pros of #4:** I could really increase my visibility and impress the of-fice account managers and senior executives by effectively mobilizing resources in my boss's absence. It's possible that this incident will help me get promoted to account manager.

✦ **Cons of #4:** I don't have a lot of experience with direct client inter-action or creative campaign development, so it will be easy to make a mistake. Also, the account managers, the senior executives, and my boss might think I'm overstepping my bounds.

Have I prioritized the best option? After analyzing the pros and cons, I believe the benefits of #4 to be the most substantial, and its drawbacks to be the most tolerable. I can mitigate the risk by collaborating with others as I take the reins.

Step Four: Implement the chosen solution.

How will I roll out and communicate the solution?

1. I will coordinate an hour-long interactive brainstorming session with all of the account managers in the office.

2. I will organize the results of our session and put together a brief action plan.

3. I will present my recommendations to senior management and await a decision.

Have I developed a contingency plan? If things get out of hand, I can always pull in a senior executive to take over (see Solution #1). At least then everyone will know that I put forth my best effort.

Once the problem is yesterday's news, take a moment to assess how things worked out before you move on to the next big thing. If you succeeded, think about what worked and why, and document everything for later use in performance reviews or discussions about your goals with your manager. Don't forget to promote your success as subtly as you can and to sincerely thank the people who helped you along the way. Return the favor by sharing your skills and resources to help your colleagues with projects in the future.

If you didn't succeed, don't look at the experience as a failure. You simply made an ineffective choice. Your career is far from over, so dust yourself off and prepare for the next challenge. As I mentioned in the section on risk-taking, if you think about why you didn't succeed and try a different approach the next time, you'll be 100 percent on track. Take responsibility for the choices you've made, but don't over-apologize. Believe in yourself and others will too!

What I Wish I'd Known

I spent the first 10 years of my career in a dead-end job. At first I just felt lucky to get something, and then I got comfortable. I never set any goals with my boss, and never really grew my skill set. It was just more of the same. I just turned 34, and I realized I was still operating at a junior level. All of my friends have masters degrees or jobs where they have a lot of responsibilities. I'm working with all 25-year-olds. I'd tell my younger self to get with the program—figure out how to move up in this company or leave so I could move up somewhere else. I can't believe how much time I've wasted.

Harry, 34, Los Angeles

Take Home Points

+ **Use your job to your advantage.** Acquire valuable skills and experience that will help you achieve your personal mission. Set specific, reasonable, and attainable goals for your present position that relate to your long-term career strategy.

+ **Determine what they need, and make sure you can provide it.** Ask yourself what your company and department need, and think about how you can use your unique set of skills and talents to aid them. Look for ways to generate and implement new ideas and make your accomplishments visible to others.

+ **Take appropriate risks.** Situations in which you have to act on the fly are excellent opportunities to prove your value. If you're indecisive, you're likely to be perceived as ineffective, whereas if you take a confident stand, you will make a powerful statement about your career potential.

+ **Learn to resolve issues effectively.** Practice the four steps of problem-solving:
  1. Define the problem in concrete terms.
  2. Generate as many potential solutions as you can.
  3. Evaluate each solution.
  4. Choose the best alternative by weighing the pros and cons.

Chapter 5

The Purposeful Workday

Setting goals, generating visibility, solving company problems in the blink of an eye—these all sound great in theory, right? But when you're a newbie in the business world, you consider yourself lucky if you can just make it through the day without dropping one of the 10 plates you have spinning in the air. Besieged by a constant influx of new assignments, you can't even stop to consider how you're using your time. Forget about managing your career and monitoring your performance to achieve optimum results. Some days, work seems so out of control that you just want to put your head down on your desk and mutter "uncle."

Wouldn't it be nice if you didn't have to live this way? What if you ruled your schedule instead of the other way around? What if you were the most effective person on the team, not wasting any energy hating the colleague who never misses a deadline or the one who always leaves the boss's office with all of his questions answered? All of this is totally possible if you take the time to develop a few new habits. In this chapter, I'll cover how to make the most out of the eight-plus hours a day you spend at work—from effective time management and organization to making every piece of communication count. Internalize these skills by reflecting on them outside the office when you have a moment to breathe, and by planning how you can implement sanity-saving processes in advance. I think you'll find that the more proactive you are in managing your workday, the more you will actually achieve—without losing your hair or your bathroom breaks!

Where Has All the Time Gone?

It took me a long time to get out of the mode of thinking that a corporate job is similar to school. When I first started working, I treated everything as though it was an assignment I would be graded on. I had no choice but to complete whatever was asked of me, because I would "fail" if I didn't. Eventually, I realized that I couldn't possibly do it all, and that I was going to have to prioritize if I was going to survive. Some things are just meant to slip under the radar. After all, if a task is relatively unimportant and no one will notice if it isn't done, is it really worth burning out over?

Leslie, 25, Ohio

It's impossible for one human being to do it all, and unless you want to spontaneously combust before the age of 30, you shouldn't try to. If you're thinking that you don't have any say in how you spend your time at work, consider whether this is a subjective state of mind or an objective reality. Is your boss really watching you every second of every day? Probably not—he's got his own work and schedule to manage. I don't care if you're inundated with assignments that could potentially keep you busy for the next decade, the only person who can truly control your schedule is you.

Here's the thing: struggling to get through each day by running frantically from one task to the next won't bring happiness or job satisfaction. You'll be exhausted, stressed, and unmotivated, and you won't have accomplished much in respect to your long-term career goals. For the first year of my career, I was so fried that you could see my hair crackling with electricity. I was so anxious for every senior person to like me that I accepted assignments indiscriminately—like a dog scarfing down table food. Boy, was I earning my $25K salary! I thought that all those days of nonstop agita would certainly earn me a promotion, so naturally I was surprised when I was passed over. At the time, I didn't understand that in the process of doing seven million unrelated and unimportant tasks, I had neglected my professional development and hadn't acquired the core skills I needed to move to the next level.

As a general rule of thumb, you must manage your time strategically if you want your efforts to translate into personal fulfillment and career advancement. You can do this by organizing your schedule around your priorities. What makes a task a priority? Think back to the personal mission statement from Chapter 1 and the goals you set in Chapter 4. For the most part, your priorities should focus on results and relate back to your master plan. Here's an example: My friend Lou's personal mission has always been to live on a farm, but he went to school for hotel management. When Lou started his first job as a hotel front desk attendant, his goal was to develop the skills and knowledge base needed to manage his own country inn. In keeping with this goal, Lou made it a priority to interact with and learn from the Guest Services staff. Several years later, Lou is living on a farm, and the visitors to the country inn he runs pay the mortgage. By leveraging his hotel experience, Lou was able to achieve his long-term vision.

Focusing on tasks that contribute to your big picture sounds like a good idea, but how do you do it? Let's look at the approach advocated by Stephen Covey, author of *The 7 Habits of Highly Effective People*. To paraphrase Covey, there are four types of tasks:

+ **Category 1:** Urgent and important tasks that allow you to keep your job (crises, deadlines, pressing problems).

+ **Category 2:** Non-urgent and important tasks that allow you to develop professionally and work toward a promotion (relationship building, new skill acquisition, opportunity assessment).

+ **Category 3:** Urgent and non-important tasks that allow you to maintain your reputation as a team player (interruptions, certain emails and phone calls, certain meetings, certain administrative work for senior team members).

+ **Category 4:** Non-urgent and non-important tasks that will get you fired if you're not careful (busywork, shooting the breeze with colleagues, instant messaging).

By "urgent," Covey means that the task is highly visible and insists on action. An important task is relevant to your personal mission and corresponding goals. If you've been spending your days running around like a chicken with its head cut off, you are probably spending 90 percent of your time in Categories 1 and 3, and you might have noticed totally irresponsible people who hang out permanently in Category 4. When you master effective time management, you stay out of Category 4 and decrease the time spent in Categories 1 and 3 to allow more time for Category 2. Do this on a regular basis by scheduling time each week to achieve Category 2 tasks that relate to your goals, leaving space for unanticipated Category 1 and Category 3 activities. Review your schedule every day and take the time to reassess it, if needed. Remember to be flexible, because, unfortunately, life doesn't always work out the way you plan, and people often don't behave consistently.

You'll feel more on top of things if you keep a running "to do" list. Mentally separate all of your tasks into their respective categories, and then decide which ones you can eliminate, delay, or delegate. As you undertake a Category 1 or 3 task, think about how you can achieve the maximum impact with the least amount of effort. Remember to keep your department's processes and your own work style in mind. For example, if your group has status meetings every Tuesday morning, you might want to schedule your personal preparation for late in the day on Monday so that you can be prepared to deliver the most up-to-date information. Alternatively, if you are a morning person and your energy is highest just after you wake up, maybe you can slot an hour before office hours on Tuesday to organize your material.

When you're an overworked and underpaid junior member of your company, it's easy to fall prey to low morale. However, by developing strong time-management skills and focusing on tasks that will help you attain your long-term goals more quickly, you'll be able to approach each new day with a sense of purpose.

Saying No

By virtue of their low rank in the organizational hierarchy, twenty-somethings are responsible for meeting the needs of the many individuals who qualify as supervisors. Work rolls downhill from all the people above you and lands in a giant heap on your plate. Many older—but not necessarily wiser—managers have no qualms about piling it on and watching an eager-to-please twenty-something scramble around like a rat in a maze. Well, even if you're an efficient multitasker, you're never going to be Superman. Don't sabotage your goals by taking on more work than you can do just because someone asks you to. Staying true to the priorities we talked about in the last section means learning to say no sometimes.

No is a tricky word in business, because you always want to be perceived as a can-do employee. In general, you should try to preempt situations in which you will have to decline an assignment. A good first step is to formalize your daily responsibilities with your official boss. Find out who on your team is authorized to delegate work to you, and note the type of assignments you can expect from each person. Let's say that Joe, who is outside this core group of delegators, gives you a bunch of client invoices to process. How should you respond? It's perfectly appropriate to politely reply that you would be glad to help, but that you would appreciate it if Joe would check with your manager first. Joe may or may not pursue the matter, but, either way, you have extricated yourself from an awkward situation and have placed the ball squarely in your boss's court. In all likelihood, your boss will say no to Joe for you, especially if processing invoices is outside your area of responsibility.

Now imagine that Jane, a member of your core group of delegators, leaves an urgent assignment on your chair that must be done by the end of the week. Jane has known about the task for a few days, but now it's Friday morning and the deadline is looming. As my mother used to say, don't let another person's lack of planning become your emergency. If your own "to do" list dictates you do something else, speak up. Tell Jane that you wish you could do the task for her, but you are currently working on a project with Tom that requires your attention. Give her the option of resolving the issue with Tom or your boss, and emphasize how much you enjoy working with her. Ideally, Jane will leave the interaction with the perception that you sincerely do want to help her, but that you can't help being caught between conflicting responsibilities.

What if your boss is the one with an urgent request that you don't have the time to attend to? In a way, this is the least painful scenario, because all you really have to do is ask her to help you prioritize your various assignments. You can say something such as, "I'd be happy to take care of that, but today I'm researching statistics for Tom's presentation. Which do you think I should do first?" If your boss wants to snatch your time at Tom's expense, that's her prerogative. Again, though, you have made someone else accountable for deciding which of the competing tasks you should direct your energy toward. Note that in all of these cases, you have declined to take on a new task. However, the actual word *no* and the phrase *I don't have time* are absent from the conversation. Always strive to present yourself as a hardworking and disciplined employee with the best interests of the department and organization at heart.

One last point: subscribing to the servant mentality is not good time management, even if you're not preoccupied with any urgent tasks. When you get into the habit of springing into action the moment a higher-up appears at your desk, people will come to expect that you are always available. Suddenly your delegators won't think twice about asking you to do all kinds of Category 3 (urgent and non-important) tasks. Meanwhile, Category 2 (non-urgent and important) priorities, such as professional development and on-the-job training, will slip further and further down your "to do" list. Remember, in the big-picture scheme of things, Category 2 should be ahead of Category 3, so no matter how busy your department is, always make time in your schedule for Category 2 activities. Have trouble doing this? Take note of the time it takes you to complete Category 3 assignments. For example, if you think it will take you an hour to create a new database for your boss, tell him you'll have it done by the end of the day. Also, instead of asking for new work the second you encounter a few free hours, spend some quality time researching your company's products, participating in training courses, or meeting with your mentor (Category 2 activities). It's probably long overdue.

It might be difficult to turn your back on a Category 3 task that's presented to you or to set aside company time for your own Category 2 needs. But think about it this way: You have to say no to something. It's either the non-important or the important things. You decide.

Battling Procrastination

We all procrastinate in one way or another. Just because something is worth doing doesn't mean it's easy to get started. Even at work, we're constantly tempted by activities that are more fun and take less effort, such as chatting with a coworker or texting a friend. However, when you're trying to stick to a schedule of prioritized tasks, repeated procrastination can wreak havoc on your master plan. It may start with a simple decision to take a longer lunch instead of making headway on your first business plan, but, next thing you know, your goals are taking longer to achieve and your upward mobility has slowed to a crawl.

To fight this battle and win, you first must acknowledge that you are procrastinating. Did you actually schedule time to play Solitaire, or are you just putting off doing work? Confront the procrastination demon head-on and ask yourself why you're avoiding the task. Could it be that the task isn't worth the effort? Maybe the benefits of completing the task don't outweigh the time and energy you'll spend on it. If this is the case, reconsider whether it's a priority. Should you decide that the task is important, however, now is the time to rally your sense of discipline and get moving. Following are reasons you might use to put off work. Arm yourself with the motivational arguments I provide, and begin the battle against procrastination.

- ✦ **You can do it later.** Think about whether a momentary reprieve is worth having to overhaul your whole calendar to reschedule a particular task. Do you want to repeat this same dance again later, or would you rather just get the task over with now?

- ✦ **The task is boring and you'd rather do something fun.** Think about the big picture. Sometimes the most worthwhile activities require the most effort, and, in turn, produce the greatest rewards. Besides, how can you really have fun when you're feeling guilty about blowing off your work?

- ✦ **You're afraid the task will be too hard or take too long.** Consider that every minute you spend procrastinating is one minute you could be using to complete the task at hand. Instead of looking at the task as a never-ending dark tunnel, break it up into a series of short, manageable assignments, and think about resources you could call on for help at each stage.

- ✦ **You don't know where to start.** Choose the least complicated part of the task, and work at completing it as swiftly and efficiently as possible. Once you've successfully finished one component, you'll gain momentum. The task will no longer seem like such a bear, and it will be much easier to move to the next component.

Don't forget to reward yourself for beating procrastination and finishing a task. Instead of moving on to the next assignment right away, block out time to do something you enjoy. Long hours of hard work will pass by much more easily when you can anticipate a fun activity at the end of the process. As I was writing this book, for example, I'd tell myself that each time I finished a section, I would spend a few hours watching a movie on cable or playing a video game. We all have our mindless vices. Remember Jack Nicholson in *The Shining*? All work and no play makes Jack a dull (not to mention psychotic) boy. So if you've earned it, go ahead and indulge!

You Too Can Be the "Organized One"

Thanks to good old Microsoft, I became a pro at scheduling meetings for my team, which was dispersed across the country in four different offices. Somehow I thought that a meeting equaled progress on a project. It took me about five meetings to realize that we were always discussing the same topics, but never making decisions or creating action plans around any of them. It was like the clock had stopped. No matter how much we talked, we never accomplished anything. The meetings were actually a huge productivity drain because they took up so much time that they prevented us from getting our individual work done.

Seth, 27, Texas

Have you ever noticed that the most stressed-out folks at work are habitually disorganized? In their defense, it's easy to lose track of an important document, project, or deadline when your smartphone is beeping every second. However, there are only so many things in the professional world that you can control, and the way you organize is one of them. When you're organized, you're more confident, efficient, and dependable. You're also much less likely to be forced into early retirement by a heart attack or a nervous breakdown.

Before I launch into a discussion of ways to preserve your sanity by incorporating organization into your daily routine, let me admit something. I do tend to believe that organization is one of those pesky inherited traits. If you have it, it's likely that you've had it all along, and you probably skipped ahead the second you saw this section's header. If you don't, these suggestions might not be as easy to implement as they sound. Take heart, though. If you can take one thing away from this section and use it to become more effective at work, reading it will have been worthwhile.

In Chapter 2, I talked about utilizing good organizational skills as you begin a new job, and I recommended starting at home base: your desk. To briefly recap: please do not buy into the misconception that an Armageddon of a cubicle makes you look super busy and hardworking. Remember that the professional world judges performance by results, not effort, and your managers will doubt that you can achieve such results in the midst of total chaos. For those of us in a constant state of information overload, keeping a neat workspace requires vigilance. I suggest thinking of every new item arriving on your desk as an insect that is infiltrating your territory. Your job is to dispose of it as quickly as possible, either by chucking it in the nearest recycling bin or putting it in its proper place. The only material on your desk should pertain to the task you're working on at that very minute. Everything else should be labeled and filed for easy access.

Treat your email inbox the same way. Delete spam and other messages you don't need as soon as they pop in, and if you know you have to respond, get in the habit of doing so immediately. When you receive a new task via email, don't let it linger. Add it to your master "to do" list. Should a message require follow-up at a later time, flag it, and place it in a subfolder that you review on a daily basis.

I'm frustrated with a few people I work with who don't read their email and always seem to be unavailable. I've tried everything from tagging messages with read receipts to automatically re-sending messages that bounce back with one of those cheerful "Out of the Office" replies. I'm sure these email neglecters have their reasons, but think about this: If I know they're not staying on top of their mail, other people, including their managers, must know it too. Even if these people haven't been seriously burned yet, their reputation is being compromised as we speak. Don't get tripped up by this one. During the business week, unless you're on vacation or in a meeting or seminar in which checking your phone would be rude, make it your business to read and respond to email several times a day.

Automate for Maximum Efficiency

These 21st-century productivity hacks will ensure that you have more time for the important things and can stay at the top of your game.

✦ **Smartphone:** If you're similar to me, sometimes the smartphone can be more trouble than its worth, especially when the old Wi-Fi connection is spotty. However, as an Android user, I recently discovered Tasker (tasker.dinglisch.net). Apps like Tasker essentially allow your phone to read your mind by using certain contexts to trigger tasks or setting changes. A context could be something as simple as the day of the week, a headset being plugged in, having a certain battery percentage, or entering a certain location. Once a context takes place, it triggers an action like turning off auto-sync, loading Pandora, or sending a text message to a certain person. Next, there is the Holy Grail of automation that is the If This Then

That, also known as the IFTTT app (ifttt.com). IFTTT connects up to Google apps and others and allows them to talk to each other without your intervention. Basically, you create your own recipes such that if a particular trigger is present, an action is generated. One example of a recipe? "If I am endorsed on LinkedIn, publish a tweet on Twitter."

✦ **Social Media:** Once you arrive at the office, take a vow against spending too much time on social media and not enough time working. Fortunately, there are tools to help. Use Hootsuite (hootsuite.com) or Tweetdeck (tweetdeck.com) to schedule social media posts, retweets, and anything else you want to publish or respond to that day. You don't have to bother logging on multiple times to see if someone mentioned you either. These apps will tell you automatically so that you can respond appropriately in real time. Real-time too much for you? Try Twilert (twilert.com) to alert you to any Twitter keywords you may want to track, several times or just once a day, just like a Google Alert.

✦ **Storage and Backup:** At the end of a busy day at work, you've probably accumulated more paperwork than is useful to anyone. How about automating your note-taking and document storage via a tool like Evernote (Evernote.com)? Evernote not only allows you to save your ideas, things you hear, and things you see throughout the day, but you can also scan the day's papers directly to an Evernote virtual notebook. Two major advantages of Evernote: it works with every kind of mobile device and computer, and it allows you to encrypt confidential data. As for all of those business cards you've collected, consider downloading an app like ScanBizCards (ScanBizCards.com) that allows you to automatically input card data right into your online contact database so you don't have to worry about losing or storing the physical cards. One hard drive crash in a lifetime is too many. At the same time, you don't want to spend your days thinking about backup. Fortunately, you can automate regular backups of your devices to an external hard drive using software such as Acronis (Acronis.com) and to the Internet using a service like CrashPlan (Crashplan.com). You should also make a habit of backing up important content to the cloud via an app like Dropbox.com

Project Management

Several twenty-somethings have told me that they have difficulty coordinating projects with multiple tasks and individuals involved. Learning to do this well is a prerequisite for getting ahead in the professional world. I have a few years of project management experience under my belt, and this has been my strategy:

Step One: Outline

As soon as I leave my boss's office with a new mission, I consider the scope of the project and the general approach I want to take. I then create a rough outline that breaks the project down into smaller components.

Step Two: Initial Project Meeting

Conducting an initial project meeting allows me to turn the assignment of tasks into a team activity. By brainstorming with my teammates about the best way to accomplish various phases of a project, I encourage them to approach the work with enthusiasm and commitment. Note that team meetings should not be called indiscriminately. As much as I love the people I work with, if I want to hang out and chitchat, we'll go to happy hour. Remember that the real project work gets done outside the conference room and that, most of the time, you do not accomplish things simply by talking about them. In general, I don't usurp an hour of my colleagues' time unless the meeting will serve a combination of the following purposes:

+ Generates ideas that will result in an appropriate project strategy.

+ Delegates each required task so that every member of the team is personally accountable for something.

+ Provides status updates so that one hand always knows what the other is doing, and so that problems and delays can be flagged before they get out of hand.

Step Three: Project Chart

After an initial project meeting, I use Basecamp (Basecamp.com) to develop a chart that displays timelines, the interrelationships of the various tasks, and the people responsible for each project component. I check the chart once a day to monitor our progress and keep track of pending deadlines.

Step Four: Communication

In order to organize a project successfully, you must make it easy for your team members to communicate with each other. My chart, which lives in the cloud, is a living document. Everyone on the team, including my supervisor, has access to view and modify the chart as we move forward on various tasks. The chart, along with ongoing status reviews, ensures that every team member understands not just his or her own responsibilities, but everyone else's as well.

Here are some traits I advise you to hone in order to become a project management superstar.

+ **Possess unofficial authority.** Often, the best project managers (PMs) do not have formal authority over those working on their teams. Instead, their natural charisma and infectious enthusiasm motivates people to follow and listen to them, and helps them develop an organization-wide reputation as a popular leader.

+ **Be a networking star.** The best PMs understand who they need to go to to get things done, and they develop strong relationships with those individuals so that cross-functional projects run more smoothly. Also, should the project run into a snag, great PMs can rely on their network to find and implement a workaround.

+ **Ask questions.** A project cannot succeed without a PM who seeks and listens to the advice of experienced partners, and then puts processes in place for soliciting feedback on a regular basis. They are clear about what needs to be done, by whom, and by what deadline, and they intuitively understand the questions to ask to ensure a project is moving in the right direction.

+ **Pay obsessive attention to detail.** When you're leading a large project with thousands of components, it's easy for small but critical pieces to get lost in the shuffle. The best PMs keep track of these details so that red flags are dealt with immediately—before they become deal-breaking issues.

+ **Understand the big picture.** At the same time, though, talented PMs can pick the areas to focus on by always keeping the end result in mind. They align the goals of the project with the overall goals of the organization, and if a project element doesn't further the big picture or impact the project in a significant way, it can be tossed out or at least back-burnered in favor of more pressing concerns.

✦ **Have thick skin.** In order to be able to sustain a complicated effort that places stress on all parties, PMs must be able to let harsh criticism roll off them. They are able to take the brunt of the fallout when a client or higher-up is upset about a delay, and put themselves in the line of fire if the project does not deliver in some way. They keep their cool and view failures as intriguing challenges rather than soul-crushing setbacks. They can make decisions quickly, without worrying about what every individual on the team is going to think.

✦ **Be an amateur psychologist.** Great PMs are able to read between the lines when team members aren't getting along, or when someone is underperforming. They are able to effectively manage the expectations of internal and external stakeholders by intuitively understanding what's important to each person. They speak to others empathetically—as fellow human beings—and diplomatically resolve conflicts when they occur.

Whether you're an experienced project manager leading a huge team or an entry-level assistant in charge of a single intern, look for ways to implement and showcase your own style. By inspiring trust, confidence, and cooperation, you'll emerge as an effective leader poised for even greater things.

Making Yourself Understood

Many people assume that communication is common sense and that there's nothing to learn about it. A manager, for example, wouldn't dream of sending a new employee on a client visit without providing in-depth training on what the employee should talk about, but that same manager will most likely ignore the specifics of *how* the rep should speak to the client. Sounds pretty dumb, huh? After all, if the employee doesn't communicate effectively with the client in the first few minutes of interaction, he might have the door slammed in his face before he has a chance to recite his product's compelling features. Your everyday work life is the same way. You could be the smartest, most qualified employee in the company, but no one will care what you have to offer if you're unable to make yourself understood. So how do you ensure that your communication style is a competitive advantage rather than a liability? I'll get to that soon. But first, let's dissect a few types of communication found in the business world.

✦ **Aggressive:** Communication that infers blame, places responsibility for a bad outcome on the other person, and takes credit for any and all successes. The aggressive communicator discourages collaboration and cooperation.

+ **Passive:** Communication that does not convey the whole picture. The passive communicator shares information with reluctance, fails to offer feedback, and responds with blanket agreement—particularly at the first sign of confrontation.

+ **Assertive:** Communication that is not accusatory, nonjudgmental, and conversational in tone. Assertive communicators are in control of themselves. They think before responding, avoid personalizing problems, and consider the big picture.

I'm sure you've had the pleasure of interacting with plenty of aggressive and passive communicators. Maybe some of them were lucky enough to advance to a high level. Usually, though, these extreme styles will handicap a career, because people don't respond well to them. If you have your eye on a VP position and want to be seen as a powerful communicator and a key influencer, assertiveness—or the ability to stand up for your rights, opinions, ideas, and desires, while respecting those of others—is the way to go.

Let me confess that I am not naturally the most assertive person in the world—I definitely lean more toward the passive style. Though I hate to admit it, I think it has something to do with growing up as a female in our society. Women are encouraged to be passive from early childhood up until we're thrust into the business world, when we're expected to promptly grow a backbone. Fortunately, communicating assertively on an everyday basis is pretty easy provided you willingly express yourself clearly, confidently, and in a tone that sounds friendly rather than fake.

It's harder to be assertive when you move beyond small talk into the realms of persuasion and confrontation. In situations in which you must communicate your point to someone who doesn't agree, assertiveness marks the difference between being perceived as a leader or as one of those "ineffective" or "difficult" people who populate the lower ranks of the professional world. Hendrie Weisinger, author of *Emotional Intelligence at Work*, makes the following suggestions for incorporating assertive communication into your problem-solving technique.

+ Use facts to justify your position.

+ Acknowledge that you understand the other person's point of view.

+ Repeat your position (be consistent and don't raise your voice).

+ Communicate emotion by using feeling statements ("I feel disappointed that you are not comfortable assigning me this project") rather than accusatory statements ("You don't trust me to work with your clients") that express an opinion as a matter of fact.

+ Strive for a compromise.

Plan for important conversations ahead of time. Assertiveness does not mean opening your mouth each and every time you have an opinion. One of the most common complaints I hear about twenty-something employees is that they think they know everything and don't hesitate to convince others of this at every opportunity. Have deference for the years of expertise in the room, and the fact that your organization is still in business for a reason. Before you speak, make sure you fully understand your own point of view, and think about the most appropriate way to communicate it. It never hurts to take an extra minute to decide whether something should be shared, and/ or if it's an appropriate time to interject your thoughts. When in doubt, err on the side of caution.

Watch people around you who are using assertiveness to their advantage. *Toronto Star* career columnist Mark Swartz recommends choosing a few role models in the office, and noting the behaviors they use to communicate effectively. Why does your coworker always seem to get the ear of your boss? How does your supervisor come out of every staff meeting with an increased budget for new projects? Try some of the successful techniques you see, keeping in mind that your communication style should match who you are personality-wise. If you stray too far from what comes naturally, you might be perceived as phony.

Now that I've talked about the role of assertiveness, let's cover specific strategies for leveraging three communication vehicles—writing, speaking, and listening—to help you connect with people in ways that will enhance your career potential.

What You Write

I learned the hard way never to write anything in an email that I wouldn't want to see on the front page of the Washington Post after I overheard my workmate talking to one of our colleagues about her recent divorce. She sounded really upset, so I wrote her an email expressing my sympathy and telling her I could totally relate to her predicament. Unfortunately, I put in all the details of my own divorce, including my ex-husband's infidelity. I really wish I had just talked to her in person, because I accidentally sent that email to the entire company. I have never been so mortified in my life.

Hilary, 29, Virginia

Word on the street is that if you're not a communications professional, you don't need to pay too much attention to your writing skills. This is not so. In fact, good writing is one of the most underrated skills in the business world. Maybe this attitude is a defense mechanism. After all, many business-people are bad writers, and how can you judge your employees on something you don't even have a clue about? If you're not the most polished writer in the world, with technology and all you might get away with it. But you're not reading this book so you can just slide by. Presumably, you want to impress the socks off your managers and come out looking better than everyone else. There's no better way to do this than to showcase the rare talent of a superior command of the written language.

I could happily devote an entire book to the craft of writing. However, because that's not what I'm here to do, I'll limit my advice to two simple rules:

✦ **Rule #1:** C&C (Clear & Concise). Most people in today's professional world have an extremely short attention span, so get right to it by prefacing your document with a brief, objective-oriented introduction, and by setting off your key points with bullets for painless consumption. Whether you're writing a routine email or a quarterly business plan, offer only the necessary information and be prepared to provide supplemental material. Your word choice should accurately convey your meaning, and your vocabulary and tone should reflect your audience. Use the active verb tense ("I wrote this plan") rather than passive ("This plan was written by me") whenever you can. Don't load Microsoft Powerpoint presentations down with too much text; instead, employ plenty of colorful graphics, charts, and photographs to keep your audience's attention.

✦ **Rule #2:** Quality Control. There is no such thing as a perfect first draft, so get into the habit of proofreading your writing and having a colleague read it over as well. Sloppiness is the enemy. Every document that leaves your desk should be carefully checked for clean formatting, proper grammar, and correct spelling. Think of your work product as little pieces of yourself sent out into the world. Even if you're the 15th person to review a document, be the one who takes responsibility for sending it forward error-free.

What if you need some help bringing your writing up to par? I suggest contacting local colleges or continuing education programs about a variety of business writing courses. These classes are typically inexpensive, and they can often be tailored to your specific needs. Don't let an inflexible schedule discourage you; many courses are now offered online.

The majority of written communication now takes place through email, which can be rather complicated. You still want to follow the C&C and Quality Control rules of regular written communication, but you also have to balance a multitude of considerations that are unique to the medium of email.

Allow me to share a true story. A student at a prestigious U.S. university was studying abroad, and emailed the dean of Undergraduate Affairs to determine the status of his Resident Advisor application. Because this particular student had been away all semester, the dean had forgotten to include his application in the pool. The student, having lost his opportunity to be a Resident Advisor, was quite upset. He shared his displeasure with the dean via email.

The dean became defensive. He intended to forward the student's email to a colleague in the office, adding the comment, "What a little snot. These spoiled brats think they're entitled to everything. Why doesn't he just transfer?" Unfortunately, the dean accidentally hit Reply, and the student received his nasty retort instead. No matter how much the dean apologized, the damage could not be undone. The already irate student had a field day distributing the dean's inappropriate and unprofessional response to everyone he knew, and, within a few months, the infamous email exchange had made its way across the country. Ask yourself this question: How many email offenses like this does it take to ruin a prominent university's reputation?

Email can be your best friend or your worst enemy. Here are a few tips to make it work for you.

Smart Email Communication Top 10

1. **Realize that email is not private.** Not only can your company's IT department access it, but you also never know to whom your messages might be forwarded—accidentally or intentionally. Avoid discussing sensitive information or writing anything negative unless it's specifically requested by your boss and/or supported by fact.

2. **Maintain a consistent professional persona.** You can achieve this by crafting friendly, polite, and grammatically correct messages. Because you can't rely on voice or nonverbal cues, always reread your emails to make sure the message you are sending is idiot-proof. Don't get too cutesy with your emoticons or acronyms (LOL, BRB).

3. **Keep emails short and to the point.** Make sure to include an informative and specific subject line (for example, don't just call the message "Update"). Begin with a call to action that encourages the person to read the message (starting with the word *you* usually does the trick). Put your key message up front, and if the information you must communicate is longer than two to three paragraphs, attach a document with the relevant details.

4. **Use email to reinforce in-person conversations.** Summarize meetings, impart helpful information (for example, FYI—"For Your Information"—messages), or respond appropriately to an important issue (for example, CYA—"Cover Your Ass"—messages) via email to reinforce face-to-face discussions you have with colleagues.

5. **Don't use email as a forum to express displeasure or criticize.** Do these things in person rather than taking the easy way out. If you must highlight a problem in email, be positive and solution-oriented.

6. **Use email sparingly.** Carbon copy (CC) your boss only on messages that clearly demonstrate that you are doing your job. Avoid sending him thousands of emails unless you want him to stop reading them.

7. **Use flags and read receipts.** When sending an important message, call it out in some way so that the recipient is not tempted to ignore it.

8. **Be courteous.** In general, older workers consider it rude to email a question to anyone sitting within 10 feet of you. Make an effort to speak to these people face to face.

9. **Know what you are sending before you send it.** Before hitting Reply, carefully read an email in its entirety. If it's preceded by a series of messages, make sure to read and understand the whole string first.

10. **Keep personal emails personal.** If you want to send personal emails at work, set up a separate account. Don't send those annoying forwards to your work friends unless they also qualify as real friends (see Chapter 3).

What if you are a business email pro, but you still can't get a response from a colleague who is holding up your progress on a project? Having been in this situation myself many times, I turned to one of my favorite workplace pundits, Alison Green of the Ask a Manager blog (AskAManager.com). This was her advice:

> *You have to be straightforward with the person and tell her, "Hey, I'm having trouble getting responses from you and it's keeping me from being able to move forward on this project. Is there something I could do differently that would help?" This way, you put her on notice that there's a problem. You could potentially find that there's something going on that you didn't know about—she's swamped with something she has been told is a higher priority, or she just didn't realize it was a high priority, etc. After that, if the problem continues, I think I'd alert her one more time: "Hey, I know we talked about this before but I'm still not getting what I need. What can we do differently so that we can move forward on this?"*
>
> *At that point, you've alerted her twice that it's a problem. If the unresponsiveness continues, you don't have much choice but to go to your manager. I realize this feels like tattling to a lot of people, but I tend to believe that the entire concept of tattling doesn't really fit in the workplace. You could even just say something like, "Could you nudge Julie for me? I'm sure she has other things on her plate, but I haven't been able to get a response from her."*

Before we move on from written communication, I'd like to say a word about texting. I hear that you can't live without it, but you must proceed carefully when using it in a business setting. For one thing, don't expect to communicate this way with your colleagues or clients unless texting has already been established as an acceptable means of interaction. When sending work-related texts, make sure your name shows up as something professional, and greet the recipient before jumping in with a request. Also, don't shorten words so much that your point gets lost, watch the level of informality, and be conscious of wasting too much time shooting messages back and forth. As with email, keep a saved log of important conversations, and always pause for a moment before you hit Send. You'd be surprised how many IT departments work their magic to monitor texts sent from company networks.

What You Say

> *I always keep my notepad handy when I go downstairs, in case I run into someone I need to talk to in the elevator. People in my company are so buried that it's nearly impossible to get them to respond to me via email or voice mail. And forget about scheduling meetings. Cornering them in the elevator is the perfect opportunity to get quick answers so that I can do my job.*
>
> *Steven, 26, North Carolina*

Author and motivational guru Dale Carnegie once said that the person who can speak acceptably is usually considered to possess greater ability than he actually has. In my experience, this is true. If you look and act as though you know what you're talking about, people will think that you do, regardless of the reality. You may not have a vast store of knowledge and years of experience to draw from, but you can get promoted just by creating the perception of being competent and informed.

I translate Carnegie's "speaking acceptably" as "effective in-person communication," because there is much more to speaking than the content that comes out of your mouth. Did you know that only 7 percent of meaning is conveyed with the words you say? People get the rest of your message from how you say it. In-person communication includes nonverbal cues, vocal style, articulateness, and sincerity, and it plays a huge role in conveying the powerful corporate persona I talked about in the beginning chapters of this book. Let's spend a moment addressing each of these components.

1. **Nonverbal cues:** Positive body language supports your message and encourages cooperation. To employ this, position yourself next to the person you're speaking to and lean toward him, but don't get so close that you invade his personal space. Sustain eye contact for several seconds throughout the course of the conversation, and always smile (unless you're delivering bad news). Take the time to focus on the other person, and don't fidget or give in to background distractions. If you want to emphasize an important point, use your hands.

2. **Vocal style:** Need something to do in the shower besides sing? Practice adjusting your tone, pace, and volume according to the situation and/or person with whom you are going to communicate. Enunciate your words so that people can understand you. Whether you are passionate about your subject or not, always convey a little enthusiasm, people will be more likely to listen.

3. **Articulateness:** Just as with written communication, practice your command of verbal communication so that you can accurately express what you mean. Improve your vocabulary in order to appear intelligent and well-educated, but don't overdo it. If you throw around too many industry terms or five-syllable GRE words, you'll look like you are trying to impress someone. A huge part of articulateness is being succinct, so learn to communicate your main points using as few words as possible. This is particularly important if you regularly participate in meetings. There is nothing worse than being the one person who goes on and on while everyone else just wants to get out of there.

4. **Sincerity:** Note that there is a fine line between portraying a strong professional persona and coming across as being fake. Although your tone should generally be confident, friendly, and conversational, you should avoid saying things you don't mean or adapting a style that is completely contrary to your personality.

Voice mail is the perfect medium to work on your in-person communication technique. Your greeting serves as an introduction to the professional you. It is the starting point from which many people will communicate with you, and if you work in nearly any kind of organization, you have to use it. Sorry.

Record your greeting before or after work hours to avoid office background noise. Politely and confidently state your name, department, and company, and invite the caller to leave a message, which you will promptly return. I would avoid saying what day it is in your message. I guarantee you will get behind in recording a new greeting each day, and, next thing you know, it will be October and your voice mail will still say it's June 5!

Public speaking is another good way to hone your in-person communication skills. Many of us fear getting up in front of a group, yet I've never known a person who was physically incapable of doing it after practicing a few times. Public speaking increases your confidence level, your poise, and your ability to flexibly convey information about your subject matter. It also pays huge dividends in terms of being taken seriously as a twenty-something in the business world. Look for opportunities to deliver formal or informal presentations whenever you can, and, as you prepare, consider using a few notes instead of a script. Extemporaneous remarks are more effective for connecting with your audience on a personal level and provide much better training for those critical one-on-one interactions.

Even if you're a master of in-person communication, people won't always welcome you in for a chat with open arms. As you well know, the professional world is a hectic environment where no one has enough hours in the day to do what they need to do. The higher the executive's title, the less time she has to speak with you. Here are a few hints for getting face time with those hard-to-pin-down senior folks.

+ Stop by her office instead of calling or sending an email.

+ Persuade her admin to give you a 10-minute slot on her calendar. (Make sure not to stay a minute longer.)

+ Catch her for a quick conversation in the hallway or elevator.

+ Invite her to have lunch in the cafeteria. (Everyone has to eat!)

Once you manage to get in front of the person, say what you have to say and get out of there. If necessary, prepare a list ahead of time of the things you want to cover so that you can whiz right through them. If the person learns that a meeting with you doesn't mean she will be held up all day, she will be more likely to respond to your meeting request next time.

One last point about speaking: if you have the opportunity to enhance your knowledge of another language, or even to start learning one from scratch, I highly recommend pursuing it. As English decreases in prominence and the economy becomes even more global, knowing additional languages will prove invaluable. Most community colleges, embassies, and consulates offer evening and weekend classes, or you could learn from the comfort of your couch with a self-directed program such as Rosetta Stone (*RosettaStone.co.uk*) or Pimsleur (*Pimsleur.com*).

When You Listen

You may have taken one look at this subhead and said, "What am I, 5 years old? I thought I learned to listen in kindergarten!" If you think about it, though, this isn't exactly the case. You learned to hear people when they talk, but you didn't necessarily get into the habit of actively listening to them. In our jobs, our relationships suffer, we miss out on a lot of information, and, ultimately, we make our jobs harder because we don't pay attention to what people are saying.

It's in your best interests to avoid unnecessary communication breakdowns caused by a failure to listen. Author Hendrie Weisinger recommends that you begin by making yourself aware of ways you might unconsciously filter out what others are saying. Filters are generated by thoughts, ideas, and feelings. They influence the type of and how much information we hear. There are four kinds of filters:

1. **The predilection filter:** Hearing what you want to hear instead of what is meant.

2. **The who filter:** Placing importance based on the person doing the talking.

3. **The facts filter:** Being oblivious to the emotional subtext of the conversation.

4. **The distracting thoughts filter:** Allowing your mind to wander.

Once you've identified what types of filters you use and under what circumstances you use them, employ these suggestions for practicing "filter prevention," and also for becoming an active and involved listener:

+ Don't interrupt.

+ Don't tune out because you think you know what's coming.

+ Read between the lines, and assess what is meant vs. what is said.

+ Acknowledge that you are paying attention by sustaining eye contact, nodding, or saying "uh huh."

+ Verbally summarize what the speaker has said, paraphrasing rather than repeating it verbatim.

+ Empathize with how the speaker is feeling.

+ Ask specific, clarifying questions.

+ Take notes to keep yourself focused and to help you remember what's being communicated.

+ Don't type on your smartphone while someone is talking to you.

✦ Don't change the subject until you're certain the speaker has concluded his or her point.

You can encourage others to listen to you by emphasizing key points, and by asking for a restatement of your message in the person's own words. Make your position relevant to the listener, and, as a general rule, listen more than you talk. You will stand out as one of the few people your colleagues consider it a pleasure to talk to!

Gender Differences in Communication

Remember *Men Are from Mars and Women Are from Venus*? Romantic relationships are one thing, but no one talks much about how Mars and Venus fare at work. In fact, there are significant verbal and nonverbal differences in the way the two genders get their messages across in a professional setting.

Verbal Communication

In the area of verbal communication, men tend to speak more concisely, whereas women tend to elaborate or explain their points of view. Men tend to assert their ideas as if they are fact, whereas women tend to phrase their ideas as questions and add disclaimers ("I might be wrong...") or hedges ("Maybe").

Men engage in verbal bantering and derogatory comments to establish rapport, whereas women think a certain level of formality is more appropriate. Men make demands of the team, whereas women try to gain consensus first. Men want to talk about plan specifics, whereas women want to talk about needs and feelings.

Men don't give positive feedback as frequently, whereas women think it's important for reports to feel valued. Men more often make decisions based on careful analysis of the facts, whereas women are more likely to spot the right decision quickly, often as a result of intuition.

Non-verbal Communication

On the non-verbal side of the equation, women tend to smile a lot, whereas men remain poker-faced. Women nod to indicate understanding, whereas men nod to indicate agreement. Women stand face-to-face to reflect engagement and shoulder-to-shoulder to reflect disengagement. Men stand face-to-face to reflect aggression and shoulder-to-shoulder to reflect collaboration. In a work setting, women often contract to make themselves seem smaller, whereas men do the opposite and often expand their presence to fill the room.

Getting on the Same Page

Fortunately, there are things both women and men can do to improve their effectiveness in communicating with the opposite gender. Let's start with the women. Women can:

+ Speak in a strong voice even when they don't feel confident.

+ Concisely explain the factual reasons behind their ideas and decisions.

+ Excuse themselves promptly if they feel their emotions getting the best of them.

+ Ask a man whose approach they are questioning to help them understand the rationale behind it.

+ Steer clear of interpersonal criticism unless it's absolutely necessary.

Suggestions for the men include:

+ Hear a woman out without interrupting.

+ Listen to and acknowledge a woman's feelings.

+ Ask for feedback as opposed to dictating.

+ Minimize the amount of teasing in group situations.

+ Avoid aggressive behavior such as raising one's voice in a disagreement.

What I Wish I'd Known

I remember getting really insulted by an executive who seemed to keep stonewalling my ideas. I was 22, and I thought that of course he should want to listen to what I had to say. I was so upset about being ignored that I talked to my boss, and she thought I was overreacting. Eventually I gave up trying to get noticed, but I got a bad taste in my mouth every time I'd see the executive. I would tell my younger self to recognize that the exec was probably just really busy and that his lack of communication was nothing personal. It would have been great to get advice from my boss or my other mentor at the time about a more effective way to get the exec's attention instead of just complaining that my way wasn't working.

Allen, 33, New York

Take-Home Points

✦ **Manage your time strategically.** Arrange your schedule around your priorities, and learn to say no to nonstrategic tasks in a way that maintains your persona as a can-do employee.

✦ **Implement effective organizational tools.** There are only so many things in the professional world you can control, and your own organizational style is one of them. Find a simple routine that works for you, and stick to it.

✦ **Be assertive.** Become a powerful communicator and key influencer by standing up for your ideas, while also respecting those of others.

✦ **Fine-tune your writing, speaking, and listening skills.** Express your ideas confidently and succinctly. If you look and act as though you know what you're talking about, people will believe that you do. Practice "filter prevention" in order to become an active and involved listener.

Chapter 6

Check Your Attitude at the Door

The most disgruntled employees in today's companies are usually the twenty-somethings. Why? I think it's because the people running the business world are of a different generation. Parents in the late 20th century were instructed to tell their children they could be anything they wanted, consuming a steady diet of "how to raise a happy, confident, socially skilled, psychologically stable, intellectually stimulated child" books. As a result, today's twenty-somethings feel as though they are the most special people in the universe. Educated on computers and the Internet, you learned rapidly or were left behind, and now that you're in the professional world, you're innovative, entrepreneurial, and devoted to changing business for the better.

Although most managers would like to believe otherwise, the business world doesn't always operate according to these values. In fact, the generation in power tends to believe that you twenty-something employees would do the world a favor if you settled down, did your jobs, and resigned yourselves to living in the "real world" of organizational bureaucracy. Naturally, this is frustrating, and it's only too common for companies to become a battleground of "us vs. them." Only, guess what? *They* are in the driver's seat for the time being. When you're running the show, perhaps you'll do things differently, but you'll never get there unless you learn to work with the system and serve with a smile.

Because this can be more challenging than any skill we've discussed so far, I'm devoting an entire chapter to strategies for combating negativity, maintaining a positive attitude, and staying motivated in the face of difficult circumstances. By the time you move on to the next chapter, you will be armed with the most powerful weapon a twenty-something can possess in the business world: the ability to harness the power of your own thinking and create a pleasant situation out of a maddening one.

No, You're Not Crazy

My department must hold the record for the company's fastest revolving door. In less than a year, we've been re-orged three times. I've had four different managers, and every new person who comes in wants to mark his territory. Meanwhile, none of these people know as much about my area as I do, so their guidance is useless. Plus, I'm changing direction so much I never get anything done. What is it they say—same sh*t, different day? If I have to be "rah rah" at yet another welcome lunch, I think I'm going to explode.

Robert, 27, Oregon

If you're reading this chapter because you're struggling with an attitude problem at work, you're not alone, and your hostility is probably justified. I've spoken to dozens of twenty-somethings, and most have spent their fair share of time banging their heads against the wall and regretting the day they signed their offer letters.

As much as I feel your pain, I don't believe it does much good to complain, because unless you're going to grad school or can successfully start your own business, you're in this world to stay. We all have to deal with business-world insanity whether we love our jobs or not, so we might as well take the necessary steps to overcome the challenges. However, because this chapter is about your emotional well-being, we need to start by recognizing the things about work that drive us nuts. Most of these points will probably sound familiar, so read on and be comforted. Warning: Do not hang this list in your cube!

Top 10 Annoying Things About the Business World

1. **Déjà vu.** It seems as though it's a requirement in the professional world that you spend huge amounts of time reporting the same information in a dozen different formats, attending status meetings in which conversation from the week before is repeated word for word, and putting out the same fires, because your department doesn't learn from its mistakes.

2. **Invoking syndrome.** The invoking syndrome occurs when colleagues try to persuade you to do what they want by name-dropping someone higher up. Whether the executive manager was actually involved or not, invoking him is a manipulative tactic used to get you to bend to your colleagues' wishes (for example, "Really? Well, I spoke to the CEO last night, and he told me we have to do the event this way.")

3. **Egomania.** When certain people reach a high level in a company, they think that they are better than everyone else and that they are entitled to be treated as a god. Regardless of the issue, they believe they are always right and that they can't possibly learn anything from someone lower on the chain.

4. **Hierarchies.** In the business world, all men are not created equal, and sometimes you can actually get in trouble just by talking to someone higher up without going through the proper channels. Unless you happen to know the right people, you're invisible.

5. **Denigration.** In some companies, it's an unspoken rule that the younger you are, the less respect you receive. Many senior managers are quick to call you on the carpet for situations that may or may not be your fault, but they say nothing when you've done superior work.

6. **Bureaucracy.** How many departments does it take to screw in a lightbulb? The professional world has a lengthy approval process for everything, and companies delight in changing those processes constantly so that you're never sure which 10 departments you need to consult before a decision can be made.

7. **Hypocrisy.** Don't you just love the way some organizations tout values such as quality, entrepreneurship, innovation, and integrity, when they would be perfectly happy if their employees just kept quiet and never strayed from their designated roles? If you've ever acted on your company's values and gotten burned for it, you are probably a victim of naked ambition (when doing what's best for the company leaves you out in the cold).

8. **Micromanagement.** Twenty-somethings thrive on independence, yet some managers will bear down on you with critical eyes at every minuscule stage of a project. Gotta sneeze? Better make sure your manager knows about it.

9. **Uncommon sense.** I've read that common sense is dead in the business world. The author almost sounded proud of this. People might make a joke of it, but this dearth of logical thought is kind of sad. It's also frustrating when the obviously correct way to do something is staring everyone right in the face, and no one sees it.

10. **Nonsensical change.** Every now and then, companies will decide to throw their departments up in the air and see where all the pieces land. Yes, it's the corporate reorganization (a.k.a. the dreaded re-org). Despite the fact that it results in mass confusion, greatly decreased productivity, and low employee morale, companies continue to do it year after year.

Combating Negativity

A week before one of our training seminars, our group manager announced that he was changing the curriculum. With one arbitrary decision, weeks of work were flushed down the toilet, and we were left scrambling. When my boss told me the news, I thought I could actually feel my blood boiling. I should have gone outside to get some air, but instead I followed my boss into the group manager's emergency planning meeting. I was so pissed off at the guy for screwing everything up that I couldn't help showing some attitude. The group manager didn't say anything about it—he just kind of frowned. But afterwards, my boss had some words for me. He said that he thought I was more mature than that, and that I needed to learn some emotional control. So much for all the great work I did on the seminar.

Donovan, 27, Michigan

When one of the professional world's realities frustrates you, you might want to stomp your foot and scream, "It's not fair! It doesn't make any sense! It's wrong!" Incident after incident convinces you that your managers are a bunch of crazy lunatics, and that every time you turn around, someone or something is keeping you from succeeding at work. You quickly develop a bad attitude without considering the consequences.

I fell into this trap at the beginning of my career. I had a clear mental picture of how the business world should operate, and I considered my company's inefficiencies to be a personal tragedy. Every time my progress toward my goals was blocked, my resentment grew (and I'm the type of person who wears my emotions on my sleeve). Pretty soon my managers didn't want to give me bad news, because they were afraid of my reaction. I was probably one of the most capable people in my group at the time, but did I get promoted? No sir. I stayed exactly where I was and watched as coworkers with half my skills moved ahead of me. Eventually I quit, believing my company was the problem. Two jobs later, I realized that the business world is the same everywhere, and that the problem was not my job, but rather my attitude.

Negativity might be a natural reaction to frustration, but that doesn't mean it's the right one. Pessimistic twenty-somethings waste a lot of energy being unhappy. They're unpopular with their colleagues because they suck the life out of everyone around them, and their professional personas suffer because they are perceived as immature. One of my first managers used to say that a bad attitude is like cholera: The person who catches it is vocal in his misery and gives the plague to everyone around him before finally kicking the bucket. Unless you want your career to end prematurely, your strategy must be to kill negativity before it kills you.

Maintaining a positive attitude when faced with demotivating situations is not easy, but it is under your control. I'm not suggesting that you suppress your bad feelings and walk around smiling when you think something is wrong. In fact, if you pay close attention to the suggestions in this chapter, you won't have to fake it at all. By learning to adjust your thoughts, let go of irrational expectations, and manage your emotions to banish anger, worry, stress, and frustration, you will genuinely become a happier and more peaceful person.

You Are What You Think

Three neighbors were standing in the road, talking about their possessions.

"I own a huge villa!" one said proudly.

"Oh yeah?" scoffed the second. "Well, I own a successful farm!"

"I don't have a villa or a big farm," the third said quietly. "But I do have optimism."

His two neighbors laughed at him. Optimism was hardly something to boast about, for what good is a possession that can't be seen or touched? Late that evening, the neighborhood experienced a violent storm. The rain destroyed the first neighbor's house. "What am I to do?" he cried, wringing his hands.

The wind ruined the second neighbor's crops. "I am finished!" he lamented.

The storm also destroyed the third neighbor's home and crops. "Well then, what should I do first?" he asked himself. After only a few minutes of consideration, he began rebuilding his home and replanting his crops. The next day, he whistled to himself as he went into his yard with some tomato seeds. His neighbors were still standing in the road feeling sorry for themselves. "We don't understand why you walk with a spring in your step," said the first neighbor. "All of your possessions have been destroyed."

"Yes," said the second. "What is your secret?"

"It is no secret," the man said. "The only thing I own is what I think."

If you take away one thing from this chapter, let it be that your thoughts control your feelings and make you who you are. As a human being, you are responsible for your own life, and you have the ability to choose your response to your environment. Have you ever stayed late at work and noticed that at least half of the janitors are smiling and whistling as they go about their cleaning? Now, objectively, these folks might not have the most stimulating job in the world, but some of them make the decision to begin each day with a positive outlook. Fulfillment, my friend, is not about the job itself—it's about one's attitude toward the job. Nothing—and no one—controls your attitude but you.

You can change your attitude for the better by recognizing that you create your feelings with the thoughts you choose to concentrate on. Let's look at a few examples of how a person might react differently in a given situation, depending on whether they choose to be negative or positive and productive.

Situation #1: A less competent coworker receives a promotion over you.

Negative Reaction: "My boss is such a jerk. He doesn't know good work when he sees it."

Positive Reaction: "I need to find out what I can do to receive the promotion next time."

Situation #2: It's 5 p.m. on Friday, and you were just given a difficult assignment that's due Monday morning.

Negative Reaction: "There's no way I can do this. I can't believe they didn't give me more notice."

Positive Reaction: "Let me think about what resources I can call on to get this done tonight, so that I can still enjoy my weekend."

Situation #3: You're given a task that doesn't exactly fit your job description.

Negative Reaction: "I didn't sign up for this. I'm totally overqualified, and they're not paying me enough."

Positive Reaction: "Maybe I can learn something new, and impress my boss in the process."

Situation #4: You just found out that your company is only giving 2 percent raises this year.

Negative Reaction: "This is how they repay all of my hard work? They can afford an expensive holiday party, but they can't reward their best employees? This company sucks."

Positive Reaction: "The economy is still recovering. At least I have a job I enjoy."

Notice that in all of these hypothetical situations, the negative reactions have some truth to them. Every situation has pluses and minuses. However, it's hazardous to your well-being to focus only on the minuses, even though they may be first to pop into your mind. Now don't get me wrong: short-lived negative reactions such as concern, regret, disappointment, annoyance, and frustration are normal and often understandable. Rather, it's the negative reactions we hold on to—rage, panic, depression, self-pity—that wreak havoc over time, and eventually result in a bad attitude. To maintain a positive attitude, you have to make a conscious effort to throw constructive thoughts into the mix.

The *Should* Patrol

Similar to negative thoughts, irrational expectations can be an attitude-buster—not just in business, but also in life in general. When we hold on to a belief that something should or must happen, we set ourselves up for inevitable disappointment. According to prominent psychologists Marvin Goldfried and Gerald Davison, much of our emotional turmoil is, in fact, self-produced when we tell ourselves that our lives will be awful if a certain expectation is not fulfilled. Recognize any of the following?

I should be able to do A...

B should not happen to me...

My company should do C...

He should understand D...

Everyone in this place should E...

This project/campaign/event should be planned like F...

...or all hell will break loose!

If you catch yourself thinking or saying the word *should*, go directly to jail and do not collect $200! *Should* often signals that you're harboring an irrational expectation. As we've talked about, life does not always play out in a logical or fair way, and you do yourself a grave disservice when you hold on to a fantasy of what work or people should be like. A case of the *shoulds* can be downright dangerous if it leads you to freak out trying to correct a maddening situation that is beyond your control. You'll appear negative and panicky to your colleagues, and the situation won't turn out any better than it would have if you'd just stayed calm and dealt with the circumstances as best as you could.

Got a bad case of negativity? Remember that all hell breaking loose is in the eye of the beholder, and ask yourself if the world is really going to come to an end if things don't go exactly as you planned. Instead of thinking that something *should* happen, reframe it as something *you would like* to happen. You're still acknowledging your own opinions and preferences, but the element of expectation is gone, so you can't be disappointed.

Make a commitment to be more tolerant and flexible, and recognize that everyone has a different point of view. Instead of creating a whole bunch of rules and judgments based on your own ideals, walk into your office each day with an open mind. Whenever you can, think about how lucky you are to be educated, to be employed, and to most likely have a standard of living that is better than 97 percent of the world's population. You'll notice an improvement in your attitude overnight, without any changes in your work situation whatsoever!

The Positive Now

Most of us spend a great deal of time obsessing about the past, the future, and how we're going to use the people and things in our lives to get what we want. What if we recognized that every moment is potentially satisfying and inspiring in and of itself? After all, the most important moment in our lives is the one we're experiencing right now, for all others are either just a memory or don't yet exist. What if we could shut out negativity by becoming deeply involved in everything we do, every day?

Even if you start off the day in a positive frame of mind, your sense of well-being can fade as the hours wear on. Should you feel yourself slipping into unproductive modes of thinking, try the following:

✦ Consider how what you're doing relates to your big-picture goals.

✦ Get up from your desk and walk around or stretch.

✦ Think about ways to make a positive difference right now.

When you routinely exist in the moment, you become more conscious of how you behave around others and how certain situations affect you. This comes in handy for coping with negative emotions that rear their ugly heads at work. In the next section, I'll talk more about how you can develop your emotional intelligence to effectively fight attitude-busters such as anger, worry, stress, and frustration.

Reach Out and Touch Your Emotions

Most of us have taken an IQ test at some point or another, but you've probably never given your EQ a second thought. Author and psychologist Hendrie Weisinger explains that EQ, or emotional intelligence, means intentionally using your emotions to guide your behavior. For example, let's say your boss just told you that his budget has been cut and your pet project must be canceled. In this situation, it's likely that negative emotions would overwhelm you. Without even thinking, you might fly off the handle and lash out at your boss. When you've honed your EQ, however, you immediately stop and consider how this development has made you feel. Once you've ascertained that you're angry, you might prevent your emotions from spilling over by talking yourself through them or taking a time-out.

Achieving Self-Awareness

High self-awareness is the basic building block of EQ. Think of it as stepping outside of your body, and then objectively observing yourself in action. Let's illustrate Weisinger's strategies for increasing self-awareness by using the previous example of the canceled project.

✦ **Strategy #1:** Examine how you make judgments about the world. Your judgments about yourself, other people, and situations are influenced by your personality, beliefs, and experiences. By becoming aware of your judgments, you learn how your thoughts influence your feelings, actions, and reactions, and you can then alter them accordingly. If you recognize that you tend to put a negative spin on your judgments, remember not to react out of anger, and try and talk yourself out of them.

  ✦ **Positive Reaction:** "I know that I have the tendency to believe that developments such as this are my fault and that they are directly related to my work. But the reality is that my boss canceled my project because our funds to pay the vendor were cut off. The decision had nothing to do with my work."

✦ **Strategy #2:** Get in touch with your feelings. When you understand and acknowledge your emotions, you are better equipped to work through them. You can identify your feelings by being on the lookout for physical manifestations such as increases in heart rate, breathing, and perspiration.

+ **Positive Reaction:** "The second the words were out of my boss's mouth, I noticed my heart was beating so fast it was almost in my throat. I didn't need to start talking to know I was really angry."

+ **Strategy #3:** Learn what your intentions are. Take the time to consider your hidden agenda, or what's really driving you to act a certain way, so that you can better strategize your course of action.

  + **Positive Reaction:** "I really want to get promoted at my next review, but I'm worried that I won't be able to build a case in time because my primary project was canceled. Maybe I should think about how I can prove myself some other way."

+ **Strategy #4:** Pay attention to your actions. Nonverbal cues such as speech patterns and body language can clue you in to your emotions and behavior. Becoming aware of these also helps you monitor how others might perceive you.

  + **Positive Reaction:** "I can tell I'm feeling really defeated by the way I'm slumping down in my chair. To my boss, it might look as though I've totally given up on my job because this project was canceled."

By using these self-awareness strategies, you'll be able to better understand your emotional hot buttons and, therefore, manage your negative emotions much more easily. Now, let's introduce some specific tools for diffusing anger, worry, and stress.

Managing Anger

Irritating circumstances often lead to feelings of anger—that's human nature. However, for the sake of your professional persona, it's in your best interests to refrain from showing anger at work. Even if you have a legitimate cause, this type of negative reaction will never reflect well on you. Whether you display your anger in the form of an irate tirade, a single rude comment, or subtle insubordination, failing to control this emotion can result in serious consequences. One friend of mine was fired on the spot when he screamed at his boss for handling a project ineptly. Another was suspended from work after sending a scathing email to a colleague. During the most stressful phase of my career, my anger masked itself as tears. I wasn't fired or suspended, but I did compromise my credibility and reputation. All it took was one supervisor to perceive me as immature, and the next thing I knew, I wasn't getting the promotion I deserved.

Regulating your thoughts, existing in the moment, and boosting your EQ are good strategies for preventing negative emotions from creeping into your workday. Despite your best efforts, though, anger may threaten to overflow at times. The key is to manage it so that you don't end up in hot water. In the midst of a heated discussion or situation, use the self-awareness strategies from the last section to determine when you're losing control. Tell the person or people you're arguing with that you need to take a break, and then temporarily remove yourself from the situation. Whether you're right or not is irrelevant. After all, winning the argument won't mean anything if you lose your temper. A month from now, your point will have been forgotten, but everyone who was within earshot will still remember your inappropriate behavior. Go back to your office or cube and decompress. Make an effort to relax, calm yourself down, and adjust your thoughts to erode some of your negativity. Consider ways to re-approach the situation anger-free, and then catch up with your colleague or colleagues to continue the discussion in a civil manner.

Sometimes we need to express our anger physically. This is fine, provided you don't destroy any company property in the process. I suggest taking a time-out and heading outside the building where no one can see you. Wrap an item of clothing around your mouth and scream as loud as you can. It works for me!

Managing Worry

One day last winter, things just weren't going my way. I'm not crazy about my job to begin with, and on this particular day, my laptop wasn't working. I was also managing a major project that was going horribly. I was totally freaking out, so I went to the cafeteria and ran into one of my coworkers. I told him how I was feeling and he said, "What's the worst thing that could happen?" My response was, "I could get fired and have to go on welfare." He went on to ask me if there was much of a chance of that happening. I felt a little silly, but from that point on I refused to let work stress me out too much. Whenever I feel anger or worry starting to overwhelm me, I always think of that conversation.

Kim, 23, Minnesota

Once upon a time, I spent huge amounts of time worrying about the past and the future. I worried when something bad happened, and I worried that something bad was going to happen. Then, one day, I visited my grandmother in the hospital. After we talked a while about my anxiety, my grandmother told me that I was wasting energy, because most of the things we worry about never come to pass. I decided to do a little experiment. I went home and wrote down all of the things I was worried about. A month later, I looked at the list and laughed. The worrisome things that had occurred were already just innocuous memories, and most of the other things had never happened. My grandmother was right. I was wrecking my mental and physical health for virtually no reason at all!

As I've talked about, you can only control the moment you're in right now. Because you can't change the past and you don't know what the future holds, what's the use of worrying? As Robert Louis Stevenson once wrote, "Let's be content to live the only time we can possibly live: from now until bedtime. Anyone can carry his burden, however hard, until nightfall." You'd be surprised how negative energy diminishes when you focus solely on the moment at hand. After all, doesn't any problem seem surmountable when you look at it from the vantage point of taking one small step at a time? Now, don't get me wrong: you should absolutely prepare for your future as best you can. But once you've done everything possible to increase the likelihood of a positive outcome, let go of your anxiety.

One summer, I worried obsessively about landing an agent to represent my novel. Every day as I drove home during my lunch break to check the mailbox for agent responses, my blood pressure zoomed into the stratosphere. Several weeks later, I finally recognized that my worry was out of control, and I talked about it with my husband, who is a psychologist. He said that I should consider the worst-case scenario and resign myself to accepting that outcome if necessary. I took his advice and imagined that I couldn't find an agent, and that my novel would never be published. I then brainstormed ways to improve the situation. This was a hard pill to swallow at first, but I actually felt better once my mind was purged of all the what-ifs. Free from worry, I was able to concentrate rationally on new strategies for obtaining an agent.

Just because you refuse to worry about a problem doesn't mean you are denying its existence. I'm just suggesting that you skip the part in which you play out a thousand variations of the same drama in your head. As soon as you become aware of a problem, consider the best way to approach it rationally.

Make a careful decision based on facts, take action, and then consider the matter over and done with.

There are always going to be bumps in the road, and if you think about it, there's no end to the things you could worry about. Remember, though, that those who break the habit of worrying live happier, longer lives. From a practical perspective, they're more productive, because they spend time resolving issues rather than fretting over them. They're also more pleasant to be around, because they're not constantly surrounded by a cloud of negativity. When you consider all of these benefits, why wouldn't you want to stop worrying?

Managing Stress

The World Health Organization calls job stress a worldwide epidemic. It costs companies billions annually. What does it cost you? During the first few years of my career in the business world, I was so stressed that I came home from work every evening and collapsed on the couch. By the time I woke up, it was almost time to go to bed again and I had missed the whole evening. I was in the doctor's office so much with aches and pains and coughs and colds that the nurses thought I was a hypochondriac. I cursed my poor health all the time until I signed up for a self-improvement class. It wasn't until then that I was able to pinpoint the problem. There was nothing wrong with my health, but my stress management did need some serious work.

Did you know that people get physically tired because of emotional factors such as boredom, frustration, and anxiety? True intellectual stimulation, on the other hand, doesn't exhaust us at all. If you are drained at the end of the day, it's not because of the mental work you have done, but rather the way in which you did it. The first time I heard this, a lightbulb went off. It occurred to me that I could write nonstop for 8 hours and then run a 5K immediately afterward, yet after spending a few hours at my corporate job I could barely drag myself to the train station. I now make reducing stress a priority, and I do not consider a day productive unless I have a substantial amount of energy left at the end of it. Here are some strategies for managing stress on a daily basis.

+ Identify what stresses you, and plan to cope with it in advance.

+ Work in a comfortable position.

+ Schedule frequent, short breaks throughout the day.

+ Take time-outs to stretch, massage your temples, or get a drink of water.

+ Join a gym and go during your lunch break.

+ Pick your battles: If it's not worth it, let it go.

There's also no substitute for leading a balanced life. Even if you love your job, remember that people who work all the time are boring, one-dimensional, and, ultimately, unsatisfied. Careers in the professional world are demanding, but don't let your intellectual, social, and spiritual needs slip through the cracks. Do family members or your old college friends live nearby? Visit them. Do you like to read for pleasure? Peruse that classic novel instead of another industry trade magazine. Spend a few hours volunteering on the weekends, because we feel better when we attempt to make our world better. And regardless of your religion, don't forget to pray. Seriously. Did you know it's been proven that people who practice religion lead more contented lives? They have faith in a power greater than themselves, and their attitudes reflect it.

My roommates once made fun of me for sleeping more hours than the average 2-year-old. Now my husband has to coax me to bed at midnight. Was my job then any harder than it is now? Definitely not. In fact, I've climbed the ladder a bit, so my current position is objectively more taxing. The difference now is that I remind myself every day how stress once destroyed my health and well-being, and I don't let it win!

Increasing Your Frustration Tolerance

A key ingredient in frustration is the lack of control that a person perceives for the outcome of their work. In psychology, this is called *locus of control*, a concept that was originally developed by Julian Rotter in the mid-20th century. One has an internal locus of control if he believes that he controls his own destiny, and he has an external locus of control if he believes that his destiny is controlled by other forces such as authority figures, fate, or God. In the last half century, psychological research has determined that males tend to be more internal than females, older people more internal than younger people, and people at higher levels in the organization more internal than junior-level staffers.

In general, having an internal locus of control is viewed as more desirable, because these individuals tend to be more achievement oriented. They are more persistent and work longer and harder to get what they need or want. It's better from a mental health perspective too, because when you feel that you can affect the outcome of your work, you are more satisfied and have a greater sense of accomplishment.

If you are a person who is prone to an external locus of control, this could be a major cause of your attitude problem at work. Fortunately, there are things you can do to develop an internal locus of control. For example, you can try a little of what psychologists call "exposure." This strategy involves making a list of the everyday situations that annoy you (driving on the highway at rush hour, waiting on hold for a customer service representative, and so on) and subjecting yourself to them gradually so that you can increase your tolerance.

As you're experiencing these situations, you might ask yourself why you're frustrated in the first place. Is it that you feel helpless or put out? If so, you might put processes in place to eliminate that negative feeling. For example, I get frustrated by sitting in meetings because they make me feel inefficient. I find that if I schedule these to last just 30 minutes (enough time for quick status updates and to-dos), I'm not nearly as anxious about my time being wasted.

One last tip is to put the frustrating situation in context. You can say, for instance, "Of all the upsetting things that have happened to me in my life, getting chastised by my boss in front of my client was a 7 on a scale of 1 to 10, but not getting a seat on the subway this morning only gets a 2."

Motivating Yourself

Whenever I start hating my job, I take on more work so I don't have time to think about it. I find that the busier I am, the less opportunity I have to consider how my company is ruining my career. Because you know what the worst feeling is? Staring at the computer screen, your mind so numb that you can't even think of a Website to surf. It's at that moment that every second of the workday feels like an eternity and all of the negative emotions—dissatisfaction, frustration, depression—come flooding in.

Robyn, 25, Nevada

Maintaining a positive attitude is much easier when you're inspired by your work and the people around you. Unfortunately, the professional world today is often not the most motivating environment. Many managers feel that their employees should consider themselves lucky to have jobs, and they see no reason to lead and encourage them. Twenty-somethings find themselves working more hours, while rewards and recognition for stellar performance are few and far between. Additionally, channels of career progression are more confusing than ever. Considering these circumstances, who could blame you for doing the bare minimum at work every day? The establishment doesn't deserve anything more.

The problem is, having an attitude similar to that only hurts you. Here's why: If you're playing your cards right, you're using your job as the means for achieving your big-picture career objectives. Therefore, when you stop giving your all because you didn't get a raise or someone didn't pat you on the back for a job well done, you're sabotaging your own goals. Meeting your own criteria for success should be motivation enough, don't you think?

Getting motivated is not as simple as it sounds when it's a rainy Monday morning, an angry client is on the phone, and you have urgent deadlines to meet. You can use this chapter's strategies to give your attitude a boost, but don't underestimate the importance of firing yourself up to do your best every day. Need a crutch? I suggest rereading a cheesy self-help book of your choice and posting some of your favorite inspirational quotes in your cube or office. Share your motivational tips with others, and you'll be surprised how much easier it is to believe in them yourself. Sign up for any personal development or leadership courses your company offers, and stay busy so you don't have time to sit around and think about how much better your job situation could be.

Always keep the big picture in the forefront of your mind, but don't forget to acknowledge your little successes along the way. Every time you master a new skill or finish a tough project, celebrate the fact that you're one step closer to your overall career goal. And just because your colleagues don't give you kudos doesn't mean your friends and family won't. Tell them!

No matter how hard you try to rally against negativity, there are going to be times when you feel like marching straight over to your boss's office and handing in your resignation. Beating yourself up for feeling this way will only upset you more. Instead, be patient and wait for the mood to pass. You might also try this suggestion from Hendrie Weisinger, author of *Emotional Intelligence at Work*: pretend it's your first day of a new job, and imagine approaching every task with confidence, eagerness, and enthusiasm. Or, you can pretend that this is the best day of your working life. You are full of energy and ideas, you're getting lots of things accomplished, and people are responding to you with praise. Maybe it will be a self-fulfilling prophecy!

Damage Control

In an ideal world, you would never cop an attitude with one of your colleagues or managers. Given that you're human, though, this is an unrealistic expectation. Sometimes you will take your aggravation out on another person, whether she deserves it or not. Provided you have a good rapport with your coworker and handle yourself correctly, one incident should not permanently affect the relationship (see Chapter 7).

When you lose your cool, you might feel embarrassed and want to pretend the incident never happened. This is not a good strategy. If you go too long without addressing the issue, the person you've offended might build up the interaction in her mind to be worse than it actually was, and she will remember it the next time the two of you talk. Before you know it, you'll have established a pattern of negative communication.

Effective damage control means taking responsibility for your actions. If you clash with a colleague, honestly assess the situation and look at it from the other person's viewpoint. Remember that being right doesn't justify rudeness or inappropriate behavior. Let go of your pride. It takes guts to go back and make it right, and your colleague will respect you for it. Approach the person and sincerely apologize for your role in the altercation. Explain that you're still learning, and assure her it won't happen again. Can't stomach an in-person conversation? Write a heartfelt card or email instead. Your colleague will likely be receptive to the overture. Instead of thinking you're a jerk, she will now perceive you as being mature beyond your years. Just another example of how a little effort on your part can turn most negative situations into positive ones!

What I Wish I'd Known

In my 20s, I was a one-trick pony. My work was my entire life, and not in a good way. Every time I would momentarily escape to go out for drinks with friends or whatever, all I could do was complain about my job. I wish I could go back and tell my younger self to cool it. Practically none of the things I vented about were of any significance in the long-term, and if I had just let more things go, I would have saved a whole lot of energy.

Nathan, 36, Washington

Take-Home Points

✦ **Choose a positive outlook.** Your thoughts make you who you are. You are responsible for your own life, and you have the ability to choose your response to your environment. If you make a conscious decision to begin each day with a positive outlook, negative conditions at work can't take that away from you.

✦ **Increase your self-awareness.** Begin to better understand your emotional hot buttons. Examine how you make judgments about the world, tune in to your senses, get in touch with your feelings, learn what your intentions are, and pay attention to your actions.

✦ **Imagine the worst-case scenario.** When you imagine the worst-case scenario and reconcile yourself to accepting that outcome if necessary, you stop worry in its tracks. Then, you will be able to rationally focus on ways to improve the situation.

✦ **Motivate yourself on a daily basis.** Motivate yourself by striving to meet your own criteria for success. Instead of relying on external validation, focus on using your job as the means for achieving your big-picture career objectives.

Chapter 7

People Management

One company I worked for offered a course designed to improve employees' interpersonal skills. I was in public relations and interacted with people all the time, so it was a no-brainer for me to sign up. On the first day of class, I was surprised to see that I was the only marketing person in the group. Most of my classmates were computer programmers and graphic designers. Later, I asked one of the programming supervisors why he wanted his people to take this class. After all, these folks sat in front of machines all day long; it wasn't unusual for them to go from morning coffee to lunch without talking to a single human being.

"Aren't some folks drawn to programming because they don't want to deal with people, because the interpersonal stuff makes them uncomfortable?" I asked.

"That's sometimes true," the supervisor said. "And it's all the more reason for them to take this class. There's no such thing as a job that doesn't require people skills. My staff might talk to a customer or colleague only once a day, but if that interaction goes badly, it will snowball, and I just can't afford that."

Let this be a lesson for all of us. Throughout this book I've talked about how being the best and the brightest won't get you very far in the professional world if you can't communicate effectively with the people around you. An individual who has mastered the art of people management gets things accomplished by leveraging his efforts in concert with the efforts of others. This is not always easy to do. How many times have we said to ourselves, "If only I didn't need to rely on Person A and could do Task X by myself, everything would be just peachy"? Well, in this chapter I'll cover strategies for enlisting your colleagues' cooperation so that you can increase the control you have over your own success. I'll also spend some time on the underrated concept of gratitude in the workplace, as well as examine strategies for creating positive relationships and coping with difficult personalities.

Enlisting Cooperation

Last year I graduated from college and took a job in a medium-sized life insurance firm. I had always considered myself pretty levelheaded, but I just couldn't figure out how to get along in the work world. I felt like my future at the company depended on the actions of other people, so every time I tried to get a colleague to do something, it was like going into the boxing ring. It turned into a vicious cycle. The more I tried to force things on people, the more I alienated them. Then they were angry, I was angry, no one got anything done, and the tension in the office became so great that someone had to go. Guess who was the lucky loser?

John, 24, Pennsylvania

During my tenure in the business world, I've seen people try all sorts of tactics, from bribery to temper tantrums, to get others to do what they want. Some use their power or position to force lower-ranking staff to comply. In today's fast-paced business culture, many middle managers are too harried and apathetic to stop and consider the best way to encourage true cooperation. In his book *The 7 Habits of Highly Effective People*, Stephen Covey outlines a number of approaches that individuals use when trying to get something from another person. Covey categorizes these approaches as Win/Win, Win/Lose, Lose/Win, Lose/Lose, and Win. Let me further explain:

+ **Win/Win** ("I love you, you love me"): The attitude that a mutually beneficial solution is the best solution because everyone feels good, and one person's success is not achieved at the expense of another.

+ **Win/Lose** ("I get my way, you don't get yours"): The attitude that someone else has to lose in order for you to win, as in football games and lawsuits.

+ **Lose/Win** ("Go ahead, have your way with me. Everyone else does"): The attitude of people who are quick to please or appease, repressing their true feelings and seeking strength from popularity or acceptance.

+ **Lose/Lose** ("I'm going to win or die trying"): The thinking that results when two Win/Lose people become stubborn, vindictive, and blind to everything except their desire for the other person to lose.

+ **Win** ("Do what you need to do; I can't be bothered"): The attitude that it doesn't matter whether the other person wins or loses, as long as you get what you want.

It's easy to fall into the trap of thinking that every interaction in the cut-throat world of business has to be Win/Lose. But because you work with the same colleagues every day, this attitude (and the manipulation and coercion tactics that often go with it) can cost you big time. Before you know it, your work relationships will have soured, and your professional persona will be seriously tarnished. In most cases, you'll be more effective at eliciting your colleagues' cooperation and, ultimately, getting what you want, if you make Win/Win your personal philosophy.

Win/Win outcomes are easier to achieve when you proactively consider ways that the other person can benefit from cooperating with you. That said, one of the biggest mistakes you can make is to enter a negotiation by expressly stating what you want. You might have heard the story of the salesman who greets a prospect by announcing, "I want to tell you about a great new product that has a thousand new features, all for the low price of...." The prospect stops listening as soon as she hears the words *I want* and slams the door in the salesman's face. If you're going to remember anything from this section, remember this: Other people don't care what you want. They want to know what's in it for them. As the initiator of a negotiation, you have to assume that although you may be looking for the Win/Win, the other person is interested only in the Win. Need her cooperation? Make her want to do what you are asking.

How do you do this? First, examine the situation from her point of view and determine her priorities. Then, in your initial approach, talk about what she wants and how your proposal can help her get it. Here's an example of this strategy in action: A former job of mine was to coordinate press interviews between executives and journalists. One afternoon, I had to persuade a high-level sales executive to postpone a visit with a client and spend an hour talking with a journalist on deadline. However, I understood that the sales executive wanted to spend his time closing deals, not chatting it up with someone who couldn't pay him. So I approached my request this way:

"You mentioned that we sometimes lose deals because we can't demonstrate to potential clients how our products are covered in the press. Here is our chance to change that. Ordinarily I wouldn't ask you to move your meeting, but the client is available for lunch on Friday. The article with your interview will have appeared online by then. Why don't I get you a copy to show him?"

In this way, the sales executive saw how talking with the journalist could help him get what he wanted: more closed deals. He realized that spending an hour now would pay huge publicity dividends later on, and that it might even help persuade the client he planned on visiting that week. I got my interview done on time, and the sales executive met the client for lunch armed with an extra weapon. Win/Win!

It doesn't matter if the other person actually wins by cooperating with you, as long as she feels like she's winning. For instance, you can frequently achieve a positive outcome by appealing to a person's moral code. In his book *How to Win Friends and Influence People*, motivational guru Dale Carnegie claims that people like to feel as though they are doing the proper, unselfish thing. If your proposal will make the other person feel good about herself, she'll be more inclined to cooperate. To take the last example one step further, suppose the sales executive needed a bit more convincing to change his schedule and meet with the journalist. I could have played to his desire to do what's best for the company with the following response:

"Our company has gotten some undeservedly negative press lately, and we're lucky to be in a position to counter it with some positive messages of our own. When unflattering articles appear, our stock goes down. But when spokespeople like you get out there and talk with the media about the good things we're doing, the reverse happens!"

Win/Win scenarios are usually within reach when you take the time to think about what you're asking of someone and how you're going to ask it. Imagine yourself in the other person's position and treat her as you would want to be treated under the same circumstances. Keeping in mind that the end goal is cooperation, remove your ego from the situation and don't insist that people do things your way. Your colleagues will be more likely to pursue a project if they have a say in how it's done, so instead of bullying them into following your lead, outline what you need and ask for feedback on the best way to accomplish it. After all, if the work gets done and everyone is happy about it, it's a Win/Win regardless of how you arrived there.

Leading Without Authority

In a business world of shrinking hierarchies and individual contributors, one of the toughest challenges for the twenty-something high achiever is leading projects without authority. In my years in the workforce, I've been responsible for several large, multi-departmental initiatives with no direct reports to engage. In addition to Covey's Win/Win approach, here are some strategies from the trenches.

+ **Let your passion shine through.** It's hard to be critical of someone earnest, and if you infuse your communication with a genuine sense of excitement about the challenge ahead, your colleagues will naturally want to follow your lead. Show them—through your behavior—why you got into this field in the first place, and what your experiences (good and bad) have shown you about what needs to be done next.

+ **Appear humble.** It's bad enough when your boss has an ego that needs some serious downsizing, but it's even less appealing when someone without power thinks too highly of himself. The manner and content of your communication must demonstrate that you are pursuing this approach because it's the right thing to do for the organization, not because you will receive personal credit or rewards.

+ **Don't be overcontrolling.** You don't have official authority, so don't get caught up in acting as though you do. Use your expertise to guide and support your colleagues, but release the need to micromanage every aspect of a project. If you share your ideas and then allow your coworkers to take partial ownership of their implementation, they will gradually put more trust in you and the approach.

A Touch of Sweetness

So many of the senior executives in my agency treat underlings like dirt. We are expected to bend over backwards for them without so much as a "thank you." One manager, however, is noticeably different. This person doesn't take for granted that we'll do whatever he says because he has the power to fire us. He's great about complimenting us for a job well done, which, in turn, motivates us to do even better for him in the future. I observed this exec for a while and noticed that no one ever seemed to praise him for being such a good manager. So, one day, I did. I told him that I didn't want him to think I was kissing up, but that I thought he deserved to know that I appreciated his efforts. You should have seen him light up. It was like my comment was the best thing that happened to him all week.

Sabrinath, 23, New Mexico

Imagine the look on a colleague's face when you hand over a tasty piece of candy, unsolicited. Appreciation is the same way. You only need a little bit to make a coworker's day and encourage her to view you in a positive light from that point on. Did someone help you out? Thank her. Was it a big deal, did she go out of her way, or did it take a lot of time? Send her a card or take her to lunch. If she really went above and beyond the call of duty, make sure her boss knows about it. And by the way, I don't subscribe to the theory that you shouldn't have to thank someone for doing her job. When a colleague does her job well and it helps you, what harm does it do to thank her? The answer is none, it just makes her like you more.

Eighteenth-century author Samuel Johnson wrote, "Gratitude is a fruit of great cultivation; you do not find it among gross people." Well, folks, times haven't changed. Most people still take good deeds and favors for granted, and you're bound to be disappointed if you do something nice and expect appreciation in return. Instead of demanding gratitude, give freely. Exhibit kindness, and go out of your way to show courtesy and consideration to each person you come in contact with. Answer your phone ready and willing to accommodate the person on the other end. Ask how you can help, listen to the answer, and then follow up quickly and cheerfully.

As we've talked about, it doesn't make sense to reserve your best behavior for your customers and your boss, because when it comes to your reputation, everyone is equally influential. Remember that people have big mouths that get even bigger when they're unhappy. All it takes is one person to complain that you were rude or uncooperative, and, next thing you know, everyone in the office will have the scoop.

People hunger for recognition. In fact, their happiness, self-esteem, and motivation depend on it. Be generous with your compliments, but make sure they're sincere. Empty flattery is, in many ways, worse than criticism. Don't praise every move someone makes, and when you do give a compliment, put substance behind the statement so it's meaningful to the person. The most effective compliments focus on specific actions or facts rather than vague generalities or assumptions. Here are a few examples:

Weak Compliment: "You did a great job on that presentation."

Strong Compliment: "The analogies you made in your presentation really engaged the audience members because they could relate what you were saying to their own lives."

Weak Compliment: "You're so organized."

Strong Compliment: "You were so prepared in that customer meeting. I appreciated the way you had supporting information to back up each of our claims."

When you receive a compliment, don't downplay or dismiss it. This makes you look insecure, and it makes the other person feel uncomfortable and stupid. You don't always have to return the compliment either. A smile and a simple "thank you" will do. If you're concerned about modesty, share the credit with someone else.

While we're on the subject of credit, always acknowledge people's achievements, both large and small. You don't appreciate when your own success is met with silence, and others don't either. And in case this wasn't obvious already, make a point of calling attention to the things people do right, not just what they do wrong. Your colleagues will be more receptive to your ideas when they don't have to brace themselves for criticism every time you open your mouth.

Sharing appreciation and praise helps those of us who lean naturally toward the "glass half empty" mentality to focus on the finer aspects of other people and their behavior. Not only does this behavior strengthen our relationships and encourage cooperation, but it also positively impacts the way we think about ourselves and the world.

Creating Positive Relationships

My expectations for myself are pretty high, and the biggest mistake I made during my first year as a manager was imposing those same expectations on the person who worked for me. This girl was very different from me. Although she still managed to get her work done on time, she was not nearly as organized or efficient about it as I am. I was frustrated with her and showed it pretty often. I even held back her promotion because she hadn't mastered, overnight, skills that come naturally to me. Nearly in tears, she told me she felt like she could never please me. Looking back, I realize she was probably right.

Marissa, 26, Ottawa

When it comes to relationship building, the professional world diverges sharply from the educational experiences of childhood and adolescence. As I've already discussed, achievement is an individual endeavor in grade school through college. Even if you didn't have a good teacher or friends to help you with your homework, you could still master the material on your own and get an A. Like it or not, the business world is a different animal. You need other people to get ahead, and each interpersonal relationship you create has the potential to do more for your career than reading 100 articles about your trade.

Most of us develop relationships every day without even thinking about it. Sometimes we select the people we want to associate with based on common interests, lifestyles, and personality traits. Other times we fall into relationships because they are convenient at a particular point in time (for example, neighbor-to-neighbor). Work relationships are similar to family relationships.

We don't necessarily choose them and we might prefer not to have them, but, for our sanity's sake, we have to make them work as best we can.

Because they don't come as naturally, work relationships can be difficult to care for and maintain if you're not paying attention. In his book *The 7 Habits of Highly Effective People*, Stephen Covey introduces the concept of the "emotional bank account" to help us consciously manage our most constant relationships. In every emotional bank account, we save trust and goodwill through deposits of kindness, honesty, and keeping our word. When the reserve of trust in an account is high, communication is instant, easy, and effective. On the other hand, if we continually show another person disrespect, the trust account diminishes, and the slightest provocation can turn into a relationship "incident." In other words, having an ongoing positive rapport with someone means that he will give you a break when you make a mistake.

Here's an example of the emotional bank account in action. I had a strong, mutually beneficial relationship with my colleague Michelle. One morning, I had to meet with a client even though I wasn't feeling well. During the meeting, Michelle justifiably asked me a question, and I bit her head off. If Michelle and I hadn't had such a good relationship, she might have been offended by my rudeness. However, when I apologized to her later, I found that she had already forgotten it. "I didn't take it personally," Michelle said. "I knew it wasn't like you and that something must be going on." Fortunately, Michelle and I had enough trust built up to cover the withdrawal to our emotional bank account. I also made an additional deposit when I apologized for my bad behavior.

Whether you make a withdrawal or not, your account reserves need constant replenishing. Old deposits evaporate with time, so a person isn't necessarily going to remember a favor you did for him months ago if the two of you haven't had another positive interaction since then. As I mentioned in the previous section, showing appreciation, praising superior work, and complimenting when appropriate are great techniques for keeping your relationships healthy and productive. Here are a few more ways you can make routine deposits to your emotional bank accounts.

- ✦ Take a sincere interest in the other person and what's meaningful to him.
- ✦ Attend to the little things, such as returning a phone call or acknowledging his birthday.
- ✦ Deliver on anything and everything you promise.

+ Make a concerted effort to keep the lines of communication open.

+ Remember his name and the names of the important people in his life.

+ Demonstrate integrity under all circumstances.

You can also improve your relationships by effectively managing your expectations of other people. Remember those evil *shoulds* from Chapter 6? Author and psychologist Hendrie Weisinger warns against expecting too much from your relationships. Consciously or unconsciously, you may want your boss to be in a good mood all the time or your admin to be as pathologically detail-oriented as you are. However, when your expectations exceed what other people can or will do, you are disappointed. You can prevent your relationships from taking a beating by ensuring that your expectations are reasonable and realistic. If you're not sure, seek advice from a mentor or trusted colleague who has been in your position before. Once you've clarified your expectations in your own mind, make certain you accurately communicate them to the other person. Solicit feedback in advance so that you can uncover potential roadblocks and avoid being caught off guard later on.

Being Mentally Present

I hate it when my coworker suggests lunch meetings in the cafeteria, because, inevitably, the two of us will be sitting there together and he'll start looking past me at everything going on and everyone around us. I know the caf's a happening place, but come on! Whatever happened to listening and making eye contact? Sometimes I wonder if he would even notice if I stopped talking. It's downright embarrassing.

Heather, 25, Georgia

Want to know an important yet significantly underrated strategy for building strong workplace relationships? Simply make a habit of being present for every person you deal with—not just physically present, mind you, but mentally present. This means actually listening to what the other person is saying, focusing on him rather than everything else going on in the room, and ignoring potential interruptions, such as beeping smartphones.

When someone comes to your office or cube, decide right then and there if you have time to talk. If you don't, say so. If you do have time, but only a little bit, ask him if it's enough. You don't necessarily have to drop every-thing for the person, but once you make the commitment to have a dialogue, please be respectful. Remember that his time is important too, and give him your full attention. Doing this will set you apart from the scores of employees who believe that sitting across the desk from another person means you're communicating.

Several years ago I had a boss who took every call and read every new email that came in while I was meeting with her. She was a great manager oth-erwise, but I get a bad taste in my mouth when I think of how every meeting took half an hour instead of five minutes, because she prioritized every inter-ruption ahead of me. I shall now retire my soapbox, but you get the point. Don't become one of them! Try to be mentally present for every person you talk to, every day.

Dealing with Difficult People

At some point in our careers, most of us are forced to work with some-one whose people skills can only be described as atrocious. Sometimes our organizations wisely get rid of these people, but they are like weeds: pluck one, and within seconds another will sprout up in its place. The dread that comes with having to regularly interact with someone who is routinely nega-tive, argumentative, stressed, or mean can make your job a wholly unpleasant experience—if you let it.

Your first instinct might be to go out of your way to avoid working with "Mr. Difficult." If you can pull it off, more power to you. Often, though, this is not an option, and whether Mr. Difficult is your boss, a colleague, or a se-nior executive, you must prepare for each meeting with him as if you are going into battle. Swallow your apprehension. Remind yourself that no one has the power to control how you feel, and suit up in your armor so that nothing he says or does wounds you deeply. Take a deep breath and walk calmly into Mr. Difficult's office. Speak to him in a controlled, cheerful, and reasonable tone. Get the information you need, and then get out as soon as possible. As we know, negativity and stress can be highly contagious, so do not allow yourself to get sucked in.

Mr. Difficult's arrows can be easier to deflect when he's an equal oppor-tunity shooter, and you realize that you are not the only target. You might even joke about him with your other colleagues who have had the pleasure to work with him directly. However, it's easy to become demoralized when Mr. Difficult saves his best poison just for you. For example, one of my first bosses couldn't stand me. To the best of my knowledge, I didn't do anything to incur her wrath. She was sweet as apple pie to the rest of our colleagues, yet, inexplicably, whenever I came around, she turned into the Wicked Witch of the West.

Unfortunately, this is not unusual. Personality clashes often happen. Your best bet in this scenario is to sit down with your Mr. Difficult and have a heart-to-heart. Tell him how you are feeling, assume that he doesn't mean to act like the devil incarnate, and give him the benefit of the doubt. Solicit his feedback regarding how the two of you can improve your relationship, and then give him a chance to do right by you. If this doesn't work and he continues to regularly use you as target practice, remove yourself from the situation (see Chapter 10). No job is worth lowering your self-esteem.

There's one caveat to all of this: human beings operate with such different styles (see the next section) that it's impossible for us to get along with all of our colleagues all of the time. You could be the most agreeable person on Earth, but I guarantee that someone at work will find a reason not to like you. Maybe she isn't blatantly obvious or malicious like Mr. Difficult, but you can feel her negativity just the same. She might walk right past your desk without saying good morning, or she might not engage in friendly conversation with you the way she does with other people in the office. For those of us with a sensitive streak, this type of behavior can be hurtful. What did you do to her anyway? Why won't she give you a fair shot? As natural as it is to fixate on the situation, if it's not affecting your daily work life or your career path, refuse to take it personally, and go about your business as usual. Focus on your reasons for being at work, and save your energy for the people in the office who deserve it.

People Styles at Work

In the classic book *People Styles at Work*, Robert Bolton and Dorothy Grover Bolton help us understand the behavioral styles that determine how colleagues think, make decisions, communicate, manage time and stress, and deal with conflict. By understanding the people style you're dealing with, you can establish rapport with a colleague more easily, become more persuasive, and avoid miscommunication and the possibility of rubbing someone the wrong way.

Industrial psychologist David Merrill found that two dimensions of behavior could explain and predict how people behave: assertiveness and responsiveness. Assertiveness is the degree to which people's behavior is seen as forceful and directive. Responsiveness is the degree to which people are seen as showing emotions or demonstrating sensitivity. Based on these behaviors, he created four people styles:

1. **Analyticals** are people who are less assertive and less responsive. Emotionally restrained, they rarely compliment others or get excited. They are organized and systematic. They crave data—the more the better. They are slow decision-makers because they want to make sure they have carefully weighed all the facts.

2. **Amiables** are, similar to analyticals, less assertive, but more responsive. Friendly and generous with their time, they are excellent team players. They aren't flamboyant creators but, rather, diligent quiet workers who do what's asked of them.

3. **Expressives** are, similar to amiables, more responsive. But they are also more assertive. They're friendly and empathetic like amiables but aren't as low-key about it. Flamboyant, energetic, and impulsive, they are the most outgoing of the people styles.

4. **Drivers** are, similar to expressives, more assertive. But they are less responsive. Decisive and task-oriented, they focus intently on the job at hand. In conversations, they get right to the point. They are purposeful and energetic, just as are expressives. But expressives are concerned about people as human beings. For drivers, there's no time for such concerns.

According to the Boltons, "When two people of different styles live or work together, one or both must adjust. If neither adapts to the other, communication will deteriorate, cooperation will decline, the relationship will be stressed, and in work situations, productivity will inevitably slump."

The Boltons advocate a four-step process to improving relationships with colleagues who may have different styles than you. They call this "style flex," and here's how you use it.

First, identify your style and the style of your colleague. To identify your own style, you have to ask the opinions of others. Only they can appropriately categorize your external behavior (in terms of assertiveness and responsiveness) without being influenced by your internal motivations or feelings. To identify your colleague's style, observe her carefully for clues such as a loud voice or flamboyant gestures.

The second step is to plan ahead, selecting the specific behaviors you will adapt and how you will adapt them. The third step is to implement your changes and monitor your colleague's reactions. Make mid-course corrections if necessary. After your next meeting with the colleague comes the last step: reviewing the process and drawing lessons for future interactions.

Criticism Incoming

The sun rises in the morning, and human beings criticize each other. Stick around the professional world for a while, and you will inevitably participate in this special ritual. What separates the strong employees from the weak, however, is how one copes with criticism. People who deny responsibility and respond with anger and defensiveness hold themselves back personally and professionally. On the other hand, the most successful individuals listen objectively, accept constructive criticism, and look for ways to grow from it. In his book *Getting Promoted: Real Strategies for Advancing Your Career*, Harry Chambers suggests the following five steps for receiving criticism productively.

✦ **Depersonalize the criticism.** Repeat to yourself, "It's a specific behavior that's the problem, not me as a person."

✦ **Assertively restate the comments for clarification.** Say to the person, "What I heard was that Behavior X is not acceptable."

✦ **Seek guidance.** Ask the person, "How could I do that differently? What change would be appropriate?"

✦ **Process the input.** Ask yourself, "Is this criticism valid? Am I willing to make the change to eliminate the contention?"

✦ **Review your progress/seek follow-up.** Say to the person, "I'm working hard to bring about the change we talked about. Do you have any other suggestions?"

Provided the criticism is meant to help you, be sensitive to what the other person is feeling. It was probably very hard for her to approach you, and you will score major points by trying to make her more comfortable. Also, there's nothing wrong with telling her how you feel. If the criticism isn't justified, say so frankly, without letting your emotions get the best of you.

One last point on criticism: Eleanor Roosevelt once said, "Do what you feel in your heart to be right—for you'll be criticized anyway." Keep in mind that if you are accomplishing something, you will most likely be criticized by someone who secretly wishes that she were as important as you are. Take it as a compliment, for it means you are worthy of attention.

Calming an Angry Person

Customer service representatives frequently have to contend with angry people, and my friend Jan, who spends all day on the telephone, offered me some valuable advice for neutralizing someone who is out of control. According to Jan, the best thing you can do is acknowledge the person's anger and listen attentively without interrupting. "If you let the customer vent, she'll eventually quiet down," Jan says. "Don't respond with defensiveness or annoyance. Show empathy for her predicament and assure her that you'll make it your business to fix the situation." Jan also clued me in on some things not to say:

+ **"Calm down":** This is bound to elicit the response "Don't tell me to calm down!"

+ **"That's not my fault":** Whether true or not, the angry person will not appreciate hearing you deny responsibility. She is looking for your help.

+ **"You're way out of line":** Needless to say, this will just prolong the argument.

+ **"If you just hold on, I'll transfer you to...":** This lack of urgency and personal ownership will annoy the angry person. She wants you to come up with an action plan now.

"The key point," Jan says, "is to remain calm. If the customer is not able to engage you in an argument, she'll eventually stop fighting. People can't be pissed off by themselves for long. Your calmness will diffuse her anger, and then the two of you can work together to solve the problem."

What I Wish I'd Known

When I was interviewing for my first job, I was very professional. Almost too professional. I wanted to be perceived as serious and knowledgeable, so every time someone would make ice breaker–type conversation, I'd shut them down. I was completely mystified as to why, with my fantastic record, I had to wait so long for an offer. Now that I've been in the business world for a decade, I realize that of course those interviewers weren't going to feel comfortable working with me—I hadn't established rapport! I didn't show personal interest in them and made it impossible for them to show personal interest in me. I wish I could tell my 21-year-old self that there's a happy medium between over- and undersharing.

Laura, 31, Missouri

Take-Home Points

✦ **Choose a Win/Win attitude.** Other people don't care what you want—they want to know what's in it for them. By approaching negotiations with a Win/Win attitude, you'll be more effective at eliciting cooperation, and, ultimately, getting what you want.

✦ **Compliment your coworkers.** People hunger for recognition. Be generous with your compliments, but make sure they're sincere. The most effective compliments focus on specific actions or facts rather than vague generalities or assumptions.

✦ **Give coworkers your undivided attention.** Being mentally present for another person means actually listening to what she is saying, focusing on her rather than everything else going on in the room, and ignoring potential interruptions, such as beeping smartphones.

✦ **Learn to handle criticism with class.** The most successful people in the business world listen objectively, accept constructive criticism, and look for ways to grow from it. Those who respond to criticism by getting defensive hold themselves back personally and professionally.

Chapter 8

Moving Up in the World

There may be no greater challenge in business than getting promoted. For every factor you can control (such as your skills and attitude), there are at least two that you can't (such as the economy and your organization's infrastructure). In this era of streamlined organizations, companies have been flattened and downsized so that there are fewer middle-management positions for twenty-somethings to be promoted into. Also, a "do more with less" mentality often translates into increases in responsibilities without additional compensation or acknowledgment. This scenario is changing baby boomer retirement, but it might not be fast enough for you.

For some, a job in the business world is just a pit stop on the way to a career in another field—such as entertainment. These individuals might define success as a check that pays for their true passion rather than a promotion that moves them to the next level. Unfortunately, there are many more twenty-somethings struggling to build careers where they are, and, as such, competition for promotion opportunities has become so intense that doing all of the right things might not necessarily get you the recognition you deserve.

If you're in the latter category, giving up is not an option. You have no choice but to ensure your promotability. If you don't move ahead now while you're young and unencumbered, you may never manage it at all. Instead, you could end up stuck at or near the bottom rung with bosses who are younger and less experienced than you. Also, your resume will look suspicious to potential new employers.

The good news is that you are much more likely to be promoted in your 20s, because, as a newbie, the whole world is open to you, and you have nowhere to go but up. Everything I've discussed in this book so far—from setting and achieving goals to maintaining strong communication and interpersonal skills—will better your chances of landing a promotion. In this chapter, I'll drill down a little deeper into strategies that will help you grab hold of that ever-elusive brass ring. I'll talk about how to troubleshoot an antipromotion situation, and how to cope when your quest for reward and recognition takes an unfavorable turn.

Acing Performance Reviews

Every time I sit down for a review with my boss, I feel like a deer caught in the headlights. Talking about myself makes me incredibly uncomfortable, so I can go the whole hour without saying a word. My boss will ramble on and on, and I'll just sit there and nod dumbly like an idiot. When he's done, he'll push the review in front of me and ask me to sign it. I'll do it, no questions asked, but as soon as I leave the room, I'll think of 20 things I should have gotten off my chest before signing that paper. By then, though, it's too late.

Debbie, 23, Texas

Most people roll their eyes when it comes time for performance reviews. This is because the review is, by nature, an uncomfortable and contrived process. In most organizations, reviews happen once or twice a year, and, during this time, every employee is forced to sit in a room with his boss and talk turkey about how he's progressed and how he's screwed up. Performance review documentation is notorious for being generic and vague, complete with ratings that are totally subjective and impossible to measure. Unfortunately, many reviews also take place in a vacuum: the items discussed are often not mentioned again until the next review.

Twenty-somethings may perceive reviews as yet another bureaucratic exercise that wastes valuable time and need not be taken seriously. However, despite a new emphasis on real-time feedback, the traditional performance review is still the only door to promotion inside much of the business world, so you must take advantage of it if you want to get ahead.

If you don't care about your review, no one else will. The worst thing you can do for your career is to go through the process passively. Whether your review cycle takes place annually or semiannually, your preparation should typically start weeks before. Think of your review as an opportunity to sell your manager on your value to the company. If you've mapped out clear career goals (see Chapter 4), and you and your boss have discussed them on an ongoing basis, you'll have a great head start. Look at your last review, including the goals and/or action steps outlined last time around, and gather facts to support how you've progressed in each area. Brainstorm concrete examples that illustrate outstanding performance, and practice communicating them so they're on the tip of your tongue. Then make a list of all the things you would like to cover in the review meeting, independent of your manager's agenda. Your objectives will probably include soliciting feedback on your progress, identifying new goals and growth opportunities, and hammering out a long-term promotion plan. This last item is particularly important. Although you can't reasonably expect to be promoted after every review, you should at least leave with an understanding of where your current responsibilities are leading.

When it comes time for the actual review, make sure your boss gives it to you. This may sound ridiculous, but you'd be surprised how many organizations will allow managers to get away with skipping the review process entirely. After all, bosses are busy, and employee reviews are not on the top of their list of priorities. Remember, though, that it's your right to request a timely appraisal. During the meeting itself, maintain a good balance between listening to what your manager has to say and playing an active role in the conversation. Just because your boss offers constructive criticism doesn't mean you won't get a promotion or a raise, so keep your defensiveness to a minimum. Even though a casual chitchat session might be more comfortable and fun than a serious conversation about your career aspirations, insist on getting through your objectives for the meeting. To paraphrase career author Harry Chambers, your performance review is your best—if not your only—opportunity to get a clear understanding of how you are perceived and what you need to do to ensure your future success.

Don't be afraid to ask questions about your boss's feedback, and make sure you read over your written review carefully before signing it. Once the cycle is complete, your manager might be perfectly happy to forget about your performance for the next five or 11 months. Don't let her. Be proactive about setting up regular meetings to review your progress, address potential problems, and incorporate new responsibilities and priorities into the master plan. If you keep the lines of communication open, nothing that comes up in your next review will be a surprise. Who knows, maybe you'll even look forward to it!

One more thing before we leave the topic of performance feedback. As we move further into the twenty-first century, some organizations are placing less emphasis on semi-annual or annual reviews and more emphasis on just-in-time, electronic feedback that's given by a variety of managers over the course of individual assignments. Be vigilant about collecting and responding to this type of feedback. It could very well help you move ahead sooner rather than later.

Asking for a Raise

If you are going to ask your boss for a raise, make sure you have a good reason—needing the money doesn't count! Your organization doesn't care if you are drowning in student loans, can't make your rent, or have to finance a wedding this year. As with everything else in the business world, the money you get paid is all about the value you add to the company. Before you sit down with your manager, you'll want to be prepared with a list of contributions that have positively impacted the bottom line. As you're putting together your case, be hard on yourself. Look at the situation from your organization's point of view. Have you honestly acquired such valuable skills, performed at such a high level, and exceeded expectations to such a degree that your organization should shell out more assets to keep you?

You also have to look at the big picture. Check out compensation surveys such as the National Compensation Survey by the U.S. Department of Labor (bls.gov/ncs) or Websites such as Salary.com or Payscale.com to determine how your salary stacks up to what other local twenty-somethings in your position are making. Don't forget to take into account other financial incentives you may receive from your company, including bonuses, stock options, insurance packages, 401(k) contributions, and tuition reimbursement.

Of course, you also have to get real and evaluate your request in the context of the current economic conditions, your company's financial status, and internal policies regarding raises. Also, some organizations have grades, or fixed salary ranges, that prevent managers from increasing compensation beyond the amount predetermined by your level or title. Still others may place the authority to decide matters of compensation in the hands of a few individuals—and your boss may not be one of them. You'll save yourself a lot of *agita* if you find out about such things ahead of time.

When is a good time to ask for a raise? Coming off a strong performance review in which your boss acknowledged your accomplishments is a good bet, because he will probably be expecting you to broach the subject of money. If you have just taken on a new role or your management has raised the bar for your performance, it is perfectly legitimate to ask for an appointment to discuss "compensation commensurate with new responsibilities."

When scheduling the meeting, pick a time when your boss's stress level and workload are as manageable as possible, and tell him what you want to talk about so that he's prepared. An informal setting such as lunch often works best, because it allows you to relate to your manager on a personal level. Before you meet face to face, decide on a number that you'd be satisfied with, and think about how you'll respond if you don't get it. You also may want to practice your tone on a family member or friend prior to the meeting, because there is a fine line separating the assertive/sincere and arrogant/entitled approaches.

Now, on to the big conversation itself. If you're underpaid and you know it, refrain from bitching. Acting bitter or angry will only put your manager on the defensive. Instead, remain calm, positive, and professional. Tell your boss how much you enjoy working for the company. Talk about your performance in a factual manner and provide concrete examples of how you add value to the organization. When it comes time to broach the topic, use the word *compensation* rather than *raise* or *money*. In the event that your boss declines your raise, don't close your ears to the rest of the discussion. He may be willing to offer you other perks instead, such as extra vacation time, flexible hours, or a nice dinner with your significant other on the company. These concessions may not be as valuable as cold cash, but they can come in handy for a twenty-something struggling to afford the good life outside of work.

Despite your best efforts, you may not get the compensation you've earned. This is not an unusual scenario for twenty-somethings. Sometimes, the only way to get a serious pay increase is to switch jobs (see Chapter 10). But if you are not willing or ready to do this, try and swallow your negativity at not getting a raise for the time being, ask your boss what you need to do in order to receive an increase, and find out if it's possible to revisit this issue in a few months. Do not give an ultimatum unless you are prepared to walk out the door right then and there. Remember, even if you have another job offer in hand that pays more, you cannot assume that your current manager will make a counteroffer.

Your boss may tell you that he would like to give you a raise, but his hands are tied. If this is the case, ask him if the two of you can schedule a meeting with the higher-up responsible for the decision. Do not go over his head without his knowledge, and make sure he is kept in the loop on all matters concerning your compensation.

Raise discussions are never easy for either party, and if your boss is the passive-aggressive type, he may tell you what you want to hear simply to get you out of his office. Make sure that you follow up appropriately on any vocal promises he makes, and, if possible, secure an effective date for your increase. The issue is not closed until you see the change in your paycheck.

Pleasing the Promotion Gods

I wasn't in with the right people at my company, so the good work that I did was constantly overlooked by the higher-ups. I watched kids five or six years younger than me getting all these high-profile assignments, and I started to get burned up about it. So I decided to try a different strategy. I love playing racquetball, so I signed up for the company tournament and just "happened" to get paired with a senior exec in my division. We got to know each other a lot during that week, and I dropped in just enough info about work so that this guy knew what I was made of. When one of his employees left the company, I asked him if he was looking for a replacement. He hadn't thought about it yet, and he didn't think about it anymore—he hired me!

Mike, 29, New Jersey

In case this wasn't obvious already, you need to do more than just master the performance review process and leave the rest to chance if you want to get promoted. According to Harry Chambers, author of *Getting Promoted: Real Strategies for Advancing Your Career*, factors that affect promotion include:

1. Yourself (your skills, your abilities, and your willingness to do what you need to do in order to get ahead).

2. Your visibility in the organization and people's perceptions of you.

3. Opportunities within the organization to move up the ladder.

Intentionally moving your career in the right direction means successfully controlling Factor #1, influencing Factor #2, and assessing Factor #3. Chambers suggests that people who want to be promoted do the following:

✦ Perform at such a high level that their candidacy cannot be denied.

✦ Demonstrate informal leadership before formal authority is attained.

✦ Keep themselves free of baggage and political skirmishes.

✦ Position themselves as agents of change who are willing to support current company policies, while also embracing future opportunities.

✦ Seek to expand their influence and challenges by broadening the scope of their responsibilities.

✦ Develop and support the people they work with by driving processes forward.

Executive Presence = Promotability

In case you haven't believed me when I've gone on and on about the importance of the professional persona and everything that goes with it...

According to a 2012 study from the Center for Talent Innovation, 268 senior executives cited executive presence, or being perceived as leadership material, as an essential component to getting ahead. In fact, executive presence accounted for, on average, 25 percent of what it takes to get promoted. The three areas that comprise executive presence are:

✦ **Gravitas:** The ability to project confidence, poise under pressure, and decisiveness. Sixty-seven percent of senior executives surveyed cited gravitas as the core characteristic of executive presence.

✦ **Communication:** Includes excellent speaking skills, assertiveness, and the ability to read an audience or situation. Twenty-eight percent of surveyed executives felt that good communication telegraphs that you're leadership material.

✦ **Appearance:** How you look and dress does affect your executive presence, but it's not as critical as the first two factors.

Sounding educated is critical if you want to ascend to the next level. Nearly 60 percent of executives felt that unprofessional, uninformed speech detracts from executive presence. And finally, you will enhance your executive presence and your chances at promotion if you hone your global competence, or the ability to understand how business is done in different countries and how to work effectively with culturally diverse teams.

When you receive feedback on your executive presence, listen and take it seriously. If the comments aren't universally positive, don't get offended. Recognize that the person is only trying to help you and that your promotability will be enhanced in the long run. No one is perfect, but the most successful leaders learn as they go along.

A few final words on promotion: I cannot emphasize enough the importance of relationships in this process. In Chapter 3, I talked about how networking can increase your visibility and establish personal connections that will help you move forward. At this stage in your career, you should be jumping at any opportunity to interact with higher-ups—from attending your company's social events and sitting in the right place in the cafeteria to volunteering to work on special projects and serving on office committees. In these situations, don't be afraid to strut your stuff. Just be sure you know what you're talking about!

It also doesn't hurt to be assertive in determining your own destiny. Just like asking for a raise, bringing up the topic of promotion with your manager is appropriate and legitimate, provided you've earned the right to move to the next level. Rather than accosting your boss in the hall during a moment of extraordinary stress and blurting out, "I want a promotion," give the matter a great deal of thought before initiating a conversation. Develop a bulletproof case for why you are entitled to advance by making a list of the weekly hours you spend doing tasks inside your job description and the weekly hours you spend doing tasks at the next level. The goal of this little exercise is to show that you are accomplishing much more than you were originally hired to do. If you're doing the work of more than one full-time employee, note that as well. Then, as you're talking to your boss, point out that your efficiency saves him money because he only has to pay one person instead of two.

Be prepared to compromise. No matter how valuable you are, chances are your boss is not going to promote you right then and there, so talk in terms of time frames and how you can ensure that you perform at a level that will warrant a promotion in three to six months. Once you and your boss agree on a promotion plan, remember to get it in writing.

At some point in your early career, it's inevitable that you will be denied advancement. The circumstances vary. Maybe you will ask your manager for a promotion, and she will turn you down outright. Perhaps a higher-level position will open up and one of your colleagues will be slated for it instead of you. It's also possible that your performance review or promotion plan says you are due for advancement, but your boss thinks you still have some work to do before moving ahead. In any case, being denied a promotion can be disappointing and hurtful. However, it does not mean that your boss doesn't like you, or that the company doesn't recognize your contributions. Often, promotion decisions have more to do with the politics of the organization than with you as an individual. It's vital that you don't demonstrate your displeasure, because the "powers that be" might be watching to see how you react. Instead, take an honest look at the reasons behind the decision, and work to overcome real and perceived weaknesses so that you can be successful at the next opportunity.

The "Unofficial" Promotion

Last year my boss increased the scope of my responsibilities without officially promoting me. My new job required me to interface with clients a lot, so my old title didn't really fit. One customer even said that my business card confused him. I was fed up, so I took the plunge and changed my title in my email signature and on my business cards. My boss eventually got the hint and promoted me.

Henry, 27, Virginia

It happens all the time: You're one of the top performers in your department, but for one reason or another, your boss doesn't promote you. Here are some suggestions for handling some of the more mystifying scenarios.

◆   Your boss keeps giving you new responsibilities, and everyone recognizes that you are operating at a higher level. Maybe your boss doesn't have the authority to promote you, or maybe *she* is at the next rung on the ladder so there's nowhere for you to go. It's also possible that your boss doesn't feel a sense of urgency when it comes to your career growth. Talk to your boss frankly about a promotion or compensation appropriate for your new level of responsibility (see "Asking for a Raise" on page X). If that doesn't work, use the visibility tactics described in Chapter 4 to alert the higher-ups to how well you're doing.

Really stuck? You may have to roll the political dice and go above your boss by asking for a meeting with your department head. Just make sure that you frame the conversation in terms of your career development rather than the promotion you want, and also ensure that you keep your boss informed.

+ You have mastered all of the responsibilities in your job description. A job well done in the professional world is not like an excellent standardized test score—it doesn't necessarily predict future success. To get promoted these days, you have to master the skills associated with your current position and, to a great extent, the responsibilities of the next level. In other words, you have to prove that you can add value to a higher-level job before your company will pay you for doing it. If you don't know what's involved in taking your skills and responsibilities up a notch, ask someone in your desired position to act as your mentor and allow you to shadow him for a bit. Don't just observe, though. You'll learn more quickly by actively participating and trying things on your own. As you grow more confident, start acting as though you've already been promoted. If you play your cards right, official recognition will be a natural conclusion.

+ You are so good at your job that you're the only person who can do it justice. It's easy for a driven twenty-something to get stuck in this trap. If you make yourself irreplaceable, how can the company afford to lose you to a new role? Get out of this one by handpicking a junior member of your team to take your place, either officially or unofficially. Training someone else to do your job as well as you serves two purposes: (1) you'll convince your boss that your job will be left in good hands, and (2) you'll show her that you're management material.

+ In the last few review cycles, you've been promoted like clockwork. Maybe you've been lucky so far and were appropriately rewarded for stellar performance. Remember that each time you take on a new position, you start from scratch. Just because you were promoted last year and have a great reputation, does not mean you have the right combination of skill, visibility, and opportunity to succeed at the next level. Harry Chambers reminds us that we are not entitled to anything, and also that dues are never paid in full. Rather, we must campaign for reelection through tangible achievement every day.

Be Careful What You Wish For

Because you're reading this book, chances are you are the type of person who can't get promoted soon enough. You probably think you're ready for the next level right now, and you might be frustrated with your management for failing to recognize this fact. The truth is, though, if people were promoted every time they thought they deserved it, everyone would be a VP by the age of 30. We all have to learn that the world doesn't work that way. The sooner we do, the happier we'll be with the way our careers are progressing.

A high school teacher of mine once said, "You don't know what you don't know." In your 20s, you don't realize that, smart as you are and quickly as you catch on, you don't have the wisdom or experience to handle the more complicated responsibilities of middle managers in the business world. It took me time to learn this, but bosses who make you wait a year or two to get to the next level are usually doing you a favor. When it comes to promotion, you have to be careful what you wish for. I've seen young employees move up and up until they are in way over their heads. The same "lucky" individuals who make you so jealous often fail outright or self-destruct from the stress of avoiding failure.

At the end of the day you have to ask yourself, "What's the rush?" Of course you want to get to the next level—as well you should. But is your career really going to fall to pieces if it doesn't happen tomorrow? Because you'll probably be in the workforce until you're in your 70s, you have the next 50 years to cope with the anxiety of answering to the big guns, being a slave to your devices, and sitting on top of a team of people who depend on you for their job satisfaction and financial livelihood. Rather than demanding that your career move at the speed of light, why not relax your grip and concentrate on learning everything you can at your current level so that you'll be better prepared for the next? And while you're at it, enjoy having zero decision-making power, relatively normal working hours, and the freedom to go to the bathroom without affecting the company's bottom line. Once you become a high-ranking superstar, you'll give anything to have these days back.

Handling Setbacks

If you've chosen a career in business, you will inevitably experience some type of setback. You'll be moving along, making great progress, and growing by leaps and bounds every day, and then, suddenly, you'll be dealt a blow. And whether your pet project is canceled, your performance review is a bust, you get turned down for a promotion, or you're asked to leave the company, setbacks hurt big-time. You're demotivated, disillusioned, and pissed as hell. You might not feel like doing anything for a few days except watching E!, munching on Doritos, and wallowing in self-pity. This response is both normal and appropriate, provided it's short-lived. In his book *Emotional Intelligence at Work*, Hendrie Weisinger tells us that resiliency, or the ability to bounce back, is what differentiates people who deal with setbacks effectively from those who don't. Everyone goes through career setbacks, but some people handle them in creative, positive, and rewarding ways, whereas others sulk, become bitter, and give up on their big-picture goals. As you can imagine, the former individuals are happier overall, and they have more successful careers too.

When you're lying on the ground and your job is stomping all over you, it can be pretty hard to pick yourself up and get moving again. Nevertheless, if you start thinking of yourself as a victim or allow yourself to lapse into prolonged negativity, you won't be hurting anyone except yourself. Worrying until you get sick, abusing alcohol or drugs, or denying that you've reached an impasse won't help either. The best strategy for making a comeback is to recognize the reality of the situation, acknowledge your feelings, and find a way to cope productively. Here are some tips that have gotten me through my darkest career days.

+ **Remind yourself that, in a month, this will be a memory.** When setbacks happen, the tendency is to feel as though your bad luck will last forever. By keeping in mind that the situation is temporary, you'll be strong enough emotionally to take the necessary steps to overcome your misfortune.

+ **Recognize that a setback does not make you a total failure.** Treat your setback as the isolated incident it is. Regardless of what happened, chances are it's not going to significantly affect your life one way or the other. And I don't know any successful people who've learned the right way to do things without trying several wrong ways first.

+ **Care for your self-esteem.** Your identity and self-worth are too precious to leave in the hands of the volatile business world. Your job does not define who you are. You existed before it, and you will exist after it. In the meantime, rather than focusing on your own inadequacies, remind yourself that you are doing the best you can under the current circumstances.

+ **Reach out to your support systems.** During a crisis, it always helps to know you are not alone and that you are justified in feeling the way you do. Instead of withdrawing from the people you care about, make an effort to connect with them and lean on them for support. Your network of friends and family is most critical, but you can receive comfort and insight from spiritual support systems and prayer as well.

+ **Look for humor in the situation.** Having a good laugh can counteract the effects of stress and restore your sense of perspective and your ability to think clearly. It's been proven that when one is happy, the body recovers more quickly from the biological arousal of upsetting emotions. Use whatever humor floats your boat—corny, silly, dry, satirical—as long as it makes you crack a smile.

+ **Be good to your body.** Regular exercise and relaxation techniques (such as stretching, meditating, or yoga) are great ways to reduce negativity and get back on track. Eating reasonable portions of healthy foods can also increase your overall well-being while you are recovering from your setback.

+ **Commit yourself to a new project.** New goals and projects provide fresh perspective and a sorely needed dose of enthusiasm. You'll be motivated to work harder, and will probably be too busy to think much about your setback.

Experiencing a setback doesn't have to be a bad thing. Gail Sheehy, author of *Pathfinders*, who spent years studying what makes happy people tick, offers this gem of optimism: The earlier we fail at something and our egos crack, the sooner we see that we won't die from it. We realize that our identities will build, show blemishes, suffer injuries, and repair themselves...again and again. Therefore, the best thing that can happen to most people is to fail a little, early in life. As we age and collect more years of experience working, the things that seem like mountains now will become smaller and smaller until they barely register as blips on the radar screen. Fortunately, this means our setbacks won't always be so traumatizing.

The Dreaded Re-org

We have a new CEO, and our entire organization is being over-turned as we speak. The worst part is that he's talking about moving corporate headquarters to another state! I don't know what I'm going

to be doing or where I'm going to be doing it, and the waiting is kill-
ing me. I haven't slept through the night since I found out about this,
and I always feel like I'm on the verge of getting sick. I've lived in
Colorado all my life, and everything I've ever known is here. I don't
know what I'll do if I have to move.

    Blair, 26, Colorado

The business world wouldn't be the fun place it is without the tribal ritual known as the reorganization (a.k.a. re-org). A re-org usually follows when new management takes over or existing management decides to change the way the company does business. What does it potentially mean to you? Oh, nothing much—except a new job, a new boss, new coworkers, and maybe even a new place to live. Re-orgs don't happen in every company, and they don't always affect everyone in the organization. Depending on management objectives, one division might be restructured while the rest are left untouched. Some companies, however, make re-org an annual event. Regardless of how the current organization is functioning, they insist that change is good and that it can't hurt to stir things up a little. Some also see regular re-orgs as an efficient way to shift talent around to best suit the company's needs.

Human beings are not big fans of change, so it shouldn't surprise anyone that the majority of employees don't like re-orgs. And life being the way it is, re-orgs tend to happen when you're cruising along in your job and everything is going just swell. They'll often strike for no discernable reason, and you'll be left to pick up the pieces of your career. When you're a driven twenty-something on the move, an unsolicited change in the landscape you've learned to navigate can be extremely frustrating. You may feel as though all of your recent achievements are for naught. Realize that re-orgs aren't personal. Organizations are huge machines, and it's likely your upper management didn't consider how the restructuring would affect you individually.

Re-orgs are tough on everyone involved, and how you conduct yourself in the aftermath says a lot about you as an employee. If you think about it, you have two choices: (1) you can leave the company, or (2) you can stay and add value to the new organization. If you choose the latter option, it's critical that you are perceived as flexible, capable, and supportive of the company's direction. When the rug has been pulled out from underneath you and you are thrust into an unfamiliar work situation, it's tempting to develop a bad attitude and express your displeasure to those around you. If there is ever a time to remember your professional persona, it's now. Re-orgs mean new faces, lots of first impressions, and extra scrutiny from senior managers watching to see how the staff is adjusting to the changes. Feel yourself slipping? Use the survival strategies I talked about in Chapter 6 (such as banishing the *shoulds* and taking care of your body) for a boost of positive energy.

If you know a re-org is coming, but you don't have the details, the best thing you can do is anticipate the change and prepare for it as best as you can. Allow yourself to get used to the idea of a new work situation gradually, and begin to think about new opportunities that could arise as a result of the re-org. Consider how you will deal with the worst-case scenario and create a plan of attack for getting through it. Once that's done, recognize that the situation is out of your control and forget about it for the time being. Worrying will not increase the likelihood of a favorable outcome. Instead, you'll most likely drive yourself nuts in the process.

Learning to roll with the punches is especially valuable when it comes to surviving re-orgs. Think about it this way: If you were in a sinking ship a few miles from the shore, would you just sit in the hull and complain? Would you wring your hands in despair and jump over the side? I think not. You would put on a life jacket and swim your heart out!

Job Uncertainty

Benjamin Franklin once said that nothing is certain except death and taxes. We might agree with him on paper, but job uncertainty still scares us, and in the last several years there's been more than enough of it to go around.

It's not good for our health either. In 2008, researchers at the University of Michigan found that uncertainty can actually be worse for us than outright bad news. The study followed 3,000 employed people younger than age 60, and divided the subjects between those who were worried about losing their jobs and those who were not so concerned.

Based on participant self-reports, the researchers discovered that people who felt chronically insecure about their jobs experienced poorer health overall and were more depressed than those who had actually lost their jobs or had even faced a serious or life-threatening illnesses!

You can cope productively with general job uncertainty the same way you would cope with an anticipated re-org, including putting out-of-your-control circumstances out of your mind, and creating a plan to manage the worst-case scenario. Here are a few other tips:

+ **Meditate daily.** The tried-and-true method is slow, deep breathing, in through the nose and out through the mouth. Doing this as well as trying to relax each part of your body one at a time has been proven to lessen the stress response.

+ **Stay off blogs and message boards.** Hypochondriacs are notorious for fueling their anxiety about whether they have a disease by scouring online health sites at all hours of the day and night. There is a psychological principle known as confirmation bias, which claims that people who are already worrying about something will value negative information they find over neutral or positive information. Don't fall into this trap.

+ **Talk to someone objective.** Find a friend or family member who understands your situation and can help you get a realistic grasp of how likely the uncertain event is to occur. Do keep in mind, though, that sometimes too much reassurance from too many people can make anxiety worse.

What I Wish I'd Known

When I was 26, I was promoted into a position that I was not ready for. I knew I didn't have enough experience to manage a multinational team of 200, but my supervisor was keen to have me in the role so I didn't feel I could say no. Besides, how can a brilliant promotion be a bad thing? Well, unfortunately, it can. I was completely lost and failed to meet any of my annual objectives. I would tell my younger self to consider whether the promotion was right for me at that time, and to ask my supervisor for more training so that I could be fully prepared for the role in a year or two.

Hadley, 39, London

Take-Home Points

+ **Prepare for performance reviews.** Objectives for your performance review should include soliciting feedback on your progress, identifying new goals and growth opportunities, and hammering out a long-term promotion plan. Although you can't reasonably expect to be promoted after every review, you should at least leave with an understanding of where your current responsibilities are leading.

+ **Do your homework before asking for a raise.** Be prepared with a list of ways you have contributed to the company that have positively impacted the bottom line. Look at the situation from your organization's point of view, and then ask yourself if you've performed at such a high level that your organization should shell out more assets to keep you.

+ **Be realistic about your career goals.** Remember that advancing to a higher level means more responsibility and less freedom. Rather than demanding that your career move at the speed of light, relax your grip and concentrate on learning everything you can at your current level so that you'll be better prepared for the next.

+ **Learn to cope with setbacks.** What differentiates people who deal with setbacks effectively from those who don't is resiliency, or the ability to bounce back and cope with life's challenges in creative, positive, and rewarding ways.

Chapter 9

You're the Boss Now!

At some point in your 20s, you will probably receive a promotion that lands you a position such that people report directly to you. You are now officially someone's boss, and you find yourself having substantial control over his or her destiny. You'll probably be ecstatic, running around your home singing, "At last! At last! I'm not the peon anymore! And I won't make the same mistakes my manager made with me. No way, I know better. I'm going to be the best boss in the world!"

There's only one problem: You don't know better. How could you? In many companies, new managers are initiated with no training whatsoever. This is why there are so many bad ones. Being an effective boss requires a skill set that few people possess naturally, and mastering it is like learning to drive: watching other people do it isn't enough. In fact, once the excitement from your promotion dies down, you may panic as you realize you have no idea what to do with your new employee. Suddenly your existence in the professional world has become more complex. Pre-promotion, it was tough enough to successfully steer your own career and keep yourself out of trouble. Now you have to do the same things times two, because you are accountable for what your new employee does—and does not—achieve. It's a big responsibility, and one that you must assume carefully if you want to sustain your upward mobility.

This chapter will help you navigate those bewildering first months as a new manager. I'll talk about how to set the stage for a good relationship with your new employee and how you can help her establish goals. I will then go through some of the important aspects of good management—from delegating tasks and communicating effectively to resolving performance issues, motivating a team, and being a great leader. If you have access to a training course to supplement what you read here, I recommend taking advantage of it. Strong leadership skills are not easy to develop or maintain, and you'd be surprised how quickly you can slip back into old habits. When it comes to being the best manager possible, there's no such thing as too many refreshers.

Starting on the Right Foot

When you are assigned a new employee, you should sit down with him for an informal conversation. Taking the employee to lunch is a nice touch, and it will give you the chance to get to know him. Establishing rapport is key, but there is a strategic purpose for this get-together. Remember what I said about first impressions in Chapter 2? Your first meeting with a new employee will demonstrate exactly what kind of boss you will be, and it will influence all interactions from that point on. Use this opportunity to let your employee know right off the bat how you prefer to work and what you expect from him. If the employee is new to the company, you are also responsible for ensuring that he understands his role in the context of the larger organization.

Similarly, you should communicate your boundaries for acceptable conduct and performance as soon as possible. For example, clue him in right away if your company is super strict about arriving to work on time. The first time he slips, subtly let him know that there will be consequences if the behavior continues. Emphasize the importance of meeting project deadlines and observing the organizational hierarchy at the start of your relationship, and no later. I know a lot of managers who desperately want their new employees to like them, so they put up with all kinds of no-no's—from insubordination to mediocre performance—without saying a word. As you can imagine, these managers are always the ones who later complain that their employees don't respect their authority or aren't meeting performance expectations.

Human nature dictates that even hardworking employees may test your boundaries to see what they can get away with. You can save yourself future frustration by guiding your new employee gently, but firmly, in the right direction. If you're worried about being perceived as the bad guy, remember that employees prefer straightforward, timely feedback to mixed messages, passive-aggressive slighting, or a bad review that comes out of nowhere. Your employee may not always love what you have to say, but he can't fault you for delivering constructive messages in the spirit of goodwill. It wasn't so long ago that you were in his shoes, so simply remember how you wanted to be treated then, and let your instinct be your guide.

A Young Life Is in Your Hands

My boss is a fantastic role model. She is so positive and encouraging that I want to do well. If I put extra effort into a project, I know she'll notice and appreciate it. I'm always a little hesitant to try new things because I'm afraid I'll screw up, but my boss is great about helping me work through the issues so that I don't have to go in cold. She's confident in my abilities, which, in turn, makes me more confident in myself.

Jori, 23, Vermont

Good management is challenging because every day you must wear a number of hats. You have to be your employee's ally, establishing a foundation of trust so that she is motivated to work hard for you. You must be a director, staying focused on your department's big-picture objectives while taking into account your employee's unique contributions. You must also be a coach, supporting your employee's development through mutual problem-solving. Once you are assigned an employee, it's not enough to be proactive about your own workload and direction. You are now also responsible for mentoring her and helping her forge a rewarding career path.

In Chapter 4, I defined a goal as an expectation of growth and achievement. As I talked about previously, meaningful career goals are devised by considering what you want to do, why and when it should be done, and how success will be measured. BlessingWhite, a New Jersey-based consulting firm (BlessingWhite.com), suggests that employee goal-setting is important to effective management because it allows your employee to:

+ Understand her responsibilities and what she is expected to achieve.

+ Know the criteria on which her performance will be assessed.

+ Participate directly in the process, which appeals to her need for collegial support, stimulation, and sharing.

Similar to your own goals, your employee's goals should be just challenging enough that she will continue to put forth effort on an ongoing basis. Early in your relationship, meet with your employee and help her draw up a list of goals. If you are a new manager, it's a good idea to think about this before you're sitting across the desk from your new employee. Taking into account her skill set and any existing goals from previous performance reviews, jot down what you think your employee's goals should be. Stuck? Ask your boss or a senior manager for help.

Write your employee's goals in the format of an informal contract, and add it to her performance review. Note what actions each of you will take to ensure that these goals are achieved. For example, suppose you and your employee agree that she needs to increase her comfort level when interacting with other departments. Suggest that she arrange and lead next's week meeting with the IT staff, and help her finalize her agenda ahead of time. Set timelines and follow-up dates for all goals so that the two of you don't forget about them once you leave the room. In between progress meetings, reinforce your employee's positive steps by rewarding productive behavior immediately and consistently.

Does your employee have a goal you've already achieved? On the job, you can help her practice new skills so that she develops the confidence to use them in her work. In his book *Emotional Intelligence at Work*, psychologist Hendrie Weisinger recommends using modeling, or demonstrating effective behaviors to be used in a particular situation, and role-playing, or simulating through live interaction how a situation might play out. *Modeling* might sound like a complex psychological term, but it can be as simple as having your employee sit next to you and listen to you call a prospective client. Role-playing in business is less fun than charades, but much more productive. Let's say your employee is nervous about presenting a new idea to a senior member of the department. Acting out the conversation (with you playing the role of senior executive and the employee acting as herself) will help her articulate her thoughts ahead of time and anticipate potential questions and issues.

If you're going to engage in either modeling or role-playing, be sincere and enthusiastic about it. It's your duty to be sensitive to your employee's development, don't ever treat it as a joke. Be cognizant of situations in which your employee may be in over her head, and suggest other alternatives if appropriate. Sometimes you might not have the personal experience needed to assist your employee with her individual goals. If you don't think you can be an effective role model in a particular situation, direct your employee to someone who can. It's always better to admit you don't know something than to lead your employee in the wrong direction.

A key part of your job now is to make sure your employee meets her goals. You may actually be measured on it. Improve her chances for success by applying all of the people-management tips from Chapter 6. When your employee achieves a goal, don't let the event slip by unnoticed. Praise her, and then encourage her to reach even higher. Basking in the glow of your appreciation and approval, your employee will be motivated to do her best.

Delegating

This one guy I work with can't delegate a task to save his life. He runs himself ragged while his staff sits around all day doing nothing. I know he does it because he thinks no one can do the job as well as he can, but what happens is that the work doesn't end up getting done at all. Everyone in the department avoids collaborating on projects with his group, which is a shame, because he has some talented people who are totally underutilized.

Terry, 27, Tennessee

You were likely assigned an employee because your workload is too much for one person. Because there are only so many hours in a day, it makes sense to hand off as many assignments as possible. However, many twenty-something managers resist delegating tasks, even if they are in danger of drowning. Some of these reasons are probably close to your heart:

 ✦ As the senior team member, you'll do a better job because you know the subject matter and the company's resources inside and out.

✦ It's easier and less time consuming to do the task yourself than to explain the assignment to your employee.

✦ You're afraid your employee will screw up the assignment and it will reflect badly on you.

✦ Your boss likes to micromanage, so you don't want to lose control over the process.

✦ You like doing a particular task and don't want to give it up.

Any or all of these factors might play a role in your particular situation. That's why delegating work is one of the most challenging managerial skills for a perfectionist twenty-something to develop. Case in point: When I first became a supervisor, I held my cards so close to the vest that my poor employee, Danny, had no idea what was going on. I didn't trust him enough to share the work, so Danny had no choice but to sit in his cube and stare at the wall. After a few months, I developed the reputation of being a bottleneck—assignments arrived in my office and never came out. No one in the department was happy with this situation. I was so stressed that my hair was standing on end, my colleagues were annoyed because they had to go around me to get things done, and Danny felt useless and demotivated.

I eventually figured out that properly leveraging Danny's contribution did not mean wasting his time with "safe" tasks, such as raiding the mailroom, or giving him ultra-specific instructions on how to do the smallest assignment. Rather, I had to invest time in helping him branch out, so that he could become a self-sufficient member of our team. The day Danny was promoted was one of the best moments of my career, because it was proof that I'd finally mastered the art of delegation. Once I offered Danny guidance based on what I knew, and then gave him the freedom to approach tasks in his own way, he actually learned something! Here is an example of the process I used to make it happen.

Step 1: Plan a task to delegate based on your employee's knowledge, skills, and willingness.

Example: "Danny is really organized and a great multitasker. He did a stellar job helping me with the Widget World booth last month, and I know he's interested in attending a trade show on the West Coast. I think I'll put him in charge of managing our booth at the Widget Symposium. I can see Danny moving into a show management role as early as next year, and I feel that this project would be an excellent jumping-off point."

Step 2: Clearly state the expectations and requirements of the project.

Example (to Danny): "I'd like for you to manage our booth at the Widget Symposium in California in October. As you know from working with me on the Widget World booth last month, we have an approved procedure for coordinating the components and staffing of the booth. However, I would love to see what creative ideas you can come up with for our corporate demo and our visitor giveaways. You'll need to be on-site October 4–8, and I expect planning for the booth to take approximately half of your time in the month leading up to the show."

Step 3: Explain why the task is important and what you hope your employee will get out of it.

Example (to Danny): "The VP of Corporate Communications considers the Widget Symposium to be one of the top five annual events for generating company visibility. I hope the project will give you valuable experience working with senior executives and managing vendor relationships. As you move into full-time show management, these skills will be critical."

Step 4: Empower your employee by asking for his feedback on the best way to accomplish the task.

Example (to Danny): "What do you think about managing this booth by yourself? How do you want to approach reviewing the show's marketing strategy and then getting everyone together for a preliminary planning meeting?"

Step 5: Suggest a few resources your employee might use to get the job done, but be careful not to micromanage.

Example (to Danny): "You should definitely take another look at the booth planning procedure document we followed for Widget

World last month. I will also email you a list of all the internal staff and vendors we worked with on last year's Widget Symposium."

Step 6: Set target dates for follow-up and completion, and ask your employee to develop an action plan.

Example (to Danny): "I know the details of planning a booth can be overwhelming. To keep the project manageable, why don't you draft an action plan? We can meet on Monday afternoon to go over it."

Step 7: Meet with your employee regularly to monitor progress, expressing confidence in his ability.

Example (to Danny): "The action plan looks great, Danny. You're doing a terrific job so far and I know the marketing people are impressed with you. Can we meet twice a week until the show, so I can answer any questions you have?"

Step 8: Evaluate the results and offer constructive feedback.

Example (to Danny): "The booth's execution was flawless and the Chapstick giveaways yielded at least 100 more leads than usual. The VP of Corporate Communications thought you'd been doing this for years! I know all of the last-minute changes were challenging, but your organization and flexibility allowed us to pull it off. Next time, I'd just suggest coordinating an on-site booth staff meeting so you can make sure everyone has their schedules in advance."

If you want your employee to be receptive to future assignments and enjoy working on your team, be appreciative of his efforts and allow him to manage projects independently. Your role is to offer direction and a supportive ear—not to get involved in all of the nitty-gritty aspects of the task. The first few times you try to delegate an important assignment will probably be difficult. Just keep in mind the end goal. The more autonomy and decision-making authority your employee has, the faster he'll acquire expertise that will make your job easier!

Countering Objections

Tasks that you assign to your employee may not always be received with open arms. However, you can't back down just because your employee objects to an assignment. She will learn that expressing displeasure will get her out of any responsibility she doesn't like, and, next thing you know, she'll be walking all over you. A successful leader is well-liked and still manages to get things done. You can become one by mastering how to handle objections. Suppose you are a sales manager for a pharmaceutical company. Your employee, a sales representative, does not want to attend an out-of-town bioscience training seminar because she is too busy. You need her to complete the course so that she has the knowledge base to take on two important accounts. Let's illustrate how you might handle this situation using a technique advocated by consulting firm BlessingWhite:

Step 1: Press for specifics to get to the heart of the concern.

You: "You mentioned that you don't want to take the seminar because you have too much on your plate. What deadlines do you have next week? If you brief me ahead of time, I'm sure that I or someone else can cover your 'to do's.' You wouldn't have to worry about your other work at all. Is there another reason you don't want to go?"

Employee: "Well, actually, the seminar just comes at a really bad time. My boyfriend just got out of the hospital. He had an appendectomy. He's fine now, but I'm worried that if I leave town, something will happen."

Step 2: Show that you understand by paraphrasing or empathizing in a warm and genuine tone.

You: "The last thing you want to do is leave someone you love when he's sick. You must be afraid that if you go to the seminar, you won't be able to check on him as often and that you'll be too far away to help if there are any complications."

Employee: "Exactly. I mean, it's not like he's alone. His mother lives a few blocks away and calls every day. It just makes me anxious, you know?"

Step 3: Respond with the appropriate facts and/or benefits about the task.

You: "Sure. Well, listen, I'd really like for you to attend this seminar. I know you really want to take on some of the higher-profile bioscience accounts. I think that you're ready, but this training is required before you can start. Unfortunately, the seminar won't be given for another six months. I would hate to hold up your progress that long."

Employee: "I really do want to move up, and those accounts will help me do it sooner rather than later. I guess I didn't realize why you were pushing me to fly out for this training. To be honest, I didn't see it as a priority. I'm going to explain the situation to my boyfriend's mother. Maybe she'll be willing to look in on him a little more often than usual."

Step 4: Test for acceptance.

You: "So is it okay if I go ahead and sign you up for the seminar? We can book your travel so that you're back on Friday in plenty of time to spend the weekend with your boyfriend."

Employee: "I think we can do that. Thanks."

Recall the Win/Win approach from Chapter 7. Your employee will be much more likely to cooperate with you if you make her want to do what you're proposing. Now, let's be real here: there won't be a Win for your employee in every task you ask her to complete. Sometimes, you will have to delegate an assignment that is just plain undesirable. When you're the bearer of bad news and you know it, it's best to get right to the point. Explain the situation and what needs to be done as positively as you can. Acknowledge your employee's feelings about what you're communicating, and encourage her to participate in finding an acceptable solution. Even if you're as frustrated as she is, don't show it. One of the hallmarks of a true leader is making the best of unfortunate scenarios without breaking a sweat.

Criticism: It's a Dirty Job

For me, the most difficult part of being a manager is delivering criticism. Even if it's given nicely, it's still criticism, and I know I've never liked receiving it from my boss. I've realized, though, that if I never suggest how my employee can improve, he won't. He'll assume that my constant positive reinforcement means he's doing everything perfectly, and he won't bother to learn the new skills required to progress. And then what kind of manager would I be?

Criticism is necessary to any manager/employee relationship, but you should never bang your subordinate over the head with it. You are not a playground bully, so always make sure to phrase your comments constructively. Begin with a positive statement about your employee's performance, and do not follow it with the word *but*. The *but* erases the good intentions behind your original comment and diminishes the credibility of the criticism to come. *But* may seem harmless, yet it has the power to anger people like nothing else. Prevent your employee's negative reaction by changing the word *but* to the word *and*. For instance:

> **Example #1:** "Dave, your site design is very sophisticated, but I'd like to see you replace the pastels with dark colors to enhance the effect."

> **Example #2:** "Dave, your site design is very sophisticated, and I'd like to see you replace the pastels with dark colors to enhance the effect."

See how much nicer Example #2 sounds?

Of course, some people are super sensitive and have trouble swallowing direct criticism of any kind. A former colleague shared a wonderful tactic that has worked for me on several occasions. If you want to improve a person in a certain respect, act as though he's already behaving the way you want him to. He will want to prove that you were right to think so highly of him. For example, suppose you want your employee to take better notes at team meetings. Take him aside and tell him that you wish you were as organized as he is. "I don't know how you keep track of everything that goes on in those meetings," you could add. "Your notes saved my life last week when the General Manager asked for the statistics that the Investor Relations Group presented." Your employee will think about your compliment every time he goes to a team meeting—and you can bet that the quality of his notes will be better for it. After all, you told him that you love his notes, and he won't want to disappoint the boss.

Addressing Performance Issues

A performance problem may be defined as a situation in which your employee's work does not meet your expectations. Maybe she turns in her weekly reports with typos, freezes up when it's her turn to present in team meetings, or lets important deadlines slide. Telling employees to shape up is such a sticky wicket that many managers steer away from it entirely. The reasons vary. Some managers genuinely like the employee with the performance problem, and they don't want to offend her. Others are simply unable to tackle uncomfortable situations head-on.

Whatever the motivation, a huge percentage of managers keep their gripes to themselves. They go about their business, allowing their disapproval to simmer while their employees continue to be ineffective. Remember that people are not mind readers. If you don't tell your employee what she's doing wrong, she won't fix it. And if she doesn't fix it, either you or your department could suffer a breakdown. Waiting until her review to discuss the performance problem is not a good idea either. By the time the assessment period rolls around, you will have had to cope with the problem for who knows how many months. A review-based conversation also means that your employee won't have the chance to correct the problem before it is noted in her permanent record.

You should address performance problems in a timely fashion, but you don't want to jump down your employee's throat every time she makes a mistake. How can you strike a good balance? The first time your employee commits an infraction (provided it's not something to fire her over), let it go. Wait and see if the incident was just a fluke or if your employee corrects it on her own. However, if the issue rears its ugly head on an ongoing basis, it may be time to sit down with her and address it. The following steps will guide you through the process.

Step 1: Begin with a positive comment—and mean it.

Example: "The General Manager was really impressed with your presentation this morning. He thought you were very articulate and natural in front of the podium."

Step 2: Explain the performance problem by citing specific instances.

Example: "You're an excellent impromptu speaker, and I'd like to see you prepare for your presentations in advance so that you can use concrete examples and statistics to back up your arguments. This morning, for example, you needed to back up your claims about growth in manufacturing with market research and third-party support. And a few weeks ago, you briefed our lobbyist partners on our product strategy without citing any specifics about our play in the government space."

Step 3: Tactfully point out potential consequences if the problem continues.

Example: "I'm concerned that if you continue to do these types of presentations on the fly, a client will call you on it and we could have an embarrassing situation on our hands. As poised as you are, I can't put you in front of customers if it could compromise the company's reputation."

Step 4: Ask for your employee's feedback in solving the problem.

Example: "What do you think is the best way to plan for your next presentation?"

Step 5: Offer any suggestions you have for solving the problem.

Example: "Can I suggest that you brainstorm an outline for each presentation a week before you're scheduled to deliver it? I think this approach will help you fill in the holes and anticipate questions ahead of time. You'll also have time to consult with the Market Research Group so that they can provide you with the supporting data you need."

Step 6: Work with your employee to develop an action plan.

Example: "If you can complete the outline for the upcoming presentation by next Tuesday, we can meet to go over it. I'll give you an extension on your other deadlines so that you have time to thoroughly research your main arguments. Once you've prepared your slides, we can rehearse the entire presentation in the conference room, and I can help you with any parts that still need some tweaking. Sound like a plan?"

Step 7: Support your employee's efforts to change.

Example: "Thanks so much for working with me here. Good public speakers are rare, and I know that you're going to become one of our best."

Step 8: Follow up, and reward improvements.

Example: "We won the new account largely due to your efforts. Your presentation was rock solid, and I know the clients were impressed with your in-depth knowledge of their business. How would you like to work directly with the General Manager on our annual briefing for the CEO?"

When it comes to addressing performance issues, the key word is *performance*. No matter what your employee's problem is, you must look at it in the context of her overall contribution. For example, suppose she does outstanding work and always hands in her assignments early, but she consistently breezes in at 10 a.m. Before you engage her in a dialogue about her tardiness, consider if it's worth it. If her lateness is not affecting the quality of her work and your boss won't notice because he works out of another office, you might be wise to avoid a confrontation. You know the old saying: If it ain't broke, don't fix it!

Encouraging Open Communication

I really couldn't tell you what my boss expects, because I never hear from him. He works out of another office, and when he does come here, he spends all of his time in meetings. We only talk so that he can review me twice a year, and so that he can tell me about the raise I'm not getting. Fortunately, I know what my role is, and I am able to do my own thing with a minor amount of direction. I think I do decent work. I just wish that my boss was more accessible, so that I could know for sure.

Anthony, 25, California

In Chapter 5, I talked extensively about techniques for good communication. I discussed the importance of assertiveness, or the ability to stand up for your rights, opinions, ideas, and desires while respecting those of others. I also covered specific strategies for leveraging three communication vehicles—writing, speaking, and listening—to sustain positive work relationships. It's in your best interests to communicate well with everyone you work with, but it's most critical when it comes to interacting with a direct employee. As the manager, the onus is on you to make sure information is shared, and if you fall down on the job, your employee's performance and morale may suffer.

Earlier in this chapter, I suggested how to set a precedent for good communication. Keeping the lines open through time, however, is more challenging than you think. When you're a busy manager, the tendency is to stop talking to your employee. You're tied up with your own assignments, and you expect your employee to be off and running with his. After you provide initial direction on a task, you assume that he knows what he's doing. You don't check in with him, and you don't ask him to check in with you.

As time goes by and your employee doesn't see you for a while, he begins to perceive you as unapproachable. He is working in a vacuum, and it's anyone's guess whether or not his performance is actually on target. In the absence of feedback from his manager, he might feel confused or demotivated. Pretty soon, he might stop making meaningful contributions to the team, and his career growth will slam to a screeching halt.

Don't get me wrong: Communication breakdowns are not always the manager's fault. Some employees are notoriously closemouthed and will refrain from volunteering any information about their work. Others will give you data that you don't need. For the sake of group performance, you must solicit timely and relevant feedback from your employee. Set up weekly or biweekly meetings with him to discuss the status of his projects and to provide guidance on issues he may be facing. Consulting firm BlessingWhite recommends asking targeted questions during these meetings to draw your employee out, and to encourage informative responses:

✦ **Factual Questions:** These questions should be asked when you are looking for specific data or statistics. Because these questions are straightforward, have a reason for asking them and don't make your inquiry sound like an interrogation. "In order for me to get an accurate picture of our team's productivity, how many reports did you complete last month?"

+ **Value Questions:** These questions should be asked to find out how your employee thinks or feels about a particular issue. They help you understand your employee's point of view and determine areas that might need further exploration. "What do you think about having two primary account managers instead of one?"

+ **Open Questions:** These questions begin with a *what, when, where, why,* or *how.* They cannot be answered with a yes or a no. These questions allow for the greatest range of responses and provide the greatest opportunity for your employee to express his ideas freely. "Why did you bill the client for hours you spent at the training seminar?"

+ **Closed Questions:** These questions can be answered with a yes or a no. They allow you to ask for more specific information and narrow the range of responses, which can help keep the discussion on track and moving forward. "Did you bill the client for the hours you spent at the training seminar?"

Finally, let your employee know that you are always there for him. Make it clear that you have an open-door policy, and if he comes by your office and you don't have time to chat, try to set aside time that day, if possible. Remember that the younger your employees are, the more sensitive they tend to be, so be gentle with your criticism. Take advantage of every opportunity to mentor your employee, and allow him to benefit from your experience. Touch base with him often—always graciously—and he will feel comfortable coming to you. I think you'll find that when you are proactive about establishing a pattern of open communication, information exchange is easy, and your team is happier and more productive.

Managing Teams

As an employee, I suffered from a certain curse: My strong work ethic compelled me to do the best job possible on every assignment—even if it was the worst assignment possible. However, some of the people in my group were particularly lazy when it came to the work no one wanted to do. After my boss got burned a few times, she started giving all the unpleasant tasks to me because she knew I would get them done. I was actually being punished for my performance, and it felt horrible. Now, as a manager, I remember that this is no way to treat people I want to keep around. All of the work is doled out equally, but the more appealing tasks are used to reward hardworking employees. My strongest people feel appreciated—and the others are motivated to do better so that they, too, can get the favorable assignments.

Susan, 28, Texas

J. Richard Hackman, author of *Leading Teams*, defines a team as a set of people who view themselves as members of the same group and who share accountability toward some outcome. As a team manager, you are responsible for ensuring that your employees understand the purpose of the group and how to leverage their own expertise to achieve the group's objectives. Previously, I talked about supervising teams in the context of project management. Your mission is raised a level when you are chosen to manage a team permanently, and when your employees rely on you for total job direction rather than individual project direction. Hackman offers the following recommendations for negotiating the team terrain:

✦ Maintain a stable group. People need to be on the team long enough to know how to work well together.

✦ Communicate a clear direction, while giving the team freedom to figure out how best to accomplish the group's objectives.

✦ Support your team by sharing information often, making training readily available, and by providing consistent rewards.

✦ Prevent organizational roadblocks by collaborating with senior executives to make sure that the right conditions are in place.

In my experience, leaders must keep in mind a few additional guidelines to effectively manage a team. First, you must treat team members equally. This might sound like a no-brainer, but you'd be surprised how easy it is to play favorites or choose to spend more time with certain individuals. After all, some of your employees will have working styles or personalities similar to yours, so you'll find it easier to coach and delegate projects to them. However, because your employees will talk to each other, make a concerted effort to share workload, information, and kudos across the board. Also, don't take advantage of the can-do people in your group by giving them twice as much work as everyone else. If some employees aren't pulling their weight, address the issue with each person individually rather than relying on the others to carry them along. And if you're going to reward a certain team member with a raise, a comp day, or a special privilege, do it discreetly so that you don't arouse resentment within the group.

Remember that your employees are not your friends. Although it's great to develop a strong rapport with them and to get to know them as individuals, you should be careful about how much information you share about your personal life and how often you get together with them socially outside the office. Your relationships with your employees should always maintain a degree of professionalism. The more the lines blur, the tougher it is to do your job as a manager. For instance, you may find yourself skirting an employee's performance problem because you don't want to jeopardize your friendship with her, or you may tell her something in confidence that she could later claim as inappropriate boss-to-employee communication. Because it's challenging to meet people in your 20s, the office is a natural place to scope out new friendships. You'd be wise, however, to look outside your reporting structure for a new buddy.

You're the Boss—And the Youngest

In the multi-generational workplace that defines the 21st century, it's not unusual for you, the twenty-something, to be suddenly managing a team of employees who are older than you. You should be prepared for some inevitable snide comments and perhaps even some long-standing resentment. Here are some strategies for overcoming your reports' initial skepticism.

✦ **Be confident, but deferential.** You were put in charge for a reason, so try not to be defensive about it. If you don't keep your head up as if you deserve to be there, your employees will perceive you as weak and immature. On the other hand, refrain from acting like a know-it-all just because you're the boss. Show respect for your reports' years of experience and go out of your way to seek out and then follow their recommendations.

✦ **Don't tip-toe around expectations.** If your older employees know what they're supposed to be doing and how they will be evaluated from the get-go, you'll avoid misunderstandings down the line. Make sure you all agree on the best way to proceed with their jobs and their careers, and encourage them to express themselves openly in the event of a conflict.

✦ **Listen and give them breathing room.** Give older employees your undivided attention (in other words, don't text while they're talking to you), and always try to understand their points of view. Make suggestions, but be conscious of their need for freedom. Older employees who have been doing a job for years may be insulted by a younger boss who insists on being involved every step of the way.

✦ **Facilitate training and mentoring opportunities.** Assume that older workers are capable of everything younger workers are, and treat them as such. Ensure that older reports are up to speed on the latest technology, especially software designed to make their jobs easier. If you have younger employees on your staff as well, consider starting a reciprocal mentoring program in which the younger reports help the older ones with technology adoption, and in turn the older ones assist the younger ones with assimilating into the company and the business world in general.

Meeting Finesse

Overseeing productive team meetings is another responsibility that separates the strong supervisors from the weak. Two of the biggest gripes I've heard about managers are that they either refuse to have team meetings or that they run them inefficiently. Recognize that team meetings serve a variety of purposes, including communicating new goals and information, building teamwork, motivating employees, and providing a forum to resolve issues. If you never call your group together as a team, your employees might feel isolated and uninformed, and problem issues may fester because there is no opportunity to clear the air. However, you don't want to have meetings just for the sake of having meetings. Here are some do's and don'ts for managing effective meetings:

DO

✦ Allow your employees to have a say in determining the agenda for the meeting.

✦ Distribute the agenda ahead of time, making sure to list the specific issues to be discussed.

✦ Plan something special every now and then, such as bringing in lunch or donuts.

✦ Have team members contribute to the meeting by having them provide a status update for their projects.

+ Keep the tone of the discussion open and positive.

+ Encourage team members to freely voice their concerns and to help one another.

+ Maintain a big-picture perspective and calmly guide the group toward a consensus or solution if a problem arises.

+ Consider your team's time pressures and keep the meeting to an hour.

DON'T

+ Have meetings too often (once a week should be the maximum).

+ Allow team members to interrupt each other or monopolize the discussion with their own opinions.

+ Allow the discussion to wander off topic for too long.

Be a Leader, Not Just a Manager

In my 10-year career in the leadership development space, I've come across the work of Development Dimensions International (DDIWorld.com) numerous times. Robert Rogers at DDI generously provided me with seven traits exhibited by *true* leaders—not merely people who are in charge because they happened to get a promotion. If you want to be in a position to shape the destiny of your organization, start honing these qualities in your first managerial position, while you're still young!

1. **Great leaders are masters of ambiguity.** The modern workplace is fraught with chaos. These leaders possess the ability to stay calm amid turmoil and to be convincingly reassuring. They keep their people focused with clear direction and goals, and view change through the lens of opportunity.

2. **Great leaders inspire confidence and believe in the future.** Leaders who make it a priority to understand and address employee needs, who can differentiate those things that are important from those that are not, and who can communicate a long-term vision that attains the buy-in of employees and customers alike, are the ones who find their organizations rewarded with long-term customer relationships and loyal, engaged employees.

3. **Great leaders have a passion for results.** These leaders place emphasis on those activities, initiatives, programs, and processes that produce the best ROI. They are able to stay the course, overcoming any obstacle thrown in their way, because they believe their focus will truly bring about the outcomes they are seeking.

4. **Great leaders express unwavering integrity.** Leaders must earn trust every day. Their values must be visible through their actions, and they must be both able and willing to be held up as an example to others. Bad news, such as the need for layoffs or budget cuts, or the failure of the organization to meet financial targets, must not be hidden or sugarcoated.

5. **Great leaders set others up for success.** Leaders who are true talent advocates understand that feeling successful is a prerequisite for ongoing engagement and that successful people are more, not less, likely to stay. But they also understand that success is about more than praise. It's about developing people, giving them room to grow, and coaching them to be their best.

6. **Great leaders have strong, rather than big, egos.** Leaders with big egos, so good at tearing others down, are often terribly insecure themselves. They lack the self-confidence that leadership demands. On the other hand, those with strong egos have a positive self-image but at the same time are able to acknowledge and value the thoughts and contributions of others.

7. **Great leaders have the courage to make tough decisions.** When faced with making difficult choices, the best leaders do not shy away from taking prompt action. They know that indecisiveness can lead to paralysis, and that popular decisions are not always the best decisions. And they understand that too many compromise decisions, although usually less painful to reach, breed mediocrity and lead to results that, in the end, please nobody.

If you're in your 20s and are already managing one or more direct reports, chances are you're on the fast track. You are obviously good at what you do and have earned a pat on the back. But as DDI alludes to, be careful of arrogance. I guarantee that you will be difficult to work with if you insist that you're always right. The people underneath you can teach you something if you're willing to pay attention. Remember this saying from Ralph Waldo Emerson, and stay humble: "Every man I meet is my superior in some way. In that, I learn from him."

What I Wish I'd Known

Now that I'm in my mid-30s and have been a manager for a lot of years, I see that it's okay not to know it all. When I got my first employee at 26, I thought I had to instantly stop asking questions because I was supposed to be the informed one. I didn't want the other managers or my employee to think I was ignorant. Some projects got pretty screwed up because I was scared to admit I didn't have all the answers. These days, I feel comfortable enough with myself to speak up!

Marcelo, 36, Sao Paulo

Take-Home Points

+ **Make expectations clear up-front.** Your first interactions with new employees demonstrate exactly what kind of boss you will be. Use the opportunity to let them know right away how you prefer to work and what you expect from them.

+ **Teach employees to be self-sufficient.** Invest time in teaching your employees what they need to know to become fully functioning members of your team. Show that you appreciate their efforts, and allow them to manage projects independently. Your role is to offer direction and a supportive ear—not to micromanage.

+ **Learn to criticize constructively.** Criticism is necessary to any manager/employee relationship, but you should never bang your employee over the head with it. Follow a positive statement about your employee's performance with the word *and* instead of the word *but*. The *but* erases the good intentions behind your original comment and diminishes the credibility of the criticism to come.

+ **Be meeting-savvy.** Set up regular meetings with each of your employees to solicit timely and relevant feedback. Ask targeted questions to prompt discussion about project status, and make sure to provide guidance on issues they may be facing.

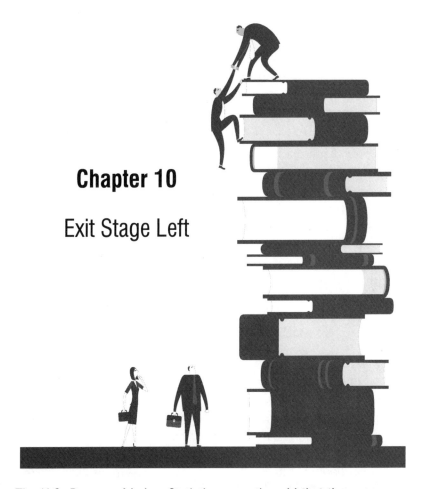

Chapter 10

Exit Stage Left

The U.S. Bureau of Labor Statistics recently said that the average young American has more than seven different employers before she reaches age 26. This means that, in general, twenty-somethings are changing jobs every 16 months. No doubt about it, this is not your parents' business world. Many people their age spent decades working their way up the ladder in the same company—a career path that is virtually unheard-of today. The job-jumping craze of the early 21st century may be over, but the market will continue to be fluid as company loyalty decreases and an upcoming labor shortage opens more opportunities for driven young workers.

Once you've been in your first position a year or two, it may be time to think about making a strategic career move. Why? No matter how well you're perceived in your current role, you'll move up more quickly if you change jobs. Now that you have some experience under your belt, you can command a higher salary, a better title, and more responsibility if you go elsewhere. Your 20s are the best time to make such a move, because you possess a certain degree of personal freedom. Most twenty-somethings don't have to worry about how a job switch will affect their children's school schedule. You uncover a new opportunity, and carpe diem!

Unfortunately, the decision to leave a job is not always one you have the luxury to make. Sometimes, for reasons you might not be able to control, you may be fired or laid off. In this chapter, I'll discuss how to detect and repair when your job may be on the line. Next, if you're ready for that strategic career move, I'll walk you through some techniques for scoping out a new career or position inside and outside your current company. I'll also cover good reasons to leave a job that aren't so strategic, such as being in an abusive situation. Finally, I'll talk about ways to make a graceful exit and preserve ties with your employer that will serve you well in the future.

Beware the Firing Squad

I had a feeling my job was in trouble when things started happening in my area that I didn't know about. All of a sudden, other people in my department were calling my clients without keeping me in the loop. This, combined with the fact that I had a new boss, clued me in that something bad was about to go down. I had been a loyal employee for three years and didn't want to leave, so I confronted my boss about it. I told him how committed I was to the new administration and asked him how I could adjust my performance to meet his needs. I think he was a little surprised that I was savvy enough to figure out what was going on. I bent over backwards to please him for a while, and he gave me a break and let me keep my job.

Orrin, 28, Washington

When my friend David was fired, he saw it coming. He had a new boss, with whom he clashed terribly. David had been an excellent employee, but after his new manager started criticizing him all the time, David lost his motivation. Eventually, he was just going through the motions. Once David's manager officially documented his poor performance, David knew his days were numbered. He was not surprised when he got the axe a month later.

Some bored or miserable employees might not have the emotional energy to consider whether they might be fired. Maybe it's all they can do to drag themselves to work in the morning. They think about quitting, but because they don't have anywhere else to go, they stick around and put in the minimum effort. Does this describe you? Let this serve as a wake-up call: If you hate it enough and don't do anything to fix the problem, your job is probably in jeopardy. Why? Long-term job dissatisfaction is difficult to hide. Your boss probably knows you're unhappy, and, if the situation continues, she'll probably find a way to get rid of you. Here are some other scenarios that should set off your smoke alarm:

+ You received a bad review or were put on probation.

+ You are no longer being consulted on new projects.

+ Your colleagues are inexplicably ignoring you.

+ You have a new boss with whom you don't get along.

+ Your boss has started giving your responsibilities to other people.

+ Your colleagues stop including you in relevant meetings.

+ You haven't kept your skills current or up to par.

+ You haven't accomplished what you were hired to do.

+ You don't adapt well to changes within the company.

+ You've been told that you need an attitude adjustment.

+ You don't fit the organizational mold.

+ You have a history of acting inappropriately in the office (for example, insubordination or gossiping).

+ You committed an unpardonable infraction (for example, cursing out a client or demonstrating overt racism or sexism).

We all go through periods of trouble on the job. Even if one or more of these warning signals applies to you, the black cloud may pass, or you may be able to work through it. Understanding when you're in danger of being fired can only empower you. Whether your job is being threatened by colleagues' perception of wrongdoing or actual wrongdoing, knowing what you're up against will help you determine a course of action. Appropriate resolutions vary. For example, if you've been chastised for bad behavior, you should cease the action immediately and show genuine remorse for any trouble you've caused. Alternatively, if your boss feels you're not producing, you should document your tangible contributions and present them to her at every opportunity. Did your manager give you a performance plan? That document should be your new bible. Live by it. Make sure you measurably improve in each designated area by the deadline noted in the plan.

In most cases, your boss won't fire you without a legitimate reason. Don't give her one. Once you discover where things are not working, swallow your pride and take the necessary steps to protect your career and your future.

Layoff Survival

In the business world today, layoffs are so common it's scary. Companies have to answer to Wall Street and their shareholders, and when an organization fails to meet its projections, a logical first step is to "trim the fat"—or eliminate jobs. Regardless of your reputation or skill set, your company might decide that your position is expendable, and they will send you packing. Usually you will have a lot of people in the same boat as you are because companies typically lay off many employees at the same time. On the one hand, being laid off is easier to stomach than being fired—it's less personal and you often can't do anything to change the decision one way or the other. However, layoffs are more disconcerting because it's harder to see the writing on the wall. Concerned? Keep on the lookout for the following danger signs:

- ✦ Top-management changes result in a new direction.
- ✦ The company message boards and blogs are rumbling about layoffs.
- ✦ Your company's or industry's financial woes are all over the news.
- ✦ Your company or department is underperforming.
- ✦ Senior executives are spending a lot of time holed up in a conference room.
- ✦ Your company has stopped investing in employees' careers via internal training or tuition reimbursement.
- ✦ Your department's budget has been drastically cut or eliminated.
- ✦ A recent re-org has left you without many of your former responsibilities.
- ✦ Your company has merged with our been bought by another company and there are now twice as many people doing your job.

Pay attention to these indicators. You must not permit yourself the luxury of denial or thinking a layoff could never happen to you. If you suspect that you are about to become a victim, take action before you are officially unemployed. Use the tactics from Chapter 1 (such as compiling a power resume and networking for job leads) to get a jump on the situation. In your 20s, you're typically not at a level that warrants a cushy severance package, so create an emergency financial plan that will carry you through a temporary loss of income. While you're at it, investigate post-employment health insurance options such as COBRA, and look into your organization's policy for rolling over 401(k) funds.

Sometimes, a layoff will take you completely by surprise. This is a traumatic experience, but do not allow it to destroy your confidence. Prospective employers recognize that companies are still downsizing as a result of the recent recession, and they will probably not hold a layoff against you. You should have no trouble landing on your feet, provided you start looking for another job right away. Interviewers will appreciate your resilience, whereas they may become skeptical if you stay off the market for too long. So if you're ever laid off, hold your head up high. Look at it as a good opportunity to find a company that truly values your talent and expertise.

Smart Career Moves

I was afraid to quit my job, even though I was beginning to hate life. I basically liked the company I worked for, so I started talking to people about opportunities in other departments. Turns out that one of the managers doing business development had noticed me during the few times we'd worked together. He was building up his team, and he'd heard that I had a good reputation. I didn't tell my current boss about it until the terms of my transfer—which included a promotion and a substantial raise—were nearly finalized. By that time, it was too late for her to try and stop me.

Seth, 24, Delaware

As I've talked about before, few employees today are lifers, or individuals who stay at the same organization for the duration of their careers. In particular, junior employees are both encouraged and expected to move around during their 20s. Even if you're happy with your job, it always pays to be on the lookout for the next big thing. This way, instead of waiting patiently to be promoted year after year, you can sell your skills to a new employer for a higher title and salary right now. In this section, I'll discuss the mechanics behind smart career moves, including how to transfer to a lateral position within your current organization, and how to scope out opportunities in a new company or in a new field.

One important caveat before I begin: Be wary of changing jobs too often. As a twenty-something in business, you should hold each job for at least a year before you consider a change. Individuals who switch more often become known as chronic job-jumpers, and employers avoid these candidates like the plague. When a hiring manager sees a resume listing four jobs in three years, he won't wait to hear your explanation. He'll think that you can't hold down a job, and he will move on to the next person.

If you are a chronic job-jumper and find yourself looking for a way out once again, you might want to do some soul-searching. A pattern of unsatisfying work experiences could mean that the problem lies not with the jobs or the companies, but with you. Here's an example: In my early career I worked with a woman named Joselyn who was a few years older than me. Joselyn tried in vain to find job satisfaction in a few different positions. Eventually she realized that, although her five work situations had been very different, her negative attitude was the one constant. She wasted a lot of time looking high and low for a better job when she should have been focusing on how she could be happier and more effective where she was. Don't let this happen to you.

As you're preparing to make a move, ask yourself the following questions, to ensure that you're leaving for the right reasons. Consider the answers carefully, and be realistic!

- ✦ Why do you want to look for a new job?
- ✦ Are you satisfied doing what you're doing?
- ✦ Are you adequately challenged? If not, do you even want to be challenged?
- ✦ Do you like the people and work environment?
- ✦ Are you fairly compensated?
- ✦ Are you treated with respect?
- ✦ Are you empowered to do your job effectively?

Transferring Inside the Company

The longer you work at a company, the more exposure you have to different functional areas. You may have even been fortunate enough to experience a job rotation, or a series of assignments in various parts of the company designed to provide a breadth of experiences. As you get to know more players and talk to them about what they do, you may find your interest piqued. There is usually no shortage of opportunities for driven and well-regarded twenty-somethings who want to transfer internally. Managers are always looking for good employees with a basic skill set and industry/company knowledge who won't come with huge salary requirements. Also, companies generally prefer to fill open positions by hiring from within. Some even have policies dictating that they *must* consider qualified internal candidates before they can expand a job search outside the company.

One type of internal transfer is the lateral move. In a lateral move, a strong employee takes on a new position at the same level as his former position. Most organizations encourage these because they are mechanisms for keeping good people happy and sufficiently challenged without promoting them. Lateral moves also save businesses the cost and risk of bringing in new employees who are unknown commodities. You may want to consider a lateral move if any of the following circumstances apply:

- ✦ You're more interested in stretching your wings and experiencing new things than moving up the ladder as fast as possible.

- ✦ You feel you are at a dead end in your current position, and you want to open a new door.

- ✦ The company is decreasing its focus on your area, and you want to better position yourself for long-term career growth.

- ✦ You're at odds with your manager or a coworker, and you have been unable to resolve the situation.

- ✦ You've discovered an opportunity to work in an area that will bring you closer to your big-picture career goals.

- ✦ You're being recruited by a manager you would love to work for.

Think a lateral move is right for you? You should certainly go for it. Just keep in mind that, in order to learn about internal opportunities, you will have to do the legwork. You may get lucky and have a savvy manager approach you with a job offer, but in most cases you'll be on your own. Start by finding out if your company publicizes job openings to employees, and review the Website religiously. If you see a position that intrigues you, discreetly follow up with the hiring manager. While this process is in motion, keep the prospects coming in by networking with as many senior managers as you can.

Get to know them on a personal level, and ask them casually what they're doing in their groups. During these discussions, never criticize your current manager, department, or position. If a manager thinks you're a spoiled brat who's running away from a difficult work situation, he won't want to bring you on board. Phrase your inquiries positively and innocently—you just want to learn, remember?

Scouting out an appropriate opportunity to transfer internally is one thing, but actually making the transition happen is quite another. Here are a couple of tips that will help you. First, just because your organization is behind your decision 100 percent doesn't mean your boss will be. Whether you're pursuing a move through human resources or directly with another manager, keep the discussions under wraps until the transfer is close to being finalized. If your boss doesn't want to lose you and finds out what you're up to too early, she may subtly—or not so subtly—block your progress. Once it's time to ink the deal, make sure HR is in the loop so that everyone involved adheres to the agreed-upon transition plan. Don't depend on your old boss and your new boss to work it out among themselves. Your old boss may try to hold on to you as long as she can, and, next thing you know, you'll have a major territory war on your hands.

Also, avoid talking about the move to your colleagues before it's official, because you might compromise your reputation in the group if the job falls through. You'll also feel like an idiot. Look at it this way: If your team were going to the Super Bowl, you wouldn't talk about the victory parade until after the game, right? Same goes for your potential hot new job down the hall!

Looking Elsewhere

It's easiest to look for a new job while you're still employed. Makes sense, right? You're more attractive to hiring managers because you're free of the unemployment stigma. And because you're still receiving a steady paycheck, you come across as more discerning. Prospective employers know you're not desperate enough to take a job that's not a good fit.

Before you start talking to anyone about a new job, crystallize your big-picture goals so that you know exactly what you're looking for. Update your resume with all of your new skills and accomplishments. Next, explore the job-search outlets described in Chapter 1 to get the ball rolling.

Ideally, you will want to do all of your job-searching research outside of business hours, but that sometimes isn't practical. Do what you need to do while on the clock—just be careful that you don't get caught! Surf discreetly. Don't blindly send your resume all over the Internet or respond to job postings without knowing where they're coming from. And if you can, register with career sites that allow you to protect your listing from your existing employer.

As far as your colleagues are concerned, it should be business as usual. Don't arouse suspicion by changing your patterns. Use sick days to go on interviews if you must, but try to stack up your appointments over a two- or three-day period so you can chalk your absence up to an actual illness. Similarly, if your company dresses in business casual attire, wearing a suit to work will send a clear signal that you're interviewing during your lunch hour. Change en route instead.

When making calls to potential employers, use a private office or conference room, and set up a separate email account for your job search. Remember that you are still receiving a paycheck from your current organization. Don't spend too much time job-searching when you should be working, and make sure you're producing on a regular basis. If anything, you should work harder than ever so that you can count on strong references down the road.

While we're on the subject of references, don't ask anyone from your current job to be one. Hopefully you have other options, because it's never a good idea to let people at your company know you're looking. Unless you want your whole office to know about your plans, don't tell a soul—even your closest colleague or your mentor.

As you interact with hiring managers and recruiters, be assertive about what you're looking for. Prospective employers prefer candidates who are in good standing with their current employers, so act as though you're happy at your job even if you're not. Your reason for leaving should always be a positive one. For example, you're looking for an opportunity to expand your skill set and take on new challenges.

If you get an offer, think through the logistics before agreeing on a start date. You still have a job and need to give two weeks' notice before departing for greener pastures. When you accept a new job, let your current boss know first, as a courtesy, and assure him that you will do everything you can to transition your responsibilities smoothly.

When to Quit Now and Worry Later

After law school, I took an associate position at a city firm. I'd been there about a month when I realized that the place was a total boy's club. All of the guys were 6 feet tall and blond, and the few women there fell all over themselves trying to get in good with the men. The senior lawyers had apparently never heard of an ambitious woman, and they were pretty vocal about putting me in my place. It was disgusting. I guess, technically, I could sue them, but it's not worth the time and effort. I'll just go somewhere that appreciates an associate who's willing to work her butt off.

Darcy, 26, Ohio

In a perfect world you would love your job to death and would only consider leaving for "good" reasons, such as the career opportunity of a lifetime or your spouse's relocation. But at some point in your early career, it's likely that a job won't work out the way you planned. For reasons beyond your control, you may find yourself in a bad work situation that mandates quitting sooner rather than later.

No matter what the trouble is, it's usually best to stick it out until you get something better and are able to jump right into another position. However, as I've talked about, finding new employment takes time. If your work is seriously compromising your mental or physical health and it's torture to go into the office every day, you might not want to wait. After all, no job is worth sacrificing your well-being. Here are some scenarios that may warrant leaving now and worrying about the consequences later.

- ✦ **You are being emotionally abused.** Is an individual at work unnecessarily unfair or cruel to you? Does she ridicule you in front of your colleagues? Does she regularly call you into her office to insult you or ream you out? Don't be fooled: Emotional abuse can be just as damaging as physical abuse. If you feel your self-esteem taking a beating, get out of the situation.

- ✦ **You are being sexually harassed.** Has someone in your organization repeatedly approached you in a way that makes you feel uncomfortable? Does he communicate in person or online in an inappropriate fashion? Has he subtly or overtly promised you advancement or perks in return for sexual favors? You should not grin and bear it, no matter how much of a big-shot your offender is.

✦ **You have been asked to compromise your integrity.** Is your boss
   or another authority figure asking you to lie, cheat, or steal? Do your
   assigned job responsibilities compromise your personal ethics? Don't
   allow yourself to be pressured into a situation that could ruin your
   career.

✦ **You don't feel safe coming to work.** Is your company located in a
   dangerous area? Are you afraid to walk to and from the office alone?
   Are the working conditions harmful or unsanitary? I don't care how
   much you're getting paid, your job should not jeopardize your health
   or security.

Under some circumstances, it might be wise to pay human resources a
visit before handing in your resignation. Sometimes, particularly in harassment cases, HR may be able to step in and quietly resolve the issue without
costing you your job. In general, though, be wary of complaining to HR.
Your HR rep's job is to side with the organization you both work for, so don't
blindly divulge information to her as though she's your therapist. Even if your
situation is objectively horrible, be positive about seeking a resolution, and
don't tell your HR rep anything that could be used against you.

Also, remember that when it comes to HR, you can't necessarily count
on confidentiality. To be safe, you should assume that anything you say in
an HR rep's office will get back to the person or people you're talking about.
And if your conflict is with a senior manager, you may not get a fair hearing.
When it's "his word against hers," many HR reps will side with the more
senior person involved, prejudicing them against you, the junior employee.
Now, don't get me wrong, certain issues, such as sexual harassment, need to be
confronted, and HR can be a useful ally in helping you do just that. Just keep
in mind that the decision to involve HR should not be made lightly, and make
sure to think through the consequences before making that call.

Know Your Rights

Life in the professional world isn't always fair, but it's helpful to know
when your workplace has crossed a legal line and when the organization is well
within its rights. For example, did you know that in most states in America,
employers have the right to discriminate against employees because they are
too young? Yes, it's true. The U.S. federal law only protects people from discrimination if they are over 40 and considered too old.

Have you ever heard the legal definition of *insubordination*? The word *insubordinate* can be dissected this way: "in" = "not," and "subordinate" = "subject to the authority of another." So someone who is legally *in-subordinate* refuses to recognize the authority of the employer, which can mean anything from cursing out your boss to refusing to complete a task that you consider unimportant.

And get a load of this one: In North America, most employees are at-will. This means that representatives of an organization hire you because they feel like it, and when your employment no longer suits their purposes, they can let you go with no strings attached. So, essentially, you can be fired for any reason or no reason at all. This is why most mass layoffs are legal.

Scary as these examples may sound, the law is generally on the employee's side. In the courts, employees are awarded millions of dollars every year for being:

+ Fired in a wrongful termination.

+ Wrongly classified as exempt from overtime pay.

+ Harassed or unfairly accused of harassment.

You don't have to have a law degree to understand your rights as an employee. Fair Measures, a company specializing in management practices that create fair workplaces for employees, has a terrific Website (FairMeasures.com) with tons of useful information about disability law, discrimination law, overtime exempt law, privacy law, sexual harassment law, and wrongful termination law.

When you're a victim, it's reasonable to feel angry and cheated. But do your homework before you take action that could backfire. If you think you've been treated unfairly, investigate the issue thoroughly before you make public accusations or hire a pricey attorney to file a suit on your behalf. Once you have the facts and understand your options, you can set out to protect your rights with confidence and conviction.

Fireproofing Your Bridges

A few years ago, I left my job in HR at a food services company because of irreconcilable differences with my manager. On my last day, I went into her office to say goodbye and brought her a little gift. I told her that I was truly sorry things didn't work out and that

I wished her the best. Boy, am I glad I went through the trouble to smooth things over, because I later went to work for a consulting firm that was competing for my old company's business! The fact that I had left on good terms made all the difference.

Violet, 29, Michigan

After the stressful process of looking for a new job while you're still employed, accepting an offer is a huge relief. At last, you're free! You probably can't wait to share your good fortune with the world and tell your boss where she can shove that evil assignment she gave you last week. You might think that because you're leaving, you don't have to worry what people think of you anymore. This is not the case. Unless you want to erase everything you've accomplished since your first day on the job, your departure must be as strategic and deliberate as your arrival.

This starts with your resignation. Under no circumstances should you let on that you're leaving before you have a signed agreement and an official start date from your new employer. If you jump the gun and blab to everyone, and then your job offer falls through, your best-case scenario is that you've got egg on your face. The worst-case scenario, of course, is that your boss is insulted enough to fire you. Here are some other suggestions for making a smooth exit.

+ **Tell your supervisor first.** You want your boss to hear the news from you, not from someone else in your department.

+ **Give two weeks' notice.** Stay for the entire two weeks, unless the company requests that you leave sooner.

+ **Be modest.** Don't alienate your colleagues by bragging or chattering incessantly about your awesome new gig.

+ **Don't insult anyone or anything.** Whether it's true or not, show that you regret leaving such wonderful people behind.

+ **Stay on top of your responsibilities.** Remember that you're accountable for your work until 5 p.m. on your last day.

+ **Continue to adhere to office protocol.** You worked hard for that professional persona, so leave them with the right impression.

+ **Review the employee handbook.** Understand what you're entitled to in regard to benefits and compensation for unused sick or vacation days.

+ **Organize your files.** Make it easy for your colleagues to find materials, so that they can transition your workload seamlessly and won't need to call you at your new job.

+ **Do a great job training your replacement.** Your current organization has paid your salary for a year or more. You owe it to them to leave your job in good hands.

+ **Don't take anything that doesn't belong to you.** This includes office supplies and work product that was not developed by you personally.

Many companies request that departing employees do exit interviews with HR. The person conducting the interview, who probably doesn't know you from a hole in the wall, will usually expect you to divulge why you are leaving and how you feel about your experience with the company. When it comes to exit interviews, stick to official business as much as possible, and in providing constructive criticism, proceed with tact and caution. Although it may be tempting to use the meeting to spill your guts about the company's difficult personalities and insufferable policies, don't give in. Once you've made the decision to leave, airing your grievances won't do you a drop of good, and the risk of offending people is too great.

The most important thing to remember when leaving a job is to fireproof your bridges. It's a smaller world than you think, and you never know when you're going to need these people again. And who knows? Maybe you won't even like your new job and will want to come back someday. At the very least, you want to be able to count on one person in the organization to serve as a reference for you in the future. During your last few weeks, do everything you can to leave behind a squeaky-clean reputation. Be conscientious and thorough as you're wrapping up or transitioning projects. Even if you're leaving because you can't stand your department, act like a team player and keep your negativity to a minimum. If your colleagues take you out for lunch or throw you a going away party, congratulate yourself. It means you've handled your departure in exactly the right way.

Getting off the Ladder

I've worked as a management consultant for two years, and I hate it. I've always been interested in philosophy, and my dad said he would pay for me to go to graduate school. I'm thinking of taking him up on it, because it would get me out of the corporate world for a few years. I'm not totally sure what I would do with that degree—there are only so many college professors, you know?—but having more education can never hurt.

Evan, 24, Illinois

So what's your course of action if you want to leave your job, and you don't want to get another one in your industry? You might have noted a few options, including going back to school, starting your own business, and making a career change. In the last several years, I've been asked for my advice on all of these paths, so read on before you decide to climb down off the ladder.

Going to Graduate School

I just heard yet another sad tale about a twenty-something with a newly minted MBA who's having a devil of a time finding a job. When employers see MBA on her resume, they assume that she should be looking for a management position. Unfortunately, because this grad's previous positions were primarily administrative and customer-service oriented, many employers don't think she has the practical experience to qualify for such a position. I've gotten dozens of emails from graduate school alumni in similar situations. After spending tens of thousands of dollars on an advanced degree, they find that they are no more marketable in their chosen field than they were before they started school. The only difference now is that their job search is more urgent because they are deeply in debt.

To me, this phenomenon speaks to the danger of going back to school without a great deal of forethought. So many people choose a graduate program because they aren't sure where they want to go with their careers, when in reality, they should first be doing a cost/benefit analysis to determine what such a program is going to bring them in terms of increased job prospects and financial compensation.

Of course, before investing an enormous amount of money, time, and effort securing an advanced degree, they should also do enough research and have enough hands-on experience to know that they actually like the field. I've heard lots of stories of twenty-somethings who graduate with a PhD, JD, or MBA only to end up deciding they want to do something else entirely. Lawyers become advertising directors, doctors become life coaches, marketing executives become journalists, and so on.

Bottom line: Although returning to the safety of books and finals might feel more comfortable than the workplace grind, graduate school is not something you should do just for the heck of it. Rather, you should first determine in concrete terms why you need the advanced degree to move ahead in your career of choice, and then map out a plan for how you'll use the training and degree to facilitate the level of success you desire.

Sometimes people ask me why I haven't gotten an MBA, and the reason is this: I now work for myself, and as such don't have a company subsidizing the $300K tuition. If I'm going to pay that kind of money out of my own pocket, then I better be sure I'm going to make it back with my post-MBA income. I know for a fact, though, that this won't happen. I'm at a point in my chosen career at which getting an MBA won't make much of a difference at all. I would like to get an advanced degree someday soon, but I don't kid myself. It's because I like to learn, not because I think it's a magic ticket into an uncharted area of the career stratosphere.

Making a Career Change

In between the first and second editions of this book, I published another career advice guide called *How'd You Score That Gig?: A Guide to the Coolest Careers and How to Get Them.* During the research phase, I interviewed more than 100 people who currently hold their dream jobs. These individuals were, among other things, travel journalists, event planners, fashion designers, forensic scientists, interior decorators, and Internet business owners, and most of them made a successful transition from another field while they were in their 20s.

In fact, the 20s are an ideal time to make a career change, for college students and recent graduates have much more flexibility when it comes to test-driving different fields. The process of self-discovery is much easier when you're unfettered by family responsibilities and substantial financial burdens, and when you haven't yet reached a level in a career where it's tougher to turn back.

People who change careers in order to do what they love have one thing in common: persistence. As unattainable as your dream job might sound, with the right amount of forethought and preparation, you can make the move as well. To get started:

✦ **Spend some time with YOU.** Follow the self-assessment steps I suggested in Chapter 1 to revisit how you like to work and what you'd be compelled to do even if you never got paid. Research careers and industries that map to your skills and interests. Hit the Internet, set up informational interviews, take relevant coursework, and arrange to go onsite at a company in your chosen field.

+ **Don't be deterred by a lack of experience.** In developing a resume and other promotional materials for the field you want to pursue, think about how your current skills and talents apply to the responsibilities you'll hold in the new job. For example, the transferable skills mentioned in Chapter 4, such as project management, client relations, information technology, and sales will take you far in most types of careers.

+ **Remember that any progress is good progress.** Make an effort to do one thing per day—such as emailing a networking contact or attending an industry event—that moves you a bit closer to your big picture goal. Perhaps this means earning a paycheck at your current job while doing a part-time internship in your new field or taking an adult education class or workshop on the weekend. The only way to find out if you're passionate about something is to try it—ideally with as little risk as you can manage.

+ **Have realistic expectations.** Even if you're lucky enough to hold your dream job, there's no such thing as the perfect work situation. Every job has its ups and downs, aspects we love and aspects we don't love. And "dream job" doesn't mean "cushy job." As your mom always told you, anything worth having in this world requires some effort. There will be some days you feel like shutting the alarm off and going back to sleep, but many more in which you feel more energized by the prospect of work than you ever thought possible!

Starting Your Own Business

The Small Business Administration (SBA) reports that there are about 28 million small businesses in the United States, and recent surveys indicate that 70 percent of Millennials want to start their own business. In addition, more than 80 percent of Americans believe they would be more passionate about their work if they owned their own enterprise.

So if you want to break out of Corporate America and forge your own destiny, you're certainly not alone. But how do you know if you have what it takes to be among the successfully self-employed? Well, to start, the personality characteristics necessary for starting and sustaining your own business include a willingness to sacrifice, a service orientation, leadership ability, business intelligence and creativity, management ability and organization, optimism, a competitive nature, a sales orientation, and confidence.

Those are some lofty traits, and it's a cold hard truth that not everyone is cut out to be self-employed. You should think long and hard about whether you want to do it, in addition to whether you could do it. Many years ago, for instance, I thought I would make my living as a freelance PR consultant. I even tried it for a while, and attracting clients and generating a steady income were actually easier than I anticipated. However, I soon realized how much I missed the camaraderie and teamwork of working in a PR organization, and how much I hated administrative tasks such as invoicing and preparing status memos. When I worked for myself, I was responsible for every aspect of my business, even the parts I wasn't great at and didn't particularly want to do. If you want to be an entrepreneur, keep this in mind. It's not just the glory, it's the guts too.

Despite limited financial resources and start-up experience, and a lack of credibility with potential investors and clients due to their age, twenty-somethings are launching their own enterprises in record numbers. There have been endless how-to books on this subject, so I'll limit my advice to a few key points.

- ✦ **Work for someone else in the field first.** How will you know what works and what doesn't without a couple of years in the trenches, where you are free to take risks and try new approaches that won't spell the end of your dreams? Look at it as a paid research endeavor, and an investment in your future business.

- ✦ **Take business-related coursework.** Sign up for college or continuing education classes in finance, management, and entrepreneurship. You can also check out free resources such as SCORE (Score.org), a nonprofit that provides advice and training to new business owners.

- ✦ **Learn from the wise.** I talked about the importance of mentors in Chapter 3, and, as a new entrepreneur, it's imperative that you look for one in your prospective field who can offer advice, connections, and moral support. You might also want to join a support group or third-party industry association in your area so that you have the opportunity to brainstorm with your peers.

+ **Write a stellar business plan.** The drafting process will help you to clarify and research your new offering, will provide a framework for growth over the first three to five years, and will be an important tool in your conversations with your mentor as well as potential partners and investors. Check out samples, and note the components of typical plans at sites such as Bplans.com.

+ **Secure financial backing.** Try to minimize your personal investment or credit card debt, opting instead for a bank loan. There are also many types of grants offered to new entrepreneurs, including individual grants, business grants, and government grants.

+ **Manage operations carefully.** Build a powerful team with strengths that complement your own, and save enough money so that you are able to live without income for the first six months of your business's life. Consult the SBA for logistical information such as how to acquire the right insurance, and enlist the services of a good lawyer and accountant.

Whether you've snagged a higher position on the organizational ladder or are planning a move that will forever change the course of your career, you can bet that the next few years will be an adventure. It is my hope that some of this book's lessons will serve you well. And now, onward and upward!

What I Wish I'd Known

I had been out of school a year when I got really excited about a business idea I had for an online women's mentoring network. After getting some encouragement from a really successful entrepreneur, I dropped everything, took out a ton of loans, and launched the site. It became apparent quickly that I was in way over my head, and pretty soon I was out of money and had no choice but to shut down. I wish I could tell my younger self that starting a business is not as easy as it looks, and what's the hurry? I have so much more knowledge today that I could bring to that initiative, and I imagine in five years I'll have even more.

Lori, 31, Arkansas

Take-Home Points

+ **Avoid job-jumping.** Hold on to each job for at least a year before you consider a change. Individuals who switch more often become known as chronic job-jumpers, and employers avoid these candidates like the plague.

+ **Master the transition between jobs.** While you're in the process of transferring to another position inside or outside the company, be discreet. Don't change your patterns, talk about a potential move, or engage in job-search activities in public. Conduct yourself as if it's business as usual.

+ **Make a graceful exit.** When leaving a company, the most important thing you can do is fireproof your bridges. It's a smaller world than you think, and you never know when you're going to need these people again. During your last few weeks, do everything you can to leave behind a squeaky-clean reputation.

+ **Consider other options thoughtfully.** If you've given your current situation a fair shot and you really desire a drastic change, plan your next move strategically. Before jumping in, think about how going back to school, making a career switch, or starting your own business can ensure your future happiness and job satisfaction.

Bibliography

Alba, Jason. *I'm on LinkedIn—Now What??? A Guide to Getting the Most out of LinkedIn*. Cupertino, Calif.: Happy About, 2012.

Alexander, Michael. *Networking: A Mentor/Apprentice Guide*. Edmonton, Alberta: Novacom International, 2000.

BlessingWhite, Inc. *Leading Successfully*. Princeton, N.J.: BlessingWhite, Inc., 2000.

Bolton, Robert, and Dorothy Grover Bolton. *People Styles at Work and Beyond: Making Bad Relationships Good and Good Relationships Better*. New York: AMACOM, 2009.

Carnegie, Dale. *How to Win Friends and Influence People*. Hauppauge, N.Y.: Dale Carnegie & Associates, Inc., 1936.

Chambers, Harry E. *Getting Promoted: Real Strategies for Advancing Your Career.* New York: Perseus Books, 1999.

Covey, Stephen R. *The 7 Habits of Highly Effective People.* New York: Simon & Schuster, 1989.

Danielson, Diane K., and Lindsey Pollak. *The Savvy Gal's Guide to Online Networking (Or What Would Jane Austen Do?).* Bangor, Maine: Booklocker, Inc., 2007.

Danielson, Diane K., and Rachel Solar-Tuttle. *Table Talk: The Savvy Girl's Alternative to Networking.* Bloomington, Ind.: 1st Books, 2003.

Dight, Clare. "How to Be an Intrapreneur." *The Times* online, *www.thetimes. co.uk/tto/business/entrepreneur/article2229896.ece* (accessed December 2013).

Ellis, Albert. *Feeling Better, Getting Better, Staying Better: Profound Self-Help Therapy For Your Emotions.* Atascadero, Calif.: Impact Publishers, Inc., 2001.

Goldfried, Marvin R., and Gerald C. Davison. *Clinical Behavior Therapy, Expanded Edition.* New York: John Wiley & Sons, Inc., 1994.

Gordon, David. "Suggested Salary Negotiation Guidelines for Recent College Graduates." Reed College Website, *www.reed.edu/beyond-reed/students/salary. html* (accessed December 2013).

Hackman, J. Richard. *Leading Teams: Setting the Stage for Great Performances.* Boston: Harvard Business School Press, 2002.

Lavington, Camille. *You've Only Got Three Seconds: How to Make the Right Impression in Your Business and Social Life.* New York: Bantam Doubleday Dell Publishing Group, Inc., 1997.

Robbins, Alexandra, and Abby Wilner. *Quarterlife Crisis: The Unique Challenges of Life in Your Twenties.* New York: Penguin Putnam, Inc., 2001.

Rogers, Robert, and Richard Wellins. "DDI's Leadership Beliefs." *www.ddiworld. com/DDIWorld/media/white-papers/leadershipbeliefs_wp_ddi.pdf* (accessed July 2013).

Sheehy, Gail. *Pathfinders.* New York: Bantam Doubleday Dell Publishing Group, Inc., 1981.

Tulgan, Bruce. *Managing the Generation Mix.* New York: HRD Press, Inc., 2006.

Weisinger, Hendrie. *Emotional Intelligence at Work.* San Francisco, Calif.: Jossey-Bass, Inc., 1998.A

Index

M

maintaining good relationships when leaving a job, 224-226

management styles, 68-69

medical benefits, 57

meeting your new coworkers, 48-49

meetings, 209-210

mentor, recruiting a, 88-89

motivating yourself, 152-153

N

negativity, 140-141

negotiating salary, 37-39

networking, 80-83

new hire documents and information, 55-59

O

observation at the workplace, 53-54

office lingo, 49-51

organization, 118-119

ownership, 101-102

P

paying compliments, 162-164

people styles, 168-170

performance reviews, 174-176

positive relationships, creating, 164-166

positive thinking, 142-145

problem-solving, 106-109

procrastination, 116-117

productivity hacks, 119-120

professional persona, 22-24

project management, 120-123

promotions, 178-183

Q

quitting because of a bad work situation, 222-223

R

raise, asking for, 176-178

relocating, 39-40

reorganization (re-org) 185-187

researching your field, 25-26

resumes, 27-30

risk-taking, 104-106

S

saying no, 114-116

self-assessment, 21-22

self-awareness, 146-147

selling your ideas internally, 100-101

setbacks, handling, 183-185

showcasing your abilities, 102-104

social networking, 83-85

starting your own business, 229-231

stress, managing, 150-151

About the Author

Alexandra Levit's goal is to help people succeed in meaningful jobs, and to build relationships between organizations and top talent. A former nationally syndicated columnist for *The Wall Street Journal* and a current writer for *The New York Times*, Alexandra has authored several books, including the bestselling *They Don't Teach Corporate in College*, as well as *How'd You Score That Gig?*; *Success for Hire*; *MillennialTweet*; *New Job, New You*; and *Blind Spots*.

Since serving as a member of Business Roundtable's Springboard Project, which advised the Obama administration on current workplace issues, Alexandra produced the critically acclaimed JobSTART101.org, a free online course that better prepares college students and graduates for the challenges of the workplace, and a U.S. Department of Labor course that helps military veterans transition to the civilian workforce.

Alexandra consults, writes, and explores leadership development and career and workplace trends on behalf of American Express, Deloitte, DeVry University, Intuit, and PepsiCo. She has spoken at hundreds of organizations around the world including the American Management Association, the Society for Human Resource Management, the Federal Reserve Bank, Campbell Soup, Microsoft, McDonald's, and Whirlpool.

Alexandra is also a frequent national media spokesperson and is regularly featured in outlets including *The New York Times*, *USA Today*, National Public Radio, CNN, *ABC News*, CNBC, *Forbes*, the Associated Press, and *Glamour*. She was recently named *Money Magazine*'s Online Career Expert of the Year and the author of one of *Forbes*' best Websites for women.

A member of the Northwestern University Council of 100 and the Young Entrepreneur Council, Alexandra recently received the prestigious Emerging Leader Award from her alma mater. The award honors a Northwestern graduate under 35 who has made a significant impact in her field and in society. She resides in Chicago, Illinois, with her husband, Stewart, and their two young children.